BOTANY BAY

# Botany Bay: The Real Story

## ALAN FROST

Published by Black Inc.,
an imprint of Schwartz Media Pty Ltd
37–39 Langridge Street
Collingwood VIC 3066 Australia
email: enquiries@blackincbooks.com
http://www.blackincbooks.com

The National Library of Australia Cataloguing-in-Publication entry:

    Frost, Alan, 1943-

    Botany bay : the real story / Alan Frost.

    2nd ed.

    ISBN: 9781863955546 (pbk.)

    Includes bibliographical references and index.

    Penal transportation--Great Britain--Colonies. Convicts--Great
    Britain--History. Penal transportation--New South Wales. Great
    Britain--Colonies--History. Australia--History.

    365.340941

Index by Michael Ramsden

# Contents

It might perhaps be practicable to direct the strict employment of a limited number of convicted felons in each of the dock-yards, in the stanneries, saltworks, mines and public buildings of the kingdom. The more enormous offenders might be sent to Tunis, Algiers, and other Mahometan ports, for the redemption of Christian slaves. Others might be compelled to dangerous expeditions; or be sent to establish new colonies, factories, and settlements on the coasts of Africa, and on small islands for the benefit of navigation.

—WILLIAM EDEN, *Principles of Penal Law*, London, 1771

*Map of Australia in relation to the East Indies and the Pacific coastlines*

# PREFACE

IN 1975, SHIFTING THE FOCUS OF my scholarly interest from
English literature to history, I began to research the reasons for the
British colonization of New South Wales in 1788.

Then, I had no real idea for how many years this quest would occupy
me, and how arduous it would prove. In the 1980s and 1990s, I published
a number of substantial studies which bore, to a greater or lesser extent,
on the general question: *Convicts and Empire* (1980); *Arthur Phillip,
1738–1814: His Voyaging* (1987); *Sir Joseph Banks and the Transfer of
Plants to and from the South Pacific, 1786–1798* (1993); *Botany Bay
Mirages* (1994). Even so, I still had only a limited sense of the magnitude
of the task, whose horizons kept expanding – witness *The Global Reach
of Empire* (2003).

The one thing above all others that I did not know when I commenced
this research was the full extent of the documentary base awaiting discovery. When I began, I naturally attended to those sources which had
either been published (as in *Historical Records of New South Wales* (1892))
or cited in what were then the standard histories of the beginning of
modern Australia (by Ernest Scott, Sir Keith Hancock, Sir Max Crawford, Manning Clark and A.G.L. Shaw). But as I investigated further,
and in particular as I came to know better the administrative practices
of British government departments in the last decades of the eighteenth
century, I uncovered more and more relevant documents.

The essays in *Botany Bay Mirages* were based on some 600 documents, and in the Introduction to that work I optimistically forecast that there might be perhaps 200 more to be collected. Even so, I still had no proper idea of the actual extent of the records. I kept searching, and kept finding more documents. When in 2003 I applied for a large ARC grant to continue the process, I thought that I should probably end up with 1000. I received the grant and went back repeatedly to the Public Record Office, now the National Archives, in London. I found more and more documents – so many that at times it seemed as though there would be no end to the business. I would utter low groans each time I opened a new file to find yet another dozen or fifty that needed to be recorded.

In the end, I gathered 2500 documents (including copies). To be sure, there is often much repetition in these as, according to the practice of the times, writers summarized or repeated at length the contents of the letters they were minuting or answering. But taken together, and when combined with other sources which also reflect government deliberations (such as secondary correspondence and newspaper reports), this base constitutes a matchless record of that moment in time's long travail that led to the emergence of Australia. (These documents are to be made available on a dedicated website at the State Library of New South Wales. It is my hope that this will become an enduring record for the future, as new documents are added to it and as other historians make use of it for different purposes.)

The greatly enlarged documentary record means that we are now in a position to understand better than ever before why the British decided to colonize New South Wales. In this volume and its forthcoming companion, *The First Fleet: The Real Story*, I analyze this decision and how it was implemented.

As has been true generally of my past writing about British imperialism in the second half of the eighteenth century, what I am most concerned with in these studies are the political and strategic decision-making processes, and the administrative procedures by which decisions were implemented. Some of what I say here I have said before, but not in such an extensive or focused way. Also, a number of my conclusions now differ markedly from some I offered thirty years ago. I understand more now than I did then.

Much of what I say, I know, contradicts what has become received wisdom in Australian history. To some readers, it may seem the height of folly – or arrogance – to gainsay what the renowned historians of Australian colonization have said; and to do so, moreover, in polemical fashion. But this is what I am doing – in these studies I am challenging the established historiography of Australia's beginnings, which I believe to be both severely limited in its perspective and wrong in a number of its central conclusions.

In disagreeing with my colleagues and predecessors, I mean no personal disrespect. However, there is no gentle way of arguing against a whole tradition of historiography. If I intend to call it into fundamental question, then it is best that I do so directly and honestly. Only in this way is the cause of history properly served; and also that of the nation, in that we shall come to a better understanding of whence we came, and therefore who we are.

## Editorial Practices

The documents I have located, and from which I quote here, have been transcribed and edited by Dr Natasha Campo and myself. Mostly, we have modernized spelling, capitalization and punctuation. (The principal exception is that we have left in their original form legal documents, such as Letters Patent and Acts of Parliament.) Sometimes, in the interest of readier comprehension, we have also broken up very long passages into shorter paragraphs (including in Letters Patent). While misspellings have been silently corrected, we have indicated where we have corrected obviously wrong words. We have standardized the spelling of personal and geographical names. However, I have retained older spellings when to alter them would lead to confusion (e.g., Bombay rather than Mumbai, as no eighteenth-century European source gives the modern Indian term).

# INTRODUCTION

BETWEEN 1718 AND 1775, British authorities transported some 50,000 male and female criminals across the Atlantic Ocean to the North American colonies (most to Virginia and Maryland), where their labour was sold to merchants and planters for terms not longer than seven years.

This distinctive penal practice came to an abrupt halt in 1776, when many of the American colonists revolted against metropolitan rule. For the next six years, hoping that the problem would be temporary, parliament instituted an alternative sentence for felonies, that of hard labour on the harbours and waterways of the kingdom, with convicts so sentenced being held on dismasted ships ('hulks') in the River Thames. When war ended, as inclination or necessity turned numbers of the tens of thousands of soldiers and sailors returning home to crime, magistrates also returned to the older sentence of transportation; but with nowhere to send them, the number of convicts being held in metropolitan and county prisons rapidly increased, and the government was forced to expand the hulks system. By 1786, there were three hulks moored in the Thames and one each in Portsmouth and Plymouth harbours, each accommodating about 250 to 280 male prisoners.

The total number of men and women sentenced to transportation to North America or Africa or, more generally, to 'beyond the Seas' then being held in the hulks and jails of the kingdom is uncertain. It is not likely to have exceeded 4000 and may have been significantly fewer. However, there were rogues and abandoned persons enough for local authorities to complain bitterly to the central government about its failure to carry out sentences of transportation. In August 1786, the administration of William Pitt the Younger decided to establish a convict colony at Botany Bay, on the eastern coast of New South Wales, along which Captain James Cook had sailed in 1770 and of which he had taken possession in the name of the King.

The British began this colonization in 1788 with 750 convicts, 200 marines and a handful of civilian officers. In the fifty or so years to 1840, they transported about 130,000 men, women and juvenile offenders to various sites in and off eastern Australia: Sydney, Newcastle, Port Macquarie, Moreton Bay, Van Diemen's Land (Tasmania) and Norfolk Island.

The government minister usually associated with the original decision was Thomas Townshend. He had been Secretary of State for Home Affairs in the Shelburne administration (July 1782–April 1783), with convicts being one of his many responsibilities. After being raised to the peerage as Lord Sydney, from December 1783 he held this position again in the Pitt administration. To avoid confusion, I shall refer to him as Lord Sydney, and to his department as the Home Office.

For decades, historians gave only one motive for the decision: the British wished to 'dump' their criminals as far away as possible. Then, in the second half of the twentieth century, some suggested that there had also been strategic and commercial motives – a suggestion the traditionalists strongly rejected. This argument among the historians is part of my story.

*

It is possible to identify a number of phases in the historiography of this curious venture, for which there is no real parallel in modern history.

The first of these extended from the commencement of European settlement to 1880. During these years, most who reflected on the convict colonization drew not on official or private records, but rather on personal experience of life in the colonies, or on descriptions by others of this life. Inevitably, the fact of convicts dominated these would-be historians' perspective, which was often overlaid with a strong theological wash.

The author of the account that appeared under the name of George Barrington, thief in England and chief constable at Parramatta in New South Wales, for example, observed that 'in contemplating the origin, rise, and fall of nations, the mind is alternately filled with a mixture of sacred pain and pleasure'. For Barrington, the pain in the colony's beginning was that there had been so many criminals in England, and that so many of these, when transported, had 'continued incorrigible'. The pleasure was that 'some in the infancy of the Colony, will be found reforming rapidly'; and he comforted himself with the thought that 'the penitence of a Few, cannot but be acceptable to Man, since in Heaven there is *Joy over even one Sinner that truly repents*'. The primary reason for the colony's existence was to create a 'School' for 'the Correction of those unfortunate Human Beings, who, urged by various depraved motives, forfeit the protection of the Laws they have failed to observe'.[1]

Another early historian of New South Wales, John Dunmore Lang, was a Presbyterian minister there from 1823 until his death in 1878. He began his 1834 account of the colony by pointing to how the earlier transportation of British convicts to North America had been disrupted by the War of Independence. The 'main objects' of the British government in colonizing New South Wales, he asserted, had been:

> To rid the mother country of the intolerable nuisance arising from the daily increasing accumulation of criminals in her jails and houses of correction;
>
> To afford a suitable place for the safe custody and the punishment of these criminals, as well as for their ultimate and progressive reformation; and,

> To form a British colony out of those materials which the refor-
> mation of these criminals might gradually supply to the government,
> in addition to the families of free emigrants who might from time to
> time be induced to settle in the newly discovered territory.[2]

This became the essential paradigm that was repeated for another fifty years. In 1862, Roderick Flanagan discussed how the successful rebellion of the American colonies had checked the British practice of transporting criminals out of the kingdom, and gave some details of the mounting of the First Fleet.[3] In 1877 Alexander and George Sutherland noted that just as Britain was presented with the problem of finding a new place to which to transport convicts, 'Captain Cook's voyages called attention to a land in every way suited for such a purpose, both by reason of its fertility and of its great distance'.[4]

But, as Babette Smith has recently shown in *Australia's Birthstain* (2008), by the middle of the nineteenth century the rhetoric of the anti-transportation movement was casting a very heavy pall over the cir-cumstances of Australia's beginnings. In *The History of Australasia* (1878) David Blair reflected this change of outlook when he waxed indignant about the British government's reprehensible approach to 'planning a settlement in the new world which the genius and enter-prise of Cook had opened up to the British people'. 'Instead of embrac-ing the opportunity to found "a new Britannia in another world"', Blair argued, the Pitt administration's only motive had been 'that Providence had shown them a favourable opening for getting rid of their surplus criminal population'. Seeing that this 'fatal purpose' cast a 'dark shadow' over European Australia's beginning, he declared that he would pass over the story 'as lightly as the exigencies of true narration will permit. Better, a thousand times, would it be for the world, if the entire record were buried in eternal forgetfulness.'[5]

The apogee of this view perhaps came with the Sydney *Bulletin*'s denunciation of the celebration in 1888 of the one hundredth anniver-sary of Governor Arthur Phillip's landing at Sydney Cove. It thundered luridly that the one day among all others which has been fixed upon as the natal-day of Australia is that which commemorates her shame and degradation, and reminds the world most emphatically of the hideous uncleanness from which she sprung. The day which gave to the New World her first jail and her first gallows – the day when the festering vileness of England was first cast ashore to putrefy upon the coasts of New South Wales – the day which inaugurated a reign of slavery and loathsomeness and moral leprosy – is the occasion for which we are called upon to rejoice with an exceeding great joy.[6]

\*

The second phase in the historiography of the decision to establish a convict colony at Botany Bay followed the recovery of original records in the Public Record Office in London and other archives.

George Rusden began this process with his research for his *History of Australia* (1883). It was soon afterwards greatly advanced when, in preparation for the centenary celebrations, New South Wales premier Henry Parkes, commissioned James Bonwick to undertake an extensive search for records in Britain, with a view to making them the basis of an official history. Bonwick executed his commission so diligently that the colonial government decided to publish the rapidly accumulating transcripts as a companion work to the commissioned history.[7] George Barton made early use of Bonwick's harvest with the first volume of *History of New South Wales from the Records*, published in 1889. The first volume of *Historical Records of New South Wales* appeared in 1892. When completed, this series consisted of seven densely printed volumes.

*Historical Records of New South Wales* provided about one hundred documents pertaining to the August 1786 decision to colonize and the mounting of the First Fleet in 1786–7. Some more were added in ensuing decades, in the various volumes of *Historical Records of Australia* and by Owen Rutter in *The First Fleet* (1937). Essentially, though, for the next sixty years and more, the documents published in *Historical Records of New South Wales* were one of the two principal pillars on which most historians' accounts of the founding of modern Australia were built.

The other consisted of complaints by English municipal and county officials to the central government about the presence in their jails of convicts sentenced to transportation. From the time peace was restored in 1783, and especially after the passage of a more comprehensive transportation act (24 Geo. III, c. 56) in August 1784, as more and more people were convicted of felonies and sentenced to transportation, these complaints grew more frequent and bitter.

The grounds of complaint were straightforward. It was the central government's responsibility to see that sentences of transportation were carried out. So long as they were not, and in the absence of any alternative means of clearing prisons, local authorities were forced to keep transport convicts in their jails. From both a security and health point of view, these jails were all too often inadequate for the purpose; moreover, there was no financial provision for the maintenance of prisoners who were not supposed to be in them. The authorities' complaints crowd the HO 42 series (George III: Domestic Papers) in the Public Record Office, and for decades historians considered them the only additional evidence needed to confirm that the 'convict problem' was the motive for colonization, reinforcing the explanation they found encapsulated in the documents in *Historical Records of New South Wales*.

The most distinguished of Australia's mid-twentieth-century historians who read these two classes of documents were convinced that Australia owed its beginning to a short-sighted government's irrational solution to an awkward domestic problem. Sir Keith Hancock held that 'the Government of Pitt chose New South Wales as a prison, commodious, conveniently distant, and, it was hoped, cheap; for prison labour, driven by prison discipline, would surely be able to keep itself'.[8] Eris O'Brien observed that the American War of Independence, bringing the 'traffic in convicts across the Atlantic to a standstill', was 'the real beginning of Australian history', and that the 'the reason given by Sydney for the necessity of making [the Botany Bay] settlement was the familiar one of jails so crowded as to give rise to the danger of wholesale escapes or an epidemic of fever'.[9] R.M. Crawford concluded that 'there was no escaping the fact that New South Wales was founded as a jail' and that 'necessity and not vision founded Australia'.[10] F.K. Crowley argued that 'the history of the first thirty years of British settlement in Australia certainly does not indicate the working out of any systematic plan for fostering new ventures in trade, colonization, or empire building'; that 'domestic needs rather than the implication of Imperial policies were the factors most evident in the determination of the English government to send a number of ships and convicts to the antipodes in 1787'; and that 'the hard-pressed ministers in Pitt's administration were little concerned with the importance of the undertaking. They were interested only in finding a solution for pressing political and penal problems in the home country'.[11] A.G.L. Shaw concluded that the satisfactory accommodation of the convicts 'seems to have been the government's principal concern, stimulated as it was by the loss of American plantations'.[12] And, displaying his propensity to take phrases and sentences holus-bolus from his sources, Manning Clark argued that 'one factor alone had convinced [Lord Sydney] of the need for a definite decision' about what to do with the convicts: 'the several jails and places for the confinement of felons were so crowded that the greatest danger was to be apprehended not only from their escape, but from infectious distempers'.[13]

\*

In this second phase of the historiography of the decision to colonize New South Wales, then, most historians concluded that the 'dumping of convicts' motive was the only one the documentary record supported.

A number of other assumptions, sometimes unstated, accompanied this one. One was that the loss of the American colonies caused British administrations of the late eighteenth and early nineteenth centuries to lose interest in empire. Another was that the young Prime Minister, William Pitt, lacked an imperial imagination. A third was that Pitt and his ministers were incapable of either envisaging the nation's future needs, or of planning to meet them. A fourth was that these politicians responded to events, rather than acted to direct them. A fifth was that they abandoned the traditional view of convicts as a cheap source of labour from which the nation might benefit, and saw them instead in their regrettable numbers only as a domestic nuisance. Finally, there was the assumption that Pitt and his ministers decided to establish a convict colony in New South Wales in a fit of despair or of absence of mind – most likely of both! The phrase 'absence of mind' was based on a mis-reading of a comment by Sir John Seely, the eminent late-nineteenth-century historian of British imperialism: 'There is something very characteristic in the indifference which we show towards this mighty phenomenon of the diffusion of our race and the expansion of our state. We seem, as it were, to have conquered and peopled half the world in a fit of absence of mind.' An oversimplified interpretation of Seeley's statement took hold and became a widely repeated mantra, used to explain the whole sorry business.[14]

Believing the decision to have arisen from inertia and incapacity, the traditionalist historians represented it as a largely gratuitous one, prompted by Britain's loss of its North American colonies and by the social and political pressure caused by the subsequent overcrowding of prisons at home. They presented it as quite unrelated to the Pitt administration's policies in such other spheres as domestic reform, the re-establishment of colonial administration or overseas security and trade. And they saw Australia as part of the broader scheme of the British empire only after the Australian colonies had, against London's inclination, slowly attained constitutional, political and economic development similar to Britain's other colonies in North America, the West Indies and the East. As Manning Clark pointed out, when he announced the decision to the new session of parliament on 23 January 1787, the King cited only the convict motive: 'a plan has been formed by my direction, for transporting a number of convicts, in order to remove the inconvenience which arose from the crowded state of the jails in different parts of the kingdom.'[15]

\*

There were occasional tinges of greenery in the otherwise dreary waste-land of official incompetence and despair described by most historians during this period.

Some of the printed records – for example, the colonization pro-posals submitted by James Matra, Sir George Young and Sir John Call – did lead a number of late-nineteenth-century writers to think that the British government may have had other motives for the decision to colonize New South Wales. Rusden thought that 'the mere providing of a jail was not the sole motive for the founding of New South Wales' and wondered if 'a desire to forestall the French' had not been a fac-tor.[16] A few years later the English historian E.C.K. Gonner noted that 'it is a serious error to mistake an incident for an all-sufficing cause'. 'While the expedition to New South Wales could always be justified on the ground of present necessity,' he wrote, 'those who sent it aimed at something more important than the mere foundation of a new crimi-nal establishment', and pointed to the commercial and political argu-ments advanced by James Matra.[17] Barton also observed that Matra and Young had argued vigorously for the 'commercial or political advantages' of colonizing New South Wales.[18] However, these writers made no detailed examination of these other possible motives, and their insights, tentatively advanced, failed to influence general understanding of the decision.

In 1937, Rutter revived this line of thought, writing:

Sometimes I wonder if those ministers of George III were indeed so blind as they appear to the advantages of Matra's first plan. Was all the talk of convicts and penal settlements a magnificent piece of subtlety, a splendid bluff designed to hoodwink the Dutch, who were jealously clutching their old colonial possessions in the Eastern Seas, and the French, who were avid for new ones? Did George III and his ministers, having lost a colony on one side of the world, really see the possibilities of a new one on the other side, as Matra would have had them see? To me that is a fascinat-ing theory: and it must remain so, for I have no evidence to adduce in its support – nothing but here and there a hint as to the working of a man's mind, an implication in a sentence which the speaker or writer may or may not have phrased to conceal his thoughts.[19]

But like those unfortunate vegetables planted at Sydney Cove in the autumn of 1788, which germinated only soon to die, these tendrils of potential insight also quickly withered.

*

So, by the middle of the twentieth century, the business seemed to rest: Australia had been founded as a jail – 'commodious, conveniently distant, and, it was hoped, cheap'.[20]

Well, not quite. Like the undercurrent that can run in opposition to the habitual roll of spectacular surf, another view was also building. Although it took some time to emerge, and although those who developed it attended to different contours, this counter-current of historical thinking had as its fundamental premise the belief that governments – even incompetent ones – seldom take a particular decision entirely in isolation from others. Understanding the true historical circumstance – that it was not cheap but rather very expensive to send a large number of convicts on a voyage of eight months to a place 20,000 kilometres away, there to start a settlement from scratch – a small number of writers went against the tide and asked: 'Might it not be that the Pitt administration hoped to obtain something in return – something, that is, more than the simple removal of criminals from Britain?'

The first serious questioning of the received wisdom came in 1952, when K.M. Dallas, a Tasmanian economic historian, published a short article in an obscure journal asserting that the 'dumping of convicts' explanation was by itself 'absurd'. Because of the 'costs and risks' involved in shipping the convicts to New South Wales, and because of the availability of suitable sites closer to Britain, Dallas supposed that there was 'some deeper reason for choosing Botany Bay'. 'The dumping of convicts view is too simple', he argued. 'The emphasis should be put on *settlement* rather than on the penal aspect; on the naval and commercial realities rather than on the legal and judicial form.' Starting with the premise that during the second half of the eighteenth century 'the wealth of nations and their power depended on the gain from foreign trade; [and] foreign trade depended on possession of strategic harbours for safe refuge, for assembling convoys and for attack on enemy shipping', Dallas linked the New South Wales venture with the possibilities of trade with China, the northwest American coast and South America, and of whaling and sealing in the Pacific Ocean. He pointed, too, to the naval significance of Norfolk Island's pines and flax. He summed up his argument: 'The First Fleet was a well-planned naval expedition sent to seize and fortify a naval base; the convicts were what they had always been – the servants of mercantilist interests.'[21]

Acute as some of these points are, Dallas lacked the gift of lucid exposition, and it wasn't until Geoffrey Blainey revived them in 1966 that Dallas's views received real attention. Blainey did more than highlight Dallas's arguments, however; he went much further in support of the idea that there had been additional motives for sending convicts to Botany Bay. He too made the important point that transporting people such a distance 'was a startlingly costly solution to the crowded British prisons', and also a very slow one; and he reiterated the usefulness of a port in the southwestern Pacific Ocean to British ships. Then, deploying his wonderful facility for conveying the essence of a historical situation in modern terms, he pointed out that in the late eighteenth century 'flax and ships' timber were as vital to seapower as steel and oil are today', and that one of the concluding paragraphs in the 'Heads of a Plan', the document which went from the Home Office to the Treasury to explain the decision, mentioned this objective. The pines and flax plants on Norfolk Island, Blainey asserted, constituted the 'key to the plan to send convicts to Australia': 'Norfolk Island was the plant nursery; Australia was to be the market garden and flax farm surrounded by jail walls.'[22]

A.G.L. Shaw and Geoffrey Bolton, historians who held to the traditional explanation, responded to Blainey's arguments with disbelief. A lively debate followed, but the question remained unresolved.[23] Into the 1970s, the 'dumping of convicts' explanation reigned supreme: as one prominent historian of Australia told me then, 'Nobody believes Blainey!'

*

It was at this point that I entered the fray. On taking up my position in the English department at La Trobe University in 1970, I became aware of the controversy among historians concerning the reasons for the British colonization of Australia. Blainey's explanation made good sense to me. While working on my doctoral thesis on 'Captain James Cook's influence on the British Romantic poets', I had read widely in the narratives of Cook's voyages – in popular abridgements of them, in extracts published in such venues as the *Monthly Magazine* and the *Gentleman's Magazine*, which had wide circulation, and in geography books intended for all levels of reader, from informed adults to young children. In these varied works, the value of the islands of the south-western Pacific Ocean (New Caledonia, Norfolk Island and New Zealand) as sources of naval materials was frequently mentioned.

Let me give just two examples from the 1780s. Anna Seward – known as the 'Swan of Lichfield' – published her *Elegy on Captain Cook* in 1780. This popular work went into a fourth edition in 1784. One of the great explorer's accomplishments, Seward pointed out, was the bringing of new botanical species to Europe:

> First gentle Flora – round her smiling brow
> Leaves of new forms, and flowers uncultured glow;
> Thin folds of vegetable silk,* behind,
> Shade her white neck …

* *Vegetable Silk*: In New Zealand is a flag [flax] of which the natives make their nets and cordage. The fibres of this vegetable are longer and stronger than our hemp and flax; and some, manufactured in London, is as white and glossy as fine silk. This valuable vegetable will probably grow in our climate.[24]

In the *Geographical Magazine*, F.W. Martyn told readers that if this plant were to be cultivated in Britain, 'it might prove of more real benefit ... than the productions of all the islands which our circumnavigators have discovered for a century past'.[25] This prospect may seem extravagant now, but at the time it accorded with the fundamental reality that Blainey highlighted. No matter how sceptically mid-twentieth-century historians viewed the possibility, it did not appear far-fetched to those who contemplated Britain's imperial needs in the 1780s.

So, when I moved into the history department, I set out to see if I could find more evidence to support this explanation. As I published the early results of my research, I received much the same reaction as Dallas and Blainey had. First Alan Atkinson and David Mackay, then Mollie Gillen, were as sceptical as the previous group of historians had been that the desire to find a new source of naval materials was a significant factor in the decision to establish the Botany Bay colony. Another lively debate followed, extending from the mid-1970s into the 1980s.[26] It is again true to say that no fundamental agreement emerged. Indeed, I must admit (somewhat ruefully) that nobody – or at least, very few – seemed to believe Frost either.

As I continued my research in the archives, mostly in Britain but also in North and South America, Europe and New Zealand, greatly expanding my knowledge of British imperialism in the last decades of the eighteenth century, I came to revise my earlier views significantly. It was not that, as you will see, I ceased to believe in the force of the 'naval materials' motive, but rather that I came to understand that this was an adjunct to a much larger plan, one developed principally by William Pitt and his closest advisers Lord Mulgrave and Henry Dundas, with the participation of Lord Hawkesbury, the president of the Board of Trade, Sir Joseph Banks and others. Their aim was to expand British commerce throughout the Indian and Pacific oceans. If this over-arching plan were to succeed, Britain would need bases and resources along or adjacent to the major sea routes, ports where ships might be resupplied and whence, in wartime, attacks against enemy colonies might be launched.

\*

As I mentioned earlier, in the course of my research over the past thirty-five years, as against the hundred or so documents printed in *Historical Records of New South Wales*, I have gathered some 2500 documents relating to the decision to colonize New South Wales and the mounting of the First Fleet. It is inevitable that historical analysis based on such a vastly expanded record will differ very significantly from that based on the old, fragmentary one.

The real story of the Botany Bay decision is much more complex than the explanation that has prevailed for two hundred years. It is also much more interesting. Australians deserve to know it. It is my story here.

# 1.

# *Eighteenth-Century England: Crime*

UNLESS THEY BE IMPOSED ON AN alien population by a conqueror, or by a group of religious zealots, the laws of a country do not function independently of the society from which they arise. It is therefore necessary that I say something about English society and laws in the eighteenth century before examining in detail the practice of convict transportation and the decision to colonize New South Wales. Elsewhere in this study, I use the term 'Britain' to signify the 'United Kingdom' of England and Scotland formed by the Act of Union in 1707. However, as there were significant regional differences, in what follows I mostly confine myself to English circumstances. (Some of the statistics I cite cover more than England; I have indicated this when it is so.) It is impossible to sketch the nature of a complex society in a brief compass without resorting to some platitudes, so you may find some in this chapter.

\*

English society in the first half of the eighteenth century still strongly reflected the medieval structures upon which it was based. At its peak were the monarch, his or her immediate family and the nobles, both secular and ecclesiastical (the Church of England having become the established church under Henry VIII). Beneath these were the prosperous landowners and merchants; the 'middling classes' of professional people, lesser merchants, tradesmen and farmers; and the sturdy yeomen-farmers who plowed their strips and ran domestic animals on the commons, and whose wives and children augmented the family income with produce and spinning. Then there were servants and labourers, and the poor (commonly classed as either 'deserving' or 'undeserving' according to their inclination to work or to be idle).

Although political power was centred on London, in the first half of the eighteenth century English society remained predominantly rural, with the village at its core. The cultivation of grains, fruits and vegetables was widespread in the south of England, while grain fields marked its fertile northern reaches. The keeping of horses, dairy cattle, sheep and the smaller domestic animals was ubiquitous.

English rural life was regulated by a complex mixture of statute law, common law and immemorial custom. To the socially and politically very conservative Edmund Burke, contemplating the havoc wreaked across the English Channel by the French Revolution, this society was just about as near to perfection as Earth might offer. 'Society is indeed a contract', he wrote:

> It is a partnership in all science; a partnership in all art; a partnership in every virtue, and in all perfection. As the ends of such a partnership cannot be obtained in many generations, it becomes a partnership not only between those who are living, but between those who are living, those who are dead, and those who are to be born. Each contract of each particular state is but a clause in the great primaeval contract of eternal society, linking the lower with the higher natures, connecting the visible and invisible world, according to a fixed compact sanctioned by the inviolable oath which holds all physical and all moral natures, each in their appointed place. This law is not subject to the will of those, who by an obligation above them, and infinitely superior, are bound to submit their will to that law … If that which is only submission to necessity should be made the object of choice, the law is broken, nature is disobeyed, and the rebellious are outlawed, cast forth, and exiled, from this world of reason, and order,

and peace, and virtue, and fruitful penitence, into the antagonist world of madness, discord, vice, confusion, and unavailing sorrow.

And were all this not true, he concluded, 'man could not by any possibility arrive at the perfection of which his nature is capable, nor even make a remote and faint approach to it'.[1]

Burke's view was impossibly rosy. For whatever its satisfactions, eighteenth-century English society was also deeply flawed. It exhibited vast extremes of wealth and privilege on the one hand and poverty on the other. Scant education – if any – was available to the majority of the population. The sick who could afford it might have the help of apothecaries (chemists) or doctors; but common folk were usually able to draw only on the resources of 'wise women' and their 'simples'. The parish might provide some relief to the old who had no family support and the destitute; but if the destitute were able-bodied they were put into the work house to earn their keep, and parishes were under no obligation to help strangers. The leisure of childhood was not available to the offspring of the labouring poor, who commonly went to work from the age of three or four.

While most statistics for the eighteenth century are uncertain, there were about 5 million people in England in 1750. There were a number of provincial towns and cities with populations in the tens of thousands (up to about 30,000, although it is possible that Bristol and Manchester had more) and one grand metropolis, London, which by mid-century contained perhaps 650,000 people. A number of these cities – Portsmouth, Plymouth, Bristol, Liverpool and, of course, London – were ports through which Britain traded with the world. Britain possessed an extensive merchant marine, which sailed to North America and the West Indies, around the coasts of Europe and the Mediterranean, and to West Africa and Asia. The Royal Navy was superior to the military marines of Britain's Continental neighbours. Unlike these rivals, however, Britain did not maintain a standing army, as prevailing wisdom held that this would be inimical to true English liberty, for it would give a tyrant the means to impose his dictatorship.

London was also the financial and manufacturing centre of the country, and it was here that the extremes of society were most starkly evident. A visitor moving westwards from Covent Garden saw the royal palaces, the imposing houses of parliament, the lavish townhouses of the nobility and the wealthy merchants, and great churches; not far in the other direction, in East London, there was the scarcely imaginable squalor of the poor, the unemployed and the criminal underclass. In 1751, the novelist and magistrate Henry Fielding offered this harrowing account of some of the city's notorious 'rookeries'. He drew first on the testimony of the High Constable of Holborn, who had reported:

That in the parish of St Giles's there are great numbers of houses set apart for the reception of idle persons and vagabonds, who have their lodgings there for twopence a night: that in the above parish, and in St George, Bloomsbury, one woman alone occupies seven of these houses, all properly accommodated with miserable beds from the cellar to the garret, for such twopenny lodgers; that in these beds, several of which are in the same room, men and women, often strangers to each other, lie promiscuously, the price of a double bed being no more than threepence, as an encouragement to them to lie together; that as these places are thus adapted to whoredom, so are they no less provided for drunkenness, gin being sold in them all at a penny a quartern; so that the smallest sum of money serves for intoxication; that in the execution of search warrants, Mr Welch rarely finds less than twenty of these houses open for receipt of all comers at the latest hours; that in one of these houses, and that not a large one, he has numbered 58 persons of both sexes, the stench of whom was so intolerable, that it compelled him in a very short time to quit the place.

Fielding went on:

I myself once saw in the parish of Shoreditch, where two little houses were emptied of near 70 men and women; amongst whom was one of the prettiest girls I had ever seen, who had been carried off by an Irishman, to consummate her marriage on her wedding night, in a room where several others were in bed at the same time.

If one considers the destruction of all morality, decency and modesty; the swearing, whoredom, and drunkenness, which is eternally carrying on in these houses, on the one hand, and the excessive poverty and misery of most of the inhabitants on the other, it seems doubtful whether they are more the objects of detestation, or compassion; for such is the poverty of these wretches, that, upon searching all the above number, the money found upon all of them (except the bride, who, as I afterwards heard, had robbed her mistress) did not amount to one shilling; and I have been credibly informed, that a single loaf has supplied a whole family with their provisions for a week. Lastly, if any of these miserable creatures fall sick (and it is almost a miracle, that stench, vermin, and want should ever suffer them to be well) they are turned out in the streets by their merciless host or hostess, where, unless some parish officer of extraordinary charity relieves them, they are sure miserably to perish, with the addition of hunger and cold to their disease.[2]

Samuel Johnson famously said, 'when a man is tired of London, he is tired of life; for there is in London all that life can afford'.[3] And it is true that eighteenth-century London teemed with life. There was a myriad employments, some of them regular, others most precarious. There were shopkeepers and skilled workers; furniture makers and watch makers; carriers, labourers and watermen; chair-men and servants; rag-and-bone gatherers; even, God help us, dog-shit gatherers (it was used to dry leather); and of course pickpockets and prostitutes.

And all about was variegated activity. At the beginning of the 1790s, for example, William Wordsworth found the city, with its rich and imperial splendour and its street-life, a great spectacle. He viewed its grand buildings, including the dozens of churches; went to its theatres; observed its shopkeepers, labourers, beggars, criminals, prostitutes and show people; heard its notable preachers; visited parliament to hear its famed speakers; discussed politics with its liberal reporters and radical intellectuals. He was struck by the energy of the people and the place, by the city's bustle of commerce and labour, and by the variety of entertainment available in it – at the theatres, where pickpockets and prostitutes found rich returns; at more popular venues such as Sadler's Wells, with its 'singers, rope-dancers, giants and dwarfs, clowns, conjurors, posture-masters, harlequins, amid the uproar of the rabblement';[4] and in the streets, where spectators might routinely see acrobats, jugglers, exotic minstrels, dancing dogs, camels ridden by monkeys, and sometimes the new-fangled hot-air balloons.

But for many men, women and children in the great city, life was a desperate struggle for survival. Food was often meagre and of poor quality – fish, for example, was usually rotten by the time it arrived from the North Sea ports; bread was easy to adulterate with such things as peas and barley or, worse, alum, chalk, lime and white lead; good meat cost too much for the poor to be able to afford it; and, as Fielding observed, gin was the oblivion of the masses. Scurvy was endemic in winter, when many of the poor simply starved. One observer commented on circumstances at the end of 1784:

> The people in general complain of the frost since Wednesday last. It has been too cold for rain … The Thames is not frozen but on the flats and edges of the shores. Thousands are however in distress, where the poor are so many and the means of subsistence so dear. The bargemen and gardeners are in the streets crying to the windows for charity.[5]

If the ubiquitous stench of cesspits and tanneries was not enough, summer's heat added that of the open sewer that was the River Thames, causing the rich to retreat to their country estates.

Death cast a heavy pall. With little town planning and no modern understanding of the causes of disease, eighteenth-century London was repeatedly swept by epidemics of smallpox, cholera, typhoid and typhus, which wreaked terrible havoc on malnourished bodies. It is estimated that one infant in three born in London died before the age of two. In the East End, 55 per cent of children died before they were five, and the average age of death was thirty. In many years deaths in the population exceeded births, so that the total was maintained only by the annual migration of up to 10,000 persons from country areas.

*

By the mid-eighteenth century, there were changes building that would in the next hundred years transform English society. First, there were marked improvements in travel and transportation infrastructure. Roads, which while the responsibility of the parishes had often been only meandering quagmires, began to improve with the introduction of Turnpike Trusts. These were bodies set up by acts of parliament to collect tolls, which were used to keep roads in good repair. Between 1748 and 1770, the number of Trusts increased from 160 to 530, and turnpike mileage was quadrupled. Then, in the last quarter of the century, came the technique of macadamisation, which also led to better roads. The first canal was opened in 1761, and the number progressively increased. (Between 1790 and 1793, for example, some fifty-three canal navigation acts passed through parliament; by 1815 there were 2600 miles of canals.)

What is known as the Agricultural Revolution also took hold. While there is much disagreement about the nature of this change and the time of its onset, it certainly involved the recognition that large-scale farming was more efficient and productive than the immemorial cultivation of small plots and commons grazing, and that the rotation of crops allowed farmlands to remain fertile. At the core of this change were the consolidation of established farms and the enclosure of common land, and the introduction of new crops that both renewed fertility and provided fodder to support larger numbers of animals, which in turn produced more manure for fertilizing fields. As each enclosure of commons had to be legislated, the parliamentary records offer a broad indication of the growth of the Agricultural Revolution. There was one enclosure act passed between 1700 and 1710, and thirty-eight between

1740 and 1750. Between 1750 and 1800 there were 5000. The amount of land enclosed or newly brought into cultivation in this period seems to have been in the order of 2 million to 3 million acres; during the course of the century, agricultural production seems to have risen by about 40 per cent.[6]

Although it led to better farming methods, which in turn supported a larger population, the Agricultural Revolution had some disastrous social consequences, impoverishing and displacing whole classes of yeomen-farmers and agricultural labourers. As the century drew to a close, this was one of the causes of the migration of people to the cities. In his articles for the *Political Register*, William Cobbett chronicled the transformation of the English countryside and the destruction of its traditional way of life:

> from one end of England to the other, the houses which formerly contained little farms and their happy families, are now seen sinking into ruins, all the windows except one or two stopped up, leaving just light enough for some labourer, whose father was, perhaps, the small farmer, to look back upon his half-naked and half-famished children, while, from this door, he surveys all around him the land teeming with the means of luxury to his opulent and overgrown master ... We are daily advancing to that state in which there are but two classes of men, *masters*, and *abject dependants*.[7]

Such accounts may be somewhat simplistic. The population of the United Kingdom as a whole seems to have increased steadily through the century, from about 9.4 million to about 15.9 million, or by 70 per cent. By the beginning of the nineteenth century there were simply more people (particularly young people) to gravitate to the cities and towns. And gravitate they did, often to find themselves living in bitter poverty. Cobbett observed of Coventry in 1817, for example, that it had a population of 20,000, of whom more than 8000 were 'miserable paupers'.[8]

The other great change that was building throughout the second half of the eighteenth century was the Industrial Revolution, but here again we need to be careful about when we locate its emergence. It is true that Matthew Boulton started his Soho Manufactory, now recognized as a proto metal-working factory, outside Birmingham in the 1760s and that, in partnership with its inventor, James Watt, he was deploying the steam engine in the Cornish coal mines from the mid-1770s. However, the substantial effects of the Industrial Revolution, with steam power driving an increased capacity for mass manufacture, really appeared only in the last two decades of the century. James Hargreaves developed his spinning jenny in the mid-1760s, which simplified, quickened and cheapened the making of cloth; in the 1770s Samuel Crompton invented his spinning mule, which when combined with the jenny allowed the manufacture of many different kinds of yarn. In 1785, James Watt patented his fourth steam engine, the one that would be harnessed to the new spinning and weaving equipment developed by Edmund Cartwright. In 1783, Henry Cort developed his puddling process, which allowed iron to be smeltered with coal and markedly improved quality.

Even if the Industrial Revolution was only beginning to gain pace in the 1780s, however, to far-sighted people the future it proclaimed was already clear. For example, in 1787 the Prime Minister, William Pitt, the president of the Board of Trade, Lord Hawkesbury, and Sir Joseph Banks developed a plan to obtain breadfruit from the Pacific islands to feed the slaves in the West Indies, who would grow cotton for Britain's mills, which would produce cloth to be sold in East Asia. This elaborate scheme revealed an understanding that the mechanization of manufacturing offered the prospect of great returns.

The evidence of this change was soon all about. As one historian has pointed out, 'after 1782, almost every available statistical series of industrial output reveals a sharp upward turn ... More than half the growth in the shipments of coal and the mining of copper, more that three-quarters of the increase of broadcloths, four-fifths of that of printed cloth, and nine-tenths of the exports of cotton goods were concentrated in the last eighteen years of the eighteenth century'. Similarly, in 1788 the annual production of pig iron was 60,000 tons; in 1796 it was 125,000 tons, the number of blast furnaces having increased from 85 to 125.[9]

By the turn of the nineteenth century, swelled by migration from the countryside, the populations of the industrializing provincial cities were growing, with those of Bristol, Birmingham, Leeds, Liverpool and Manchester now exceeding 50,000.

*

While some of the structures of authority that controlled eighteenth-century English life are quite familiar to us (the monarchy, parliament, the courts, the church), others are very strange. By and large, ours is a highly regulated society, what with the imposing role of central government, including welfare support; a plethora of laws and very extensive legal practices to govern both public and private behaviour; extensive police forces with highly sophisticated surveillance methods; and town and local councils, which provide what we have come to consider essential goods and services, and which are in turn governed by networks of laws, by-laws and regulations.

In eighteenth-century England, however, central government was only just beginning what would become in the nineteenth century and afterwards its ever-increasing regulation of public and private life. Police forces existed only in embryonic form and the law's operation was, to our eyes, perfunctory. Much more then than now, what social cohesion there was usually depended on the recognition of customary rights and the maintenance of long-standing practices that bound together servants and masters, tenants and landlords, yeomen and gentry, nobles and the monarch. Those who lay claim to authority had to negotiate it rather than assume or enforce it. Nicholas Rodger has made this point eloquently of the Royal Navy:

> In the eyes of a modern officer, the discipline of the mid-eighteenth-century Navy would appear lax to the point of anarchy. Insubordination in every form and from every rank and rating in the Service was a daily part of life. Where modern officers expect to command, mid-eighteenth-century officers hoped to persuade. The fact that this did not alarm them was partly because it was a

feature of Service life to which they were completely accustomed, and no different from the weakness of civil authority on shore.[10]

Consider this example of indiscipline. Jacob Nagle was an American who sailed on the *Sirius* to Botany Bay. In 1797, after returning to England, he enlisted in the *Blanche*, one of Nelson's Mediterranean squadron. The captain of the *Blanche* was superseded by a more senior officer, Henry Hotham. In Jacob Nagle's barely literate prose (too colourful to modernize), Hotham bore

> the name of such a tarter [i.e., one of Genghis Khan's horde] by his own ships crew, that our ship mutinised and entierly refused him. He came on board [7 January 1797], had all the officers armed on the quarter deck and all hands turned aft to hear his commission read at the capstain head. They [i.e., the seamen] all cried out, 'No, no, no'. He asked what they had to say against [him]. One of the petty officers replyed that his ships company informed us that he was a dam'd tarter and we would not have him and went forward and turned the two forecastle guns aft with canester shot.

In the face of this tumult, Hotham retired to Nelson's ship and returned with the commodore's first lieutentant. Nagle continues:

> When on b[oar]d [the lieutentant] ordered all hands aft. The ship's company came aft. He called all the petty officers out, which ware call'd by name, and pareded them in a line on the quarter deck. 'Now, my lads, if you resist taking Capt[ain] Hotham as your capt[ain], every third man shall be hung'. The crew flew in a body forward to the guns with match in hand, likewise crowbars, handspikes, and all kinds of weapons they could get holt of and left him, Capt[ain] Hotham, and the officers standing looking at us. They consulted for a moment and returned on b[oar]d Commodere Nelson's [ship].

The standoff was only resolved when Nelson himself came on board and assured the crew that if Hotham mistreated them, he would rectify the situation. As Nagle recorded triumphantly: 'Ameditely there was three chears given and Capt[ain] Hotham shed tears'.[11]

As at sea, so on land. As R.W. Malcolmson has pointed out:

The exercise of established authority in eighteenth-century England was not only subtle and complex, it was also very uneven in its impact and effectiveness. In some parts of the country authority was unchallenged and securely enforced; in other areas the exercise of authority was tenuous, uncertain and often ineffectual … In one type of community – perhaps a small market-town or a dominant squire's parish – we detect evidence of firm social discipline, outward deference and quiescence; in other places we uncover a social reality of dissent, frequent social conflict and plebeian independence … For in many parts of England the formal institutions of power were neither deeply rooted nor widely respected; the populations of these places were partly withdrawn from, and sometimes resistant to, the exercise of 'lawful' authority.[12]

Let me summarize the behaviour of that class of persons that Malcolmson researched in detail. The area of Gloucester to the east of Bristol, known as the Kingswood Chase, was partly deforested and rich in coal. In the first half of the eighteenth century, the men who mined the coal and those who transported it to Bristol were notorious for their refusal to accept authority and for their more general lawlessness – notorious for, as John Wesley succinctly put it, 'neither fearing God nor regarding man'. Repeatedly, since they did not believe that they should have to pay tolls to get their coal to market, they gathered in their hundreds to destroy turnpike gates. They counterfeited coins. They broke into houses. They stole horses and sheep. They robbed travellers on the Bath and Bristol roads. They threatened violence (at one point promising to set fire to houses, and even to a whole town) to obtain the release of 'brethren' who had been arrested. Armed with clubs, staves and even muskets, they turned out in large numbers in support of other groups with popular grievances, such as the Bristol labourers and Wiltshire weavers, defying magistrates who read them the riot act. The Kingswood Chase colliers were, all in all, 'a set of ungovernable people'.[13]

*

In eighteenth-century English society, then, the bonds of civility were often fragile and easily broken, and authority was often weak or absent. It was therefore a society in which crime might easily flourish. There has probably never been an age since the beginning of the world when respectable citizens have not lamented that crime was increasing; but given the fewer checks to its progress in eighteenth-century England, it is difficult to avoid the conclusion that it impinged more on daily life then than it does now.

The greatest offence was treason – the high treason of rebellion against, or violence upon the person of the King, and the lesser treason of wife against husband, or servant against master. Below treason in the hierarchy of enormous offences were murder with malicious intent (that is, premeditated), manslaughter, rape (which, because of evidentiary difficulties, was often tried as attempted rape), infanticide, robbery with violence, burglary (heinous because it caught householders unawares at night) and horse-stealing. The common denominator linking this group of offences was violence against the person; contemporaries condemned them particularly because 'they endanger life and safety, as well as property; and … render the condition of society wretched, by a sense of personal insecurity'.[14]

Then there were clusters of lesser crimes: breaking into a house (i.e., when no one was present); stealing without violence from the person (i.e., picking pockets); stealing from a shop or from ships in the river; receiving stolen goods; sheep- and cattle-stealing; theft of small animals and items, such as hens and ducks, turnips and fruit; sexual assault, particularly of children; coining and debasing the coinage (i.e., adding to the number in circulation, whether by forging coins or by combining fragments chipped from several coins to create new ones); forging bank

27

drafts and wills; stealing from the post office; doing business on the Sabbath; keeping a bawdy house; poaching and the taking of wood from forests; shooting at someone, even if that person was not wounded; rioting; and vagrancy, particularly where idle and dissolute persons were suspected of 'pilfering'.

Inevitably, the great metropolis of London was where crime in all its varieties flourished. There were more people and a greater range of goods to be stolen than in smaller towns and the countryside. The buildings and narrow streets provided greater opportunity for escape and concealment, while the 'bawdy houses' and 'flash taverns' made it easier to pass on stolen goods. And crucially, the influx into the city of large numbers of feckless labourers and young people from all over the country meant that vice was more widespread and social bonds weaker than in more settled communities, where people might have known each other for decades and families lived side by side for generations.

Prostitution provides a case in point. Contemporary estimates of the number of prostitutes in London in the second half of the eighteenth century range from 50,000 to 62,000. A large proportion of these women perhaps sold themselves only occasionally; but even if we then reduce the total by half, we are left with something like 25,000 to 30,000 'working girls' servicing a male population of about 350,000, which suggests a very high incidence of paid-for sex (and this does not take into account courtesans or official mistresses). In these circumstances, it was inevitable that family and community bonds be weaker than those who lived in villages were accustomed to, and society therefore less stable.

*

In 1785 the *Edinburgh Magazine* listed the various sets and subsets of thieves, both in the metropolis and in the countryside, each of which had its particular skills and mystique.[15] At their head were the 'high-pads' or 'highwaymen', who operated on the major roads of the kingdom, frequently just outside town limits (because highwaymen too needed taverns at which to refresh, and beds in which to sleep). 'This class sit at the head of the table, pay a double share of the bill; and whenever it is necessary or expedient that one die for the credit or conveniency of the rest, the high-pads claim a preference.' Often, highwaymen went about in small gangs, such as that led by Ralph Wilson, who claimed to have operated along all the coach routes servicing London:

> One Morning we robbed the Cirencester, the Worcester, the Gloucester, the Oxford, and Bristol stage-coaches, all together; the next morning the Ipswich and Colchester, and a third morning perhaps the Portsmouth coach. The Bury coach has been our constant customer. I think we have touched that coach ten times.[16]

A romantic tinge of the Robin Hood sort often attached to these 'gentlemen of the road' or 'of the shade'. One young practitioner presented himself to a group of travellers 'dressed in a blue surtout coat, brown cut wig, a black crepe mask over his face, mounted on a bright bay gelding'. Two others, who in the space of a week 'committed many robberies on Blackheath and the Kentish roads', were 'handsome young men' who had 'all the exterior appearance of gentlemen'.[17] Crowds would gather at the haunts of highwaymen to watch them setting out on their business.

Sometimes highwaymen did conduct themselves with a peculiar sense of honour, as shown by this December 1786 story:

> A gentleman, from the west of England, went to London a few weeks ago to receive a legacy of £500, which he proposed to bring with him into the country. His servant, apprised of his master's errand, imprudently talked of it at an inn upon the road. A person in the room, in appearance a tradesman, but in reality a highwayman, overheard the conversation, and determined to possess himself of the booty. Pursuing the gentleman to London, he watched all his motions, and on his return into the country, was ready to follow him. On the other side of Hounslow, near the turnpike on Smallberry Green, the robber came up with the chaise, and passed it full gallop, but was stopped at the gate, not having a single penny to pay the toll. He appeared greatly confused, took out his handkerchief,

and begged the turnpikeman to take it as a pledge. The gentleman in the chaise having observed the transaction, on his coming up, enquired the cause; and promising to return the handkerchief to the owner, paid the penny for him. He presently overtook the highwayman, and, ordering his chaise to stop, 'Pray Sir', said he, 'is this your handkerchief? If so, I fear you are in great distress.' 'I am indeed, sir', replied the man, 'in the greatest, that is possible.' 'Allow me, then', rejoined the gentleman, 'to relieve your immediate wants'; and pulling out his purse, presented him with five guineas. 'Your generosity', said the highwayman, 'disarms me. Your five guineas have saved your five hundred'; and turning his horse, immediately rode off.[18]

But the highwaymen's strikes were not always benign. Witnessing an attack by a group of three men, a woman called out that 'she knew the rogues', who thereupon cut out her tongue.[19]

Then there were the 'collectors', the 'low robbers', or 'foot-pads', 'those who take charge of the cross ways, concurrent departments of the road, by-lanes, or wherever a purse may be taken, a pocket rifled, or a stab given with security'. These sorts of thieves, the *Edinburgh Magazine* explained, 'are bloody, cowardly villains, who lurk in the dark, loiter about hedges and old houses, and stroll out in the evenings in groups. Their orders are to take whatever they can, to strip rich and poor, and to murder or mangle whoever has nothing, gives what he has with reluctance, or makes the least resistance.' The London newspapers of the time are rife with reports of good citizens being assaulted, robbed and sometime maimed in the street, often in broad daylight, even while crossing London Bridge.

Then there was the 'rifleman' or 'budge', the person 'who is always strolling about, down lanes, up courts, lounging in unfrequented streets, and hanging in markets, or about stalls, where those who sell, and those who buy, are often over-busy, or over-careless; and he generally take aim so well, that he seldom or never misses the mark'.

The 'diver', or 'pick-pocket', 'occupies a situation of infinite danger and address. The practitioners in this branch of the system formerly went single. They were then called *bung-nippers;* because with a *horn thumb* and a *sharp knife*, they generally cut off the pocket and its contents.' These thieves were often 'well-dressed, and are constant frequenters of the theatres, the chapels-royal, both houses of parliament, and all other public places'.

The 'diver' often worked in tandem with the 'bulk'. This person's role 'was to create quarrels, in order that, by gathering a crowd, their enterprises may be carried on with effect, and without observation'.

Then there was the 'jilt' or 'ferret' or 'house-bug', a woman who, 'connected with some of the gang, takes lodgings, especially in alehouses or taverns, and with pick-locks opens all the chests and trunks to which she has access; and having selected what she likes, fastens them, discharges her lodgings, and goes off without suspicion'.

The 'prigger' or 'prancer' was he who confined his activities to stealing horses. 'This line is recruited from Newmarket, and the various mews and livery stables in the metropolis.'

The 'ken-miller' 'robs houses in the night-time, by breaking them open, getting in at the window, sprawling down the chimney, and nestling under the beds. These expeditions are generally executed by stout and resolute parties, who carry on their depredations with great system. Their implements of forcible entrance, when that is necessary, are altogether irresistible; but they generally prefer that mode which is accompanied with as little noise as possible. A watch is carefully set on every pass, and their retreat, in the event of discovery or disturbance, effectually secured.'

The 'scourers' 'are a set of people who have lately infested the houses situated on the side of the river'. Most of these were reportedly unemployed sailors, who robbed from ships and lighters.

Finally, there were the 'petty hawkers' or 'shop-lifters', 'whose chief employ is to cheapen [that is, to ask the price of or barter for] goods from place to place, till an opportunity offers of secreting such articles as are most commodious for carrying off without detection'.

*

The provincial cities, market towns, farms and sheep-walks of the country were also the scenes of other varieties of crime: riots by the labouring poor; the stealing or maiming of domestic animals; the poaching of game from gentlemen's parks; the illicit gathering of fuel; the cutting down of orchards and forest plantations. Poaching was often carried out by gangs whose members, like their city confreres, might swear oaths not to betray each other. And all along the southern coasts of England there operated smugglers intent on defrauding His Majesty's customs revenues, who frequently resorted to violence to avoid arrest.

Sometimes, as E.P. Thompson has shown,[20] this rural lawlessness arose from a sense of injustice (for instance, at sharp increases in food prices in times of dearth), or from the removal of a customary right by a rapacious landlord (such as the traditional right to gather wood in forests 'by hook or by crook'), or as a conscious act of class rebellion. At other times, however, it was simply vicious.

\*

The closest contemporary Australian equivalent of eighteenth-century English society is not to be found in our well-ordered suburbs or our by and large tranquil country towns, but in the inner city of Melbourne on a Friday or Saturday night, or in the western suburbs of Sydney, with their raucous violence and warring criminal gangs.

Lord Sydney gave one indication of just how unruly life in London could be in March 1778, when he complained in parliament that crime was increasing, and that 'in the course of the winter every day furnished a fresh account of some daring robbery or burglary ... Scarcely a night passed in which there were not robberies committed in Park Lane, and firing of pistols heard'.[21] With his lavish houses, servants and carriages, however, Sydney was largely cocooned from the violence all about him. At this time, as old Bow Street officers later remembered, gangs terrorized Londoners. A constable could not 'walk in Duck Lane, Gravel Lane or Cock Lane, without a party of five or six men along with him, they would have cut him to pieces if he was alone', reported one officer. Another recalled that the members of these gangs 'used to be ready to pop at a man as soon as he let down his glass'.[22] Typical of the all-too-frequent 'atrocious' assaults was an occasion when three foot-pads slashed their victim's face with a sword ('so that his teeth and jaw-bone could be seen'), knocked him down and stole one shilling from him before running off.[23]

Mayhem was not confined to the metropolis, however. At the beginning of January 1784, 'on Monday morning early the house of Philip Martin, Esquire, near Epping, was broke open by some villains, three of whom entered the apartments, while the other stood sentry at the door. Their faces were all blacked; they were well-armed, and after behaving in a very inhuman manner to the servants, carried off plate and other valuable articles to a very considerable amount.' In January 1787, William Fitzgerald and John Millan were convicted of assaulting James Richards in the main street of Exeter and 'robbing him of a linen handkerchief and 6 shillings'.[24]

These were minor instances of the ever-present lawlessness. The two following stories show how extreme this might become. Lewis Gunner was a Hampshire gamekeeper and gang leader who terrorised his community with arrogant violence. He was, as one magistrate put it, 'of a proud, insulting and revengeful temper'. He always carried loaded pistols, and he and his men shot dogs, seized nets, lit fires and maimed farm animals. He was arrested and sentenced for shooting at an enemy, a capital offence. In response, his men rampaged, burning houses and barns. He was reprieved on condition that he transport himself out of England for fourteen years. But once he was released, he and his men intensified their violence, threatening more fires, stabbing animals and shooting at people. They coerced some of the community into signing a petition for him to receive a full pardon. As one frightened citizen complained to authorities, 'No doubt he will add names enough ... for very few would have the courage to deny him. Our thatched buildings and enclosed country, my Lord, lay both our lives and fortunes at the mercy of such desperate villains.'[25]

After the Maidstone quarter sessions in January 1785, the chairman wrote to Sydney (now Home Secretary) of the particularly troubling case of Alexander Rimington, 'formerly a notorious smuggler in the neighbourhood … but later employed by the Excise officers as an assistant', who had committed a long series of outrages:

[He] was indicted at the Michaelmas sessions for an assault, and the bill found by the grand jury [that is, the indictment was found to be 'true' – valid in legal form and having substance]. He was apprehended and committed to jail; and then on finding securities for his appearance to answer the complaint, was discharged. He surrendered this session, and on his appearance in the town a man seized him, and charged him with robbing him on the highway in June last. He was accordingly tried for this fact and found guilty, and sentenced to transportation for seven years. On his return to prison, he confessed the fact.

One great reason for my troubling your Lordship with this story is that strong hints have been given that our sentence signified not a pin, for that such application would be made for him to the King, as would ensure his pardon. And as he has long been a terror to this part of the country, I thought it proper that, if such application should be made, your Lordship might not be a stranger to the story. For this man, under pretence of being an assistant to the Excise officers, but without any officer in his company – and I think it clear they cannot delegate their authority – has stopped and searched innocent persons, totally unconcerned with smuggling, with great rudeness and barbarity. He has often broke open barns at a distance from any house, and stolen corn and hay for his and his companions' horses. He has seized goods from smugglers without any authority, and converted them to his own use. And there are two miserable men, who with their families are now kept by the parish, owing to their having been totally disabled by him, having been almost hacked to pieces. These men were indeed smugglers, but unarmed, and made no resistance. In a word, the outrages he has committed in this part of the country have been so enormous, that if he is not totally removed, nobody can be safe. The sense of

the people was fully shown by a burst of applause at his being convicted and sentenced, which I was never witness to before in a court
of justice.[26]

This prevailing lawlessness intensified with the demobilization of
tens of thousands of soldiers and sailors at the end of war. During conflict, as rogues were absorbed into the army and navy, the incidence of
assaults and property crimes diminished; after it, it rose sharply. Put
ashore at the Channel ports, far away from family and friends and with
no other means of support, many of the demobilized men soon squan-
dered their pay on women, alcohol and gambling; for such men, the
temptation to turn their martial skills to assault and robbery could be
irresistible. Stephen Janssen, who was Lord Mayor of London in 1755,
observed:

> As a great many idle men and lads are taken into the sea and land
> service during a war, so we then find the gangs of robbers soon bro-
> ken and the business at the Old Bailey gradually diminished to half
> its duration in time of peace nor are half the number of criminals
> condemned. For in some years of war they have not amounted to
> twenty, whereas in peace they have arisen to seventy, eighty and
> ninety. It is farther observable that at the conclusion of a war, through
> very bad policy, when we turn adrift so many thousand men, great
> numbers fall heedlessly to thieving as soon as their pockets are
> empty, and are at once brought to the gallows. The wiser ones survive
> a while by listing with experienced associates, by which means in a
> few years, those numerous and desperate gangs of murderers, house-
> breakers and highwaymen have been formed, which have of late
> stuck such a terror within the metropolis and twenty miles around.[27]

After the war of 1776–83, for example, an estimated 160,000 soldiers
and sailors returned to England. Numbers of these were soon committing depredations. To give just a few examples from in and around
London in 1782–3: in Dorking, a female miller was set upon by five

sailors with pistols and cutlasses; two marines, similarly armed, robbed a higler (a person who sold provisions and other small items door to door); two soldiers and four sailors committed a number of robberies in Chelsea; and ten men 'armed with cutlasses and pistols, in two boats, boarded a vessel near Union Stairs, Wapping ... and stole thereabout two bales of woollens'.[28]

This lawlessness was general; as one country newspaper reported in October 1783, 'a great number of disbanded militiamen, who are too idle to return to their farming business, are robbing in all parts of the country; in Oxfordshire and Berkshire the highways are particularly infested with them'.[29] At least some of those responsible for this crime wave were soon filling the hulks and jails, and their swelling numbers was one of the factors that led the Pitt administration to resume transportation.

*

In 1751, Henry Fielding published *An Enquiry into the Causes of the Late Increase of Robbers*. Among other things, he pointed to the lower incidence of crime in the countryside than in London, where there was both more temptation and greater probability of escaping detection. Understanding that there would be less crime if people found it more difficult to profit from it, he proposed much stronger penalties for receivers of stolen goods (known as 'fences'). He urged the strengthening of community policing and recommended compensation for those bringing prosecutions, to compensate them for loss of income while they attended court.

Fielding opened his study with this striking assertion: 'I make no doubt, but that the streets of [London], and the roads leading to it, will shortly be impassable without the utmost hazard; nor are we threatened with seeing less dangerous gangs of rogues among us, than those which the Italians call the Banditti.'[30]

There are earlier instances of this word in English,[31] but Fielding's work gave it widespread currency and by the 1780s 'banditti' had become a commonplace term. In May 1781, Richard Camplin used it to describe the convict soldiers sent to Africa. One Bow Street constable spoke of the London street gangs of the time as 'the bandittis'. Another commentator complained bitterly of the 'tribes of banditti who lay the rest of the community under continual contributions'. A third bemoaned the existence of 'the dreadful banditti that infest this kingdom', 'the most formidable and dreadful number of abandoned wretches, that for a series of years have committed their depredations on the public'. Another called the foresters of Selwood, in Somerset, 'a desperate clan of banditti', and Admiral Milbanke described the Irish convicts landed at Newfoundland in 1789 as 'a Banditti'.[32] In the public imagination, 'banditti' was short-hand for those rogues who preferred a life of crime to honest labour, who as often as not operated in gangs, and who were willing to use violence, either to rob or to effect their escape. These were men who held the law in contempt, who might form 'leagues of friendship' and swear diabolical oaths, who were feared by respectable citizens and who were considered by judges to be incorrigible.

# 2.

# *Eighteenth-Century England: Punishment*

IT IS NOTORIOUS THAT IN THE middle of the eighteenth century English law contained some 160 crimes punishable by death, and that this number had increased to about 200 by the beginning of the nineteenth century. These totals suggest a frightful 'bloody code'. However, simply stating the number does not represent the situation properly. As various historians have pointed out, English law was not codified, and therefore punishment needed to be specified for each variant of a general crime – for instance, the punishment for each variety of larceny needed to be stated. In the nineteenth century, as the criminal code was overhauled and more comprehensive definitions developed, the number of crimes to which the death penalty was attached fell significantly.[1]

Before discussing the punishments given for the range of crimes prevalent in eighteenth-century England, I need to explain the peculiarity in English law known as the 'benefit of clergy'. Originating in medieval times, this device permitted members of religious orders who were convicted of public offences to claim the 'benefit' of clergy, and thereby escape being severely punished by secular courts.

Applying at first only to ordained priests, it was gradually extended to include religious clerks, and then to persons who were literate. (These were required to demonstrate this ability by reading a verse from the Psalms before they were sentenced.) The extension of this practice – a legal fiction, really – allowed those convicted of felonies to escape a mandatory death sentence.

In the course of the sixteenth century, authorities removed the benefit of clergy from the most serious crimes, including treason, murder and accessory to murder, infanticide, rape, highway robbery, robbery with violence, burglary, horse-stealing, and some forms of larceny. For these offences, conviction brought the death sentence regardless of literacy.

The list of crimes punishable by death and without the benefit of clergy was expanded in the eighteenth century to include appearing armed and with face blackened in public; shooting at someone; poaching deer, hares and other animals; stealing sheep or cattle; the theft of linen or cotton cloth valued at 10 shillings or more; the theft from a ship or wharf of goods valued at 40 shillings or more; grand larceny (where the goods taken were worth more than 1 shilling); theft from a shop, warehouse or stable of goods valued at more than 5 shillings; and forgery.

For the grand and petty larcenies that remained 'clergyable', there were fundamentally two punishments. For grand larceny, this was branding on the base of the thumb, with release immediately afterwards. For petty larceny, it was whipping, either at a post or at the tail of a cart that travelled a prescribed distance in public. For some slight thefts and assault, there was the possibility of fining, which effectively involved the offender making some financial restitution to the victim. For some other forms of assault and for sexual offences there was a comparatively short imprisonment, which might also entail one period or more of 'exposure' in the pillory, a lockable wooden frame with holes for neck and arms. This last punishment might or might not be relatively benign, depending on whether the public sympathized with the criminal or not. If they did, then their throwing of rotten fruit or loose dirt might not have much effect beyond the humiliation involved. However, if the crowd was hostile, the consequences of being exposed in the pillory could be gruesome. In 1762, for example, the public turned on one old man convicted of a homosexual act, 'tore off his coat, waistcoat, shirt, hat, wig, and breeches, and then pelted and whipped him till he had scarcely any signs of life left; he was once pulled off the pillory, but hung by his arms till he was set up again and stood in that naked condition, covered with mud, till the hour was out, and then was carried back to Newgate'.[2] On another occasion, the London public threw rocks at a mannish woman who had been sentenced to the pillory for going through forms of marriage with two other women, causing her to lose her sight.

*

By the beginning of the eighteenth century, the view was widespread that the law was defective because it offered only a few punishments intermediate between death and branding or whipping. It was to remedy this defect that in 1718 parliament enacted legislation providing for felons whose crimes had not been of the most extreme nature to be transported to Britain's colonies in America for terms of seven years, fourteen years or life.

While there had earlier been some expulsions of felons from the kingdom, this act systematized the practice. The government let contracts to merchants to transport the convicts across the Atlantic Ocean on ships run and supplied at the merchant's expense. In the early 1720s, a merchant received £3 from the government for each convict taken. In 1727, this was raised to £5, though at times, when the demand for labour was strong in the colonies, the merchant might transport the convicts for no fee, knowing that he could cover his costs and make a profit by selling the labour of his charges at a higher than usual rate.[3]

On taking custody of convicts sentenced to transportation ('transports') the merchant had to sign certificates of 'jail delivery' and bonds for their safe conveyance to their destination, and for not assisting them to return to England before their sentences had expired. When he had delivered his cargo, he had to obtain certificates from the customs officer or the governor confirming that he had done so, for without these he would not receive his fees from the Treasury in London. Once in the American colonies, the merchant was able to sell the convicts' labour for the unexpired term of their sentences, up to the maximum of seven years that colonial laws permitted. Duncan Campbell, who was one of the principal merchants engaged in transportation in the 1760s and 1770s, recorded that he received on average £10 per man and £8 or £9 per woman, though for younger men, particularly those with skills such as carpentry or blacksmithing, he might receive £15 to £25.[4] And then there was the profit to be made from the return cargo, which might be timber or tobacco, or rum and sugar from the West Indies.

It was obviously in the merchants' interest to land their human cargo in as good health as possible, as the colonial merchants and planters seeking labourers did not wish to pay for those who were old or ill. And there is evidence that most of the merchants involved in the trade were usually diligent in this regard. Campbell estimated that about one-seventh of the men he transported, and one-fourteenth of the women, died between the time of jail delivery and disembarkation, mostly from smallpox and the prison scourge of typhus fever.

There were some other developments in the regimen of punishment in the course of the eighteenth century, the principal of which was imprisonment in a 'house of correction' with hard labour for periods of between three and twelve months. But for those felonies deemed not serious enough to warrant the death sentence, transportation remained the predominant form of intermediate punishment from 1718 until 1775, when the American colonies revolted.

In view of later Australian circumstances, there are other points worth making about transportation to North America. First, it was essentially a private business, for the role of central government ceased once merchants had signed contracts and taken custody of the convicts. Second, unless they did something in the colonies (such as absconding or assaulting or robbing) to give rise to a fresh record, most of the transports were simply absorbed into the general population. Presumably many of them eventually returned to Britain, but there are no figures. Third, the punishment involved in the sentence of transportation was essentially exile from Britain. From 1718, early return constituted a felony bearing the death sentence, with little prospect of reprieve.

There were ways of avoiding the forced labour that usually accompanied transportation, but these were in practice available only to those with money and influential friends. Felons might receive a reprieve if they undertook to transport themselves. For example, in 1775 Jonathan Biggott was convicted of highway robbery. He received a pardon of his death sentence on condition that he leave Britain 'within the space of two months' and not return for fourteen years.[5] Then there was the case of Nicholas Greenwell, embarked on the *Alexander*, one of the First Fleet ships. As they were on the point of sailing, he received a pardon 'on condition that he shall depart this kingdom within one month from the day on which he shall be discharged out of custody, and not to return to or be found within the same for the term of seven years'.[6] Or, persons might buy themselves out of servitude on disembarkation, by paying the contractor what he would have received for them on the labour market.

Although some authorities were expressing dissatisfaction with the practice of transportation to the American colonies in the 1760s, on the grounds that exiled felons could represent no lesson to would-be offenders at home and that it was too easy for them to return before their term was up, it was in the main a well-regarded punishment. The House of Commons committee that enquired into the resumption of transportation in 1785 reported:

that the old system of transporting to America answered every good purpose which could be expected from it; that it tended directly to reclaim the objects on which it was inflicted, and to render them good citizens; that the climate being temperate, and the means of gaining a livelihood easy, it was safe to entrust country magistrates with the discretionary power of inflicting it; that the operation of it was thus universally diffused over the whole island, as well as this metropolis; that it tended to break, in their infancy, those gangs and combinations which have since proved so injurious to the community; that it was not attended with much expense to the public, the convicts being carried out in vessels employed in the Jamaica or tobacco trade; ... that the colonies seem to have been sensible of the beneficial consequences of this

42

practice; that the convicts whose labour was so purchased were usually removed into the back country, and finding none of the temptations, in that new state of things, which occasioned their offences at home, it does not appear that the police or peace of the colonies suffered in any considerable degree by them.[7]

\*

What of the courts which sentenced criminals? To put the situation more simply than it was in some jurisdictions, there were essentially two levels of courts in the English counties in the eighteenth century. These were the quarter sessions, which, as the name suggests, were held four times a year. They were staffed by magistrates, who were also justices of the peace, and heard cases involving breaches of the peace, minor thefts such as of fruit and vegetables, less serious assaults, vagrancy and fraud. Often juries participated in these hearings, but sometimes cases might be heard in a 'summary' fashion by one or two magistrates sitting alone. The quarter session courts might sentence offenders to brief periods in 'houses of correction', or they might assess fines. The magistrates might also negotiate a private settlement between perpetrator and victim, which most often involved some payment in reparation, thus avoiding the need for a court hearing. As the quarter session courts did not deal with felonies carrying the death sentence, I shall not describe their workings in further detail.

The assizes constituted the second level of courts. Judges from the country's central (superior) courts conducted these hearings, twice a year in most counties (in spring and summer) but eight times a year at the Old Bailey, which had jurisdiction over London and Middlesex. In holding these hearings, the judges exercised four commissions – those of assize and of *nisi prius* (i.e., before an assize court rather than a superior one), which empowered them to deal with civil cases; and those of *oyer and terminer* ('to hear and determine') and jail delivery, which enabled them to deal with all criminal cases.

The procedure of a case coming before the assize judges was significantly different from that which we are used to, for our system employs mechanisms that were only just coming into use at the end of the eighteenth century. In effect, the victim of an assault or theft or serious fraud was also the prosecutor. He or she had to make a complaint to a magistrate, identify the nature of the crime and its perpetrator and, if possible, provide witnesses. The magistrate then turned the complainant's oral testimony into depositions. He also took depositions from the person or persons accused of the crime, without telling them of the charges against them. If the purported crime constituted a felony, the accused was imprisoned until the next assize hearing, which meant that the period of waiting for the trial might be as short as two or as long as eight months.

The assizes were conducted with a good deal of pomp, and were also the occasion of social events such as dinners and balls. Leading citizens of the municipality and county would welcome the judges on their arrival. After their commissions had been read formally in public ('published'), the judges would give the depositions to a grand jury, to determine if there was a *prima facie* case to answer. If the decision was yes, then the matter went to trial by jury, with the victim appearing to repeat their complaint and confirm their identification of the accused, and with the accused having the opportunity to challenge this identification, to question witnesses, provide an alibi, and present evidence of good character. Only late in the century did the habit develop of the accused employing a lawyer to help them challenge the evidence against them.

The English legal system in the eighteenth century was never so bloody as it now on the face of things appears. When a person was charged with and convicted of a crime (excepting the most serious offences), there was the potential for the final punishment to be mitigated. At each step the victim/prosecutor, judge and jury might collude to see that the full rigour of the law was not applied. For example, if in the indictment the stolen goods were wrongly identified as the property of William Jones rather than of his brother John Jones, the rightful owner, the case foundered. William Smith, the former chief justice of New York, attended various courts while in England after the Revolutionary War. He reported this case heard in December 1784:

Count Duroure was tried this morning at the Old Bailey on an indictment for attempting to kill Huxley Sandon by firing a pistol at him as he entered to take his wife. It was death by the Black Act ... The jury acquitted him agreeable to the charge of Baron Notham, the judge. The shooting was stated to be done 4 October in a hotel kept by John Sundy and James Brewer and the proof was that it was kept by James Sundy and John Brewer. Notham said the prosecutor was not obliged to say who kept the house, but since he had undertaken it he must prove the charge as made. The Count had seduced the wife of a man who had shown him civilities.[8]

Again, if the judge and the grand jury found that while a group of poachers had been taken beside a dead deer, and while the barrel of the musket used to shoot it was still warm, if there was no witness to identify which of the poachers had pulled the trigger, none of them had a case to answer. Or a judge might advise a victim or effectively instruct a jury that the evidence was insufficient to sustain a full charge, and that a lesser one should therefore be sought. Or, out of friendship or compassion, a prosecutor might deliberately understate the value of the goods stolen, so that a guilty verdict would not bring the mandatory death sentence. Or, a jury might convict not on the whole charge, but rather on a lesser one contained within it.

These habits of 'down-charging' or bringing in a 'partial' verdict were pervasive in the eighteenth-century legal system. For example, stating the value of the goods stolen from the person at 10 pence rather than 1 shilling (12 pence) meant that a jury avoided the need to find the criminal guilty of a capital felony, as did stating the value of goods taken from a shop at under 5 shillings or from a house or a ship in the River Thames at under 40 shillings. A jury finding someone guilty of the theft of a single spoon rather than the whole dinner service they had actually taken would have the same effect.

There was often a deliberate manipulation of the legal system. For example, one woman in Sussex stole sixty-one yards of lace, which would have been worth about £100. In the indictment, however, this was valued at 8 pence and a silk girdle at 2 pence, for a total of 10 pence. Another woman who had items taken from her house 'very humanely refused to say' that they were worth more than 39 shillings. The judge at one Shropshire assize told the jury dealing with a charge of the theft of twenty-four fowls 'that the matter of fact was so fully proved that they must find the prisoner guilty, but they would do well to consider of the value'; so that the jury found him guilty of 'felony to the value of 11 pence, at which the judge laughed heartily and said he was glad to hear that cocks and hens were cheap in this country'.[9]

Even when a crime had been adjudged so serious that it mandated a capital sentence, this might still be avoided by the exercise of the 'royal mercy', whereby, having learned of mitigating circumstances, or prominent citizens having come forward with character references, a judge might recommend to the Secretary of State that the King pardon the convicted felon on condition that a secondary punishment (usually transportation) be substituted.

Sir Dudley Ryder was chief justice of the Court of King's Bench in London. He presided over four sessions at the Old Bailey between 1754 and 1756, and at various assize hearings in the Home Counties. He kept detailed notes of the cases he heard and a diary, which together give a very good insight into the sentencing system then and the exercise of the royal prerogative of mercy.[10]

At Guildford in the summer of 1754, for example, Ryder refused to mitigate the death sentences of two burglars, because 'it was a very plain and bad case', but he reprieved two men guilty of the theft of animals because the evidence was 'not clear'. He refused to accept requests for clemency from two employers of twenty-year-old Richard Gilbert, convicted of highway robbery, because Gilbert had robbed twice on the same day. Similarly, in the case of Richard Tichner, he refused requests to recommend mercy from very powerful patrons who had made a direct plea to the King, because there was 'no reason to doubt' Tichner's guilt and 'there were no circumstances of alleviation'.[11]

Ryder was certainly not uncaring, however, when he saw a clear case of necessity driving a person to serious crime. Charged with the highway robbery of a woman, Thomas Rolf came before Ryder at the Old Bailey in October 1754. As he had been apprehended at the scene, the evidence against Rolf was clear; but during the trial it emerged that he had behaved courteously towards his victim, apologizing for his action and explaining that he was destitute, with a heavily pregnant wife and two small children. Ryder told the jury that, since 'compassion could not justify finding contrary to the truth', they must convict Rolf. However, when the jurors asked Ryder to intercede on the unfortunate man's behalf, he informed the Recorder of London of the circumstances. Rolf received a free pardon.[12]

It is clear that Ryder's practice was the norm. In 1772, Theodore Janssen published details of convictions and death sentences at the Old Bailey for the period 1749–71. Of 1121 persons sentenced to death, 443 were reprieved (or died before the sentence was carried out). The breakdown of these totals shows a steady application of mercy according to the descending seriousness of the crime. For example, 72 of 81 murderers were executed; 15 of 17 attempted murderers; 251 of 362 highway robbers; 118 of 208 burglars. Conversely, only 6 of 23 shop-lifters hanged; 22 of 90 animal thieves; 27 of 63 guilty of stealing from a house; and only 27 of 80 pickpockets.[13]

The use of the royal mercy to reduce the number of death sentences continued until the end of the century. For example, in September 1772, ten persons convicted of capital felonies at the Norfolk assize had their sentences altered to transportation on the recommendation of the justices.[14] Then, the following were convicted at the Oxford assize in the spring of 1787: Thomas Court, Thomas Roberts, Thomas Gilbert, William Jenkins, Isaac Williams of horse-stealing; John Aston, Luke Mapp, John Owen, David Jones and William Watkins of sheep-stealing; William Brooks of stealing cattle; Henry Foulk and William Garrett of having returned to England before their previous sentence of transportation had expired; James Gibbard of robbery and John Ashby of being an accessory to it; Thomas Holland, Robert Crumplin, James Murphy, Annan Hudson and Thomas Spencer of highway robbery; William Smith of picking pockets; Henry Gardiner of the theft of cloth; James

Cleaver of burglary; Hugh Pincot and Thomas Parker of theft from a dwelling place. These felons were all guilty of capital offences. However, since the judges recommended them 'as fit objects of the royal mercy', they were spared death on condition that they be transported to New South Wales.[15]

Indeed, sometimes a felon might receive more than one mark of His Majesty's mercy. Joseph Hall, for example, was twice reprieved from death sentences.[16] But this was unusual. More commonly, felons for whom someone was willing to speak up might expect only one mark of royal mercy. As the Under-Secretary of State commented about one criminal on whose behalf an influential friend had petitioned:

> I can see the propriety of omitting to propose any other punishment than that which Aylett is sentenced to suffer. If the Lord Chancellor thinks the man should not be exposed to the pillory, I dare say he will point out some other mode for punishing him. I think that in the course of my life I never heard of so infamous a character.[17]

Sometimes, too, such requests rankled with the officials in the Secretary of State's office, as in this October 1786 case:

> Since the receipt of your letter of the 1st inst, I have examined the report of the judge upon the case of James Hedding, in whose behalf Mr Rishton has so warmly interested himself, and I am very sorry to inform you that according to the judge's opinion it would not be proper to extend to the unfortunate convict any further mark of the King's mercy.
>
> I expect that the ships will proceed with the convicts to Botany Bay early in the next month, and I shall take care to provide for Hedding's conveyance thither in one of them, which I observe by his letter he desires may be his fate if a pardon cannot be obtained.[18]

But then, there were also instances when authorities acted to produce a result that was clearly justified. In April 1784 the *Mercury* was taking 170 convicts to North America. In a very violent rebellion, a group of the prisoners seized the ship as it was passing down the English Channel, wounding and imprisoning those transporting them. They ran it into Torbay and attempted to escape inland. William Jones, however, 'distinguished himself from the rest by a peaceable, quiet behaviour. He did not join in the insurrection and after it happened he conducted himself with humanity, sobriety and honesty'. The ship's officers recommended that he be pardoned.[19]

There were other ways for justices to determine a lesser sentence than might ordinarily have been recorded. For example, while there could be no value-mitigation where the theft of animals was concerned (that is, the crime was theft of a horse, not of one worth more or less than £10), as this crime did not usually involve violence, those convicted of it were frequently recommended for the royal mercy on condition of being transported. Persons under twenty years of age (for whom there might be some hopes of reform) and those over thirty (who were likely to have families to support) were less likely to be sentenced to transportation than unmarried, able-bodied men in their twenties. Women who were likely to have dependent children might also escape the harsher penalties.[20]

*

Let us now look at some of the felons convicted at the Old Bailey assize sessions in the 1780s who were transported to New South Wales.

Simon Hughes went to a boarding house where he was given a bed to share with two other men. After he had fallen asleep, Robert Forrester and Richard McDale robbed him of 6 guineas (£6.6.0). When he awoke at 3 a.m., Hughes found one of the robbers gone and the other preparing to leave. He also found his money gone. He told the court: 'I halloed, and made a noise in the room, which alarmed the landlady and her daughter, they came upstairs and brought a light, and I dressed myself, and the two women went down to the houses where they thought to find the prisoners, but they could not find them then.'

When taken, the prisoners tried to do a deal with their victim by offering him 4 guineas not to appear in court. At their trial, they both denied having robbed Hughes and produced witnesses who said McDale had received 3½ guineas as part of his pension. They also found a woman to testify that Hughes had asked if he might stay with her that night. She told the court that this had not been 'convenient' since her husband was at home, so she had given him 2 pence so that he might find a bed elsewhere. But Hughes said he had never seen her before, and another witness said that she had offered him 'anything in the world' if he would help get the indictment thrown out. The accused were disbelieved and sentenced to death, but were recommended for the royal mercy on condition of being transported for seven years.[21]

Ann Green was charged with stealing nineteen china plates and a china bowl from the workshop of William Moody, valued at a total of 8 shillings. Moody's wife testified that 'I heard a noise in the back shop a few minutes after six; when I opened the door, I saw the prisoner turning from the workboard; I was in the middle room; I caught her by the cloak; she said she had made a mistake; I told her I would see what it was; I saw the nineteen plates in her hand; I immediately secured her as well as I could; I opened her apron, and found a china bowl'. Green had a very young child, and her husband had died shortly before the birth. She told the court that she did not know which had been her husband's parish – i.e., she did not know where to go for charity – and that 'I have not a friend in the world'. Clearly, all believed her story, for the prosecutor requested the court show her mercy, and the jury made the same recommendation. She was sentenced to seven years' transportation.[22] (Of course, by our standards, this was scarcely merciful; but the point is that the court pleaded successfully for her life.)

Mary Greenwood was indicted with George Partridge for the highway robbery with assault of Adam Mills, 'putting him in corporal fear and danger of his life' and stealing from him goods to a combined value of 12 shillings. However, the offence was much greater. A group of six or seven men and women first stole a £10 bank note, 7 guineas in gold, and about 15 shillings' worth of silver from Mills's pockets. When he chased them and seized one woman, Greenwood and Partridge came to her aid, striking him 'a violent blow on the side'. They then took from him a bundle of clothes also mentioned in the indictment, saying: 'Damn your eyes, you bloody bugger! If you do not give us this bundle, we will cut your bloody milt [spleen] out; I then received a hard blow on my knee, which has been very black.' Some witnesses helped him get the assailants to the watch house. The jury asked Mills if he had been sober that night, and he assured them that he had. They also asked him if Greenwood did 'aid and assist' in the robbery. He asserted that she had, and that she had 'made use of worse imprecations than the man did'. Both were found guilty and sentenced to death, but were recommended for mercy on condition of being transported for seven years.[23]

Together with James Beach and Francis Burke, Joseph Hall was charged with assaulting and robbing Sarah Stockden and her husband John in a field near a highway, putting her 'in corporal fear and danger of her life, and taking from her person, one pair of silver shoe buckles, value 7 shillings, one pocket-book, value 6 pence, and 5 shillings in money, her property'. The Stockdens were walking to Covent Garden at 6 a.m. when the thieves passed them. She deposed:

Mr Stockden said I believe they are thieves; they are bad ones; they came back immediately, and took hold of us, and set my husband's face to Tottenham Court, and mine to Islington; I said I had a family of children; they blasted my eyes, and said, they did not care if I had twenty, they said money they wanted, and money they would have, and said my buckles were plated; they were going to sea, and blasted my bloody eyes, and said if I would not give them my money they would blow my brains out.

One took her buckles and money as another menaced her with a cutlass.[24] The Stockdens reported the assault and theft to a constable, who located the culprits at Holborn. He testified:

I took hold of Burke by the collar, and another, and told them I had a charge against them for a footpad robbery; there were four in company; then with that they immediately blasted my bloody eyes; they gave me a blow, and drawed their knives, and fell cutting away, I scuffled with them, and we took two; the other two made their escape; I pursued Burke and Mowatt; he is not here; I took Burke; Beach, the tall one, gave me a violent blow with the butt end of a pistol; I was hit about so, I almost lost my senses; the Bow Street people secured the other.

The three were found guilty and sentenced to death. They were pardoned on condition of fourteen years' transportation to America. Put on board the *Swift* to be carried across the Atlantic, they joined in the mutiny and Hall and another escaped into Sussex. After capture, these two were again sentenced to death (for the felony of returning before their first sentences had expired). Hall was again reprieved, on condition of fourteen years' transportation to America. Shipped out on the *Mercury* in 1784, Hall joined in the mutiny on that ship too and landed at Torbay, only to be recaptured. He was once more sentenced to death, then once more reprieved on condition of transportation for life.

Margaret Hall and Elizabeth Coleman were charged with the theft from John Jackson of a box containing '8 gold rings, value 40 shillings; 3 silver buttons, value 12 pence; 4 guineas, value £4.4.0; 6 light guineas, value £6; 1 half-guinea, value 10 shillings 6 pence; 1 light half-guinea, value 9 shillings; one moidore, value 27 shillings; 1 gold medal, value 2 guineas; 16 pieces of old silver coin, value 20 shillings ... and one promissory note of £20 from the Governor and Company of the Bank of England'. Jackson met the women at St Giles's and went to a tavern with them. He testified: 'After we had drunk, she took me to her lodgings, as I understood it to be, it was just opposite the public house; we went up stairs, and had a cup or two of some liquor, purl, or gin-hot, or something of that sort; they teased me for money ... I gave them one half-guinea, and they brought me the change ... Soon after I went to bed ... [and] I was asleep in five minutes. I slept till daybreak; when I awoke, I found nobody with me; I missed the two boxes and the silver.'

Under hard questioning from the judge, Jackson conceded that he had been 'very much in liquor', and that otherwise he would have shown 'more prudence'. Nonetheless, he maintained that he could positively identify the women charged as those who robbed him. But a witness said that Coleman had not been the second woman whom Johnson had said he wished to have sex with; and Coleman denied ever having seen him before she was charged. Coleman was acquitted, while Hall was found guilty and sentenced to death, then reprieved on condition of being transported for seven years. She too was on the *Mercury* and escaped into Exeter, only to be quickly recaptured and to have the sentence of transportation reaffirmed. Put on board the *Friendship* at Portsmouth as it waited to sail with the First Fleet, she and two others broke out of their quarters and joined the sailors. During the voyage, she was put in irons for ten days for fighting with other women.[25]

George Lisk was tried for 'feloniously assaulting John Jeffries on the King's highway ... and putting him in fear and danger of his life, and taking from his person and against his will 9 shillings in monies ..., his property'.

Jeffries, who was a poor old man, testified:

as I was coming, very nigh 11 o'clock at night, along the New Cut, that goes from John's Hill to Wapping church, the way from the New Tavern, up jumps two sailors, they came over to me directly; they were smothered with rubbish before I came, I never saw them till I came up, they threw me down at once, and I had 9 shillings and I lost it all, that man that got my money he got off, and this is the gentleman that kept me down.

He added that Lisk had held him down, and by the throat, so that he was scarcely able to cry out. Solomon Williams, who seized Lisk after hearing the watchman's alarm, said that he then found 'the old gentleman almost senseless, he kept crying out for God's sake do not hurt me, do not hurt me, he did not know what he was about, he begged he might go home to his wife and family'.

On identifying Lisk, Jeffries very magnaminously said, 'I would not have him hanged neither, because I have children of my own, and I do not know what they may come to; there is nothing too hard for God to do, he may make a good man of him yet'. Lisk was found guilty of the felony (assault), but not guilty of robbery. The judge told him:

> From the mercy of your prosecutor and the lenity of the jury, you have escaped with your life, which the offence as stated certainly affects. Considering the age and infirmity of the prosecutor and taking his all from him, your offence is very heinous. The jury have not gone to the extent of the law, but the Court thinks proper to transport you to America for seven years, and if you return and are found at large within that time, you suffer death without the benefit of clergy.[26]

\*

It is one of the abiding myths of Australian history that many of those sentenced to transportation were poor people convicted for stealing a loaf of bread to feed their starving family, or a handkerchief worth a few pennies; that they were the hapless victims of a savage penal code and an uncaring, class-driven society. It seems not to matter how often or with what clarity the real situation is explained. This myth is, it seems, necessary to the maintenance of our identity as a nation forged out of dastardly oppression.

It would be silly to claim that there were never miscarriages of justice, or that harsh penalties were not given for what we should now consider minor offences. Long sentences given to children or to those made desperate by poverty still trouble the mind and hurt the heart. However, the plain fact is that the majority of eighteenth-century convicts sentenced to transportation were convicted of crimes that we continue to consider serious. When you think about it, this only makes the emergence of modern Australia the more remarkable: somehow, people not used to acting for the common good came to form a cohesive and prosperous society.

# 3.

# Dealing with the Convict Problem: Hulks and Enlistment, 1776–83

BETWEEN 1718 AND 1775 PERHAPS AS many as 50,000 British men, women and adolescents 'left [their] country for [their] country's good',[1] the majority from London and the West Country port of Bristol. In the New World, 'planters, mechanics, and ... such as choose to retain them for domestic service' used their labour to produce raw materials cheaply for export to the mother country or in local services.[2] In the twelve years before the American Revolution, an average of about 1000 transport convicts a year made the crossing. Merchants prominent in the business at that time included Messrs Stevenson, Randolph and Cheston of Bristol and Messrs John Stewart and Duncan Campbell of London. Since they could not sell the labour of dead convicts, and were able to obtain more for that of healthy ones, it was decidedly in these contractors' interest to handle the business carefully and to attend to the welfare of those whom they transported. The most recent studies show that they did so.[3] Nonetheless, the often deplorable condition of prisoners when they were taken from the jails and the nature of the ocean passage made it inevitable that there be deaths *en route*. Campbell told the 1778 House of Commons committee enquiring into the hulks that:

on an American voyage in the transport service he has lost only 5 or 6 men out of 150; but he remembers one ship that lost 50 or 60 out of the same number; that upon an average 10 is considered a moderate loss out of 100; that upon an average of seven years, the loss of convicts in jail and on board will be one-seventh.[4]

The studies of the operations of the Bristol merchants confirm this figure.

Since he played such a large part in the creation of the system that temporarily replaced transportation to America, it is worth looking at Duncan Campbell in detail.[5] He was born in 1736 and served as a midshipman in the Royal Navy before setting up in the West India trade. In 1753 he married Rebecca Campbell, whose father owned a plantation in Jamaica, which he subsequently inherited. In 1758 he acquainted himself with circumstances in the North American colonies, at the same time as he became a junior partner of John Stewart, who possessed the government contract to transport convicts from London and the Home Counties. On Stewart's death in 1772 Campbell took over the firm and continued transporting convicts until the American Revolution. It was this association that enabled him to claim justly in 1776 that he had been 'nearly twenty years in the management of the same sort of people'.[6]

Campbell was punctilious, processing business efficiently, keeping precisely to his agreements and expecting others to do the same. But while he was meticulous, he was not grasping. In 1782, when convict numbers had fallen significantly below those he had agreed to, he offered to reduce the amount claimed at the end of his contract. And he told the Treasury in January 1785 that he had accommodated more people than he had contracted for, but that 'as the additional expense of this excess is only in clothing and provisions, which may perhaps in [the] course of my reports for the year fall as much short of that complement, I do not mean to claim on this occasion more than was paid me for the last quarter'.[7] One basis of Campbell's plain dealing was a deeply Christian outlook. After the death of a female member of his household, he described how 'without pain or fear she resigned herself to his hands who gave her life. I never saw a nobler instance of the consequence of an innocent and virtuous life. She knew herself dying and seemed much pleased at the approaching summons to her eternal happiness'.[8] Campbell brought this religious outlook to bear on his supervision of convicts.

\*

From the central government's point of view, transportation to the American colonies was a neat penal practice that brought three distinct benefits. First, it 'exported' a social problem; second, it did so at comparatively small cost; and third, it benefited the nation by helping to create a supply of materials needed in Britain.

When the American colonists revolted, these smiles stopped together. Developing over more than a decade, the revolt of the American colonies had many and complex causes. By mid-1775 colonists were showing their opposition to British authority by refusing admittance to their ports of British ships and goods – and convicts. By the end of that year the British government, led by Prime Minister Frederick (Lord) North, had recognized that it must cease transporting convicts across the Atlantic, at least while circumstances in the American colonies remained unsettled.

The presence of convicts awaiting transportation in the kingdom constituted a real (if, in terms of numbers, slight) problem for the administration. While these prisoners might be pardoned or obtain remission of their sentences by the exercise of the royal prerogative, the sentence of transportation in itself could not be altered, and the administration had a legal obligation to carry it out. The sensible answer was to substitute another punishment. As the administration moved to do so, it concentrated all transport convicts in one place. In late November 1775, William Eden, the Under-Secretary of State at the Northern Department, told the Recorder of London (the most senior judge of the Old Bailey, London's central criminal court) that those in Newgate prison should be sent on board 'a proper vessel in the river [Thames] in the usual manner and as if in due course for transportation'.[9] The ship in question was Duncan Campbell's *Tayloe*. Campbell began receiving transport convicts there in January 1776 and continued to do so throughout the year. However, the administration simultaneously acted to solve the immediate problem by pardoning those men who agreed either to enter the King's service or to transport themselves beyond the seas for the remaining term of their sentence. A number of women were pardoned absolutely.[10] By December, Eden advised Campbell that there were no more transport convicts in British jails. With the last ones on the *Tayloe* having enlisted in the army or navy, left England or been pardoned, Campbell terminated his contract with the Treasury and closed the ship down.[11]

The new punishment for felonies that the North administration now adopted involved hard labour on the harbours and waterways of the kingdom. In practice at this time, however, the only place of labour was the River Thames, where the convicts were accommodated on unrigged ships moored to the east of the city.

These convict 'hulks' have had a very bad press. For 150 years, the belief that these ships quickly became extremely overcrowded and were scandalously unhealthy has underpinned the conventional explanation of the decision to colonize New South Wales. In 1916 Ernest Scott, for example, wrote:

> The prisons were wholly insufficient to hold the condemned persons … Thousands of prisoners were crowded into wretchedly insanitary hulks which were purchased to serve as receptacles. Every month saw more and more sentences of transportation inflicted, more hulks filled with offenders, and still there was no place to which they could be exiled.[12]

(In passing, consider the ludicrousness of the statement that 'Every month saw … more hulks filled with offenders'. Were this true, by the mid-1780s there would have been dozens of these convict ships. The reality is that by late 1784 there were *three* in the Thames, with one at Plymouth; later, another was added at Portsmouth.)

Historian after historian has since reiterated this view. R.M. Crawford wrote in 1952:

> So the number of convicted persons continued to rise, particularly in the more depressed areas of southern England and Ireland; and the former outlet by way of transportation to the American colonies was closed. When the jails were crowded, hulks were pressed into service, to become crowded in their turn. This was the situation which pressed Lord Sydney – not given to long views – into the action which founded Australia.[13]

In 1955 Frank Crowley claimed: 'By 1783 it was clear that the hulks had rapidly become "reservoirs and hotbeds of criminals"'.[14] Manning Clark wrote in 1962 that by early 1784, 'the escapes of felons from the hulks, as well as anxiety about the spread of jail distemper and smallpox, enabled the philanthropists and charity workers to play on the fears of those in high places, while hints and complaints of the hulks as schools of villainy and vice tweaked consciences into action'. He also stated that 'one factor alone' persuaded Lord Sydney of the need for the Botany Bay decision: 'the several jails and places for the confinement of felons were so crowded that the greatest danger was to be apprehended not only from their escape, but from infectious distempers'.[15] In 1966, A.G.L. Shaw repeated this interpretation, writing that in 1778 the hulks 'were supposed to hold only 380; but before the war nearly a thousand felons had been shipped to the plantations every year'.[16]

In 1985, writing of the recruitment of criminals into the armed forces, Stephen Conway observed, 'It was still found necessary periodically to clear both the putrid and congested jails and the equally overcrowded and insanitary hulks'.[17] In 1987, Robert Hughes claimed that when Sydney replaced North as Home Secretary in December 1783, 'he faced a rising clamour over the problem of criminal confinement – the shamefully over-crowded hulks and prisons'. The same year, John Molony wrote: 'The problem of what to do with English prisoners demanded action because of the growth in the number of persons being sentenced had resulted in crowded and unhealthy jails, particularly those in the old hulks of vessels moored on the Thames'. And in 1985 David Mackay stated that, as the number of convicts rose after 1776, one of the government's responses 'was to increase the number of hulks'. 'Another', he went on, 'was to increase the number in the hulks until they were dangerously overcrowded.'[18]

Together, these statements exemplify James Blackburn's observation (made concerning another egregious error in Australian historiography): 'Let an erroneous statement of fact, either invented or taken upon rumour, but once appear in print, and it is ever after regarded as a truth requiring no further verification, so that it is adopted by the next historian, who is copied by a third, and so on *ad infinitum*.'[19] It is also striking that *none* of these historians – commonly supposed to be pre-eminent in the field – *actually counted* the numbers of felons on the hulks during the ten years between 1776 and 1786, though Campbell's precise quarterly returns were readily available. (He was bound by law to report to the Secretary of State and the Treasury every three months; if he had not done so, he would not have been paid.) No. One writer having said that the hulks were 'shamefully overcrowded', over the next seventy years the others simply accepted the claim as fact, and repeated it.

I have counted the numbers. Here is the real story.

*

The North administration's new system for punishing felons emerged principally from discussions between Duncan Campbell and William Eden, who had a few years earlier publicized his view that the nation should receive some economic or strategic benefit from the transportation of the 'more enormous offenders'.[20] Under this new system, men who would previously have been sentenced to transportation to America would instead be sentenced to hard labour for between three and ten years. The administration enacted the legislation to make these provisions legal in April and May 1776 (16 Geo. III c. 43), to have effect for two years. With these changes, central government assumed a much greater role in the punishment of felons than it had previously taken.

Campbell had proposed that he accommodate hard-labour convicts on a ship in the Thames, where, under careful supervision, they would work from lighters (small, flat-bottomed barges) on the water and on the river bank. For £3560 a year (or some £30 per person), he offered to provide a ship of at least 240 tons to accommodate 120 convicts, together with guards, six lighters and the necessary tools, and 'to find every reasonable necessary for the people under their circumstances, medicines, vinegar etc, to wash and fumigate the vessel, for their healthful preservation'. On 12 July 1776 Campbell was formally appointed for three years as Overseer of Convicts on the Thames. For accommodation, he offered one of his own ships, the *Justitia*, of 260 tons.[21] In August he took in 85 convicts, and thereafter progressively filled up his complement of 120.

In March 1777 the administration asked him to take an additional 130 convicts. Initially he used the *Tayloe* again but in June he purchased a French frigate, the *Censor*, of 731 tons, which he fitted out 'for the accommodation and safe custody of 240 convicts and upwards'. In February 1778 he contracted for another 130, after which he accordingly filled the *Censor* to capacity, to reach a total contracted number of 380. It was arranged that these three contracts should end together on 12 July 1779.[22]

Between March and May 1778, parliament enquired into conditions on these ships and extended the 1776 act for another year (18 Geo. III c. 62). In July the Treasury asked Campbell to provide for an additional 130 convicts; he agreed, and this new contract was scheduled to conclude, like the others, on 12 July 1779. He purchased 'an old Indiaman', which he also named *Justitia*, and fitted it out to accommodate 250 people. From this point on, he was contracted to provide accommodation for 510 inmates. The actual number of prisoners aboard fluctuated around this figure for the following fifteen months.[23]

Before all four of Campbell's contracts expired together in July 1779, parliament conducted another inquiry, not only into the workings of the hulks system, but also into punishment more broadly. Sir Charles Bunbury chaired the House of Commons committee, which heard evidence about conditions in the prisons and on the hulks, about the prospects of resuming transportation variously to West Africa, the East Indies and New South Wales, and about the desirability of developing a third mode of punishment, to involve solitary confinement in 'penitentiary houses' and hard labour.[24] Parliament renewed the original 1776 legislation until 1 July 1779 (19 Geo. III c. 54) as a prelude to the introduction of a more comprehensive measure. With this new legislation, parliament extended servitude on the hulks for five years, with the term reduced (at Campbell's suggestion) to between one and five years. The place specified for transportation was amended to 'any Parts beyond the Seas', and three supervisors were appointed to oversee the building of two penitentiary houses in one of the Home Counties.

From mid-1779, then, there existed two modes of punishing those pardoned of capital offences or convicted of non-capital felonies – servitude on the hulks, or transportation to anywhere outside Britain, even though there was no obvious alternative to North America at this time. How soon justices resumed sentencing felons to transportation, and in what numbers, is unclear. In November, Campbell concluded a new contract with the Treasury whereby he agreed to provide accommodation for 510 convicts on ships on the Thames, together with a 'receiving ship' (*Reception*) and a hospital ship (the first *Justitia*) for twelve months.[25]

For a combination of reasons – expirations of sentences, enlistment in the armed forces – the number of hard-labour convicts on the hulks began to fall from the middle of 1780, to reach a low of 176 in mid-1783. Campbell's annual contracts reflected this decline: in July 1780 he agreed to accommodate 460; in July 1781, 440. In 1782 and 1783, he seems not to have concluded formal contracts, but rather to have adjusted his claims for payment according to the numbers actually borne.

In the absence of his detailed returns, it is impossible to be precise about the base complements in these years. That for 1782 seems to have been about 250, and that for 1783 about 200. (The average numbers were 284 in 1782 and 200 in 1783.[26]) Campbell took the *Censor* out of use in July 1782, so that the second *Justitia* was the sole receptacle for convicts sentenced to hard labour on the Thames.

With the return of tens of thousands of soldiers and sailors when the wars of 1776–83 ended, however, the numbers of people convicted of felonies increased rapidly and the hulks system expanded again. By 1786, Campbell was running three on the Thames, and there was one each at Portsmouth and Plymouth. Altogether, there were about 1200 transport convicts in these ships by this time, and more were being held in county jails. But this is a story for another time. For now, I wish to tell you something about the hulks system as Campbell developed it.

*

In the beginning, achieving satisfactory conditions was very much a matter of trial and error. Campbell told the 1778 House of Commons committee that in the absence of any specific directions from the Secretary of State's department, he had fitted the first *Justitia* out in the manner of ships used to carry troops, with cabins having two tiers of beds five feet, ten inches apart, providing each man with a sleeping space eighteen inches wide. This still made for crowded conditions. Other aspects of the accommodation were also undesirable. The sick were separated from the healthy only by a partition, and the sick bay was located at the upstream end of the ship, so that patients' excrement drifted past the sleeping quarters of the others.[27] The weekly food ration, which was calculated for a 'mess' of six persons, consisted of – for five days out of seven – five pounds of biscuit, half an ox cheek and three pints of peas in a soup. For the other two ('burgoo') days, each mess received three pints of oatmeal in the form of porridge, five pounds of bread and two pounds of cheese. This ration was modelled on that given in the navy, but there were certain differences. The navy diet included butter and some pork and beer (e.g., the convicts were dependent on the largesse of friends for milk and green vegetables).

This situation was one in which disease might spread rapidly, as it did in October 1776, when sixty-four convicts from Maidstone and other jails brought typhus fever with them. When the prison reformer John Howard inspected the ship at the time he found the inmates in bad circumstances, with many poorly clothed and fed, numbers of them ill and a very disagreeable smell in the sick bay. Not surprisingly, eleven of the inmates died between October 1776 and January 1777.[28]

Genuinely concerned about the welfare of his charges, Campbell moved to improve conditions. To enlarge the cramped accommodation on the first *Justitia*, he knocked down the cabins to form an open space, in which he erected a communal sleeping platform fitted with mats that allowed each person a width of two feet. Then, he replaced the mats with beds for two, six feet by four feet, with straw mattresses that were folded against the walls when not in use. He provided the convicts with more and better clothing, and more comprehensive and more regular medical attention. Simultaneously he developed a regimen of care, which he subsequently described to one of his supervisors:

> I would have you keep the convicts as dry as possible in theirs berths and let them have plenty of fresh air, but not partially as at ports; when it blows strong on the side of the ship much mischief is sometimes done by keeping the windward ports open. Have them frequently upon deck, but as they are inactive, not too long in cold and windy weather. The colds they receive by that means often create disease and serious disease too. Endeavour ever to prevent sickness, it is easier done than to cure it.[29]

These changes certainly improved matters. Visiting the *Justitia* in July 1777, Dr Solander – the Swedish naturalist who assisted Joseph Banks aboard the *Endeavour* – found the sleeping accommodation still rather cramped, but the foul smell was mostly gone, the food was good and there were few sick. When Howard inspected both ships in January 1778 the convicts told him 'that they were better used than when he saw them last', a fact he thought 'very evident by their looks'. He was impressed by their rations and the medical attention. Jeremy Bentham also reported at this time that 'no fire or candle allowed at night but the place is abundantly warm; fires kept burning all day; the ship often washed with vinegar, hardly any disagreeable smell between decks, bathing allowed at first but now prohibited as unwholesome'.[30]

Despite these measures, according to Jeremy Bentham, there was 'a very considerable sickness which Campbell says is concealed as much as possible – chiefly putrid fever and low spirits and some swelled legs, no ague'. Because of these health problems, Campbell had fitted out 'the forecastle of the *Censor* … tolerably neat and clean for a hospital, beds very close, almost touching'. Modern knowledge shows us that such crowding is scarcely conducive to good health, and it is telling that Campbell 'declined going down' with Bentham and Howard 'into the hospital and soon called us out'. The testimony of these witnesses leaves no doubt about the improvements, but at this stage the hulks system was still not good so far as the health of the inmates was concerned. Between August 1776 and March 1778, 176 of the 632 convicts (28 per cent) received on board the ships died, but in the period of the filling of the vessels, Campbell was not responsible for the condition of those arriving from metropolitan and country jails – and as he told Bentham and the Commons committee, the mortality was 'greatest among country convicts'.[31]

In the second phase of the hulks (April 1778 to mid-1780) Campbell continued to improve conditions as he expanded overall capacity. He increased the bread ration to seven pounds per person per week in summer and six pounds in winter; he added 'small beer' to the menu, offered porridge for both breakfast and supper on 'burgoo' days, and gave each mess half an ox head per day. With these changes, he considered the whole ration to be 'better than labouring men usually had'. He began a vegetable garden on an acre of adjacent ground. He instituted a 'receiving' ship, where convicts were stripped of their vermin-laced clothes, bathed and held for four days while surgeons inspected them for signs of infection. He set up a separate hospital ship and employed three surgeons on a regular basis. He also employed a clergyman. Initially, the death rate remained high, with some 165 out of a total of 724 inmates (23 per cent) dying in the twelve months from April 1778 to April 1779. Again this rate was in large part attributable to men arriving sick – about 90, for example, died from typhus fever, 'chiefly brought by persons who came on board the hulks from the different jails'. Once the hulks' complements were reached, and the proportion of new inmates each quarter dropped, so too did the death rate. In the third phase, in the twelve months from 1 January 1782 to 9 January 1783 (as numbers declined) some 89 out of 486 died (19 per cent).[32]

In the fourth phase, the death rate was much lower. In the twelve months from 12 January 1785 to 12 January 1786, 66 of the 379 admitted to the second *Justitia* died (17 per cent), but this figure included an unusually high figure of 34 in one quarter. For the first three quarters of 1786, 20 out of 356 died (5.6 per cent). For the last three quarters of 1785, 25 out of 291 admitted to the *Censor* died (9 per cent), and for the first three quarters of 1786, 26 out of 282 (9.2 per cent).[33] These rates compare more than favourably with those from the period of transportation to North America when, as noted earlier, a 14 per cent death rate between embarkation and landing was the norm. In a more general way, and while such comparisons are notoriously difficult, it may well be that the convicts on the hulks were healthier than peer groups elsewhere in the kingdom, and certainly in London. It is also quite possible that they were better fed.

*

Contrary to long-standing belief, Campbell did not crowd convicts relentlessly into his hulks. Rather, he controlled the numbers carefully, keeping them as much as possible around the stated complements. At times, in response to 'pressing' applications from county officials, he did take on more, but this was always a strictly limited gesture. More often than not, he told importuning officials and jailers that he '[could] not at present give you directions when to bring up your people, as there are already as many convicts engaged as there is room for in the vessels'.[34]

The returns for the first and second *Justitia, Censor* and *Ceres* entirely confirm this point. In the twenty-four months before the decision to send convicts to Botany Bay, the second *Justitia*'s stated complement was exceeded by no more than thirty-three, and the *Censor*'s by no more than twelve. In 1786 the *Ceres*' complement was not exceeded by more than fourteen. In presenting the return for the *Justitia* for the quarter 12 October 1784 to 12 January 1785, Campbell observed that 'the pressing applications from clerks of the peace and jailers, stating their difficulties from time to time, has obliged me to exceed the number considerably, which I had limited for that vessel'.[35] He thereafter decreased this excess, although in his own defence he said he 'never failed' to relieve the county jails 'as fast as vacancies happen'.[36] Generally, however, he was punctilious about not exceeding the stated complements significantly. One reason for this was that he had contracted on the basis of a fixed number and was paid accordingly. From time to time the Treasury did lend a sympathetic ear to his requests for additional payment for the extra men, so money was not Campbell's sole reason for keeping numbers down. As we shall see, he cared for the welfare of his charges more than for profit, and successive administrations were willing to bear the cost.

When it came to transporting the convicts to their place of labour and overseeing their work, Campbell gradually developed a regimen. At first, arrangements were rather haphazard. When in October 1776 Eden asked how much sand and gravel had been raised, Campbell replied that he had so far attended rather to 'the mode than the quantity of labour'.[37] But the Under-Secretary's query stirred Campbell to place the employment of the convicts on a more regular footing. Ten days later he wrote that he would moor the vessel next to the work site at Woolwich, 'in order to make our first trial for raising sand and gravel from the banks of the Thames contiguous thereto, as being the *safest* and fittest [spot] for that purpose'. He added that the site selected was then of 'little or no utility, being nearly all overflowed every tide', so that it was 'a very convenient place for us to throw our soil upon when training the people to this labour', and that their improvements would render the area 'more valuable to the Board of Ordnance'.[38]

With experience, Campbell came to understand better what was needed. He provided lighters of 'from 35 to 45 tons burden fitted up for the employing and sheltering of twelve convicts each with the necessary bolts and securities, ballast engines to each lighter and all other implements necessary for the raising [of] sand and gravel from the River Thames', together with an appropriate number of supervisors.[39] Someone who observed the convicts at work in mid-1777 described how

There are upwards of two hundred of them, who are employed as follows. Some are sent about a mile below Woolwich in lighters to raise ballast, and to row it back to the embankment at Woolwich Warren, close to the end of the Target walk; others are there employed in throwing it from the lighters. Some wheel it to different parts to be sifted; others wheel it from the screen, and spread it for the embankment. A party is continually busied in turning round a machine for driving piles to secure the embankment from the rapidity of the tides. Carpenters, etc, are employed in repairing the *Justitia* and the [*Censor*] hulks, that lie hard by for the nightly reception of those objects, who have fetters on each leg, with a chain between, that ties variously, some round their middle, others upright to the throat. Some are chained two and two; and others, whose crimes have been enormous, with heavy fetters. Six or seven are continually walking about with them with drawn cutlasses, to prevent their escape and likewise to prevent idleness.[40]

To guard further against escape, Campbell built a high brick wall on the landward side of the site, which also served the useful function of keeping away the curious who came to see the convicts at work. So as to allow the men to work more freely and effectively he removed the irons from all but the most recalcitrant.

The new regimen of labour meant that, in spring, the convicts worked from 7 a.m. to 12 noon, and from 1 p.m. to 6 p.m., and longer in summer. In winter they worked from 8.30 a.m. to 2 or 3 p.m. Directly or indirectly, the work they did always had a naval aspect – dredging the Thames to improve its navigation and using some of the gravel to build a new road to the Seamen's Hospital at Greenwich; building a new wharf for the Board of Ordnance at the Woolwich Arsenal; or digging moats and ditches there and performing 'other useful works', which included building new 'proof and practice butts of large extent', 'cleaning cannon' and sawing timber.[41] Always Campbell impressed on his overseers the great desirability of keeping strict control. 'Constant attention, coolness and firmness', he counselled,

> will be the sure means of keeping good order, not only amongst the convicts but amongst the ship's company. You will require to be very strict at the outset in order to obtain good habits, which if once established [are] easily maintained, while on the other hand bad habits are difficult to get the better of. In short your giving close attention to duty yourself will be an example for everybody about you to follow.[42]

Evidently Campbell had considerable success in this. The 1777 observer described with amazement how, 'so far from being permitted to speak to anyone, [the convicts] hardly dare speak to each other. But what is most surprising, is the revolution in manners: not an oath is to be heard; and each criminal performs the task assigned to him with industry, and without murmuring'.[43]

Still, the convicts did not always behave. It was sometimes necessary to flog fractious individuals, and those who threatened violence were put in irons. There were occasional riots, when desperate men sought freedom. Late in September 1778, more than 150 attempted to rush their guards and escape, but only a few succeeded in doing so. With the help of forces from the Warren, the guards put the insurrection down, killing two prisoners and severely wounding eight in the process. The next day, thirty-six convicts attempted to escape, with the result that one more man was killed and another eighteen wounded. Despite such incidents, however, most convicts seem to have behaved reasonably well in this period. Campbell's deputy, Stewart Erskine, told the 1779 House of Commons committee that they 'had behaved very well for some time'.[44] Later, the absence of any subsequent striking comment to the contrary suggests that this situation continued to prevail, though in the mid-1780s there was the inherent problem that the act under which the transport convicts were sentenced did not compel them to hard labour and they knew it.

Campbell and Erskine assessed the labour undertaken by the convicts as moderately hard, with Campbell saying that they worked as hard as labourers employed on highways, but not so hard as 'common labourers'. The real worth of the work they performed is unclear. The 1778 Commons committee accepted the estimate of £6053 as the value of their labour in the period January 1777 to March 1778. In December 1778 Campbell stated that 2680 tons of ballast had been raised in the previous seven weeks. One of the witnesses to the 1779 committee stated that:

> they had removed a mud bank, and made a very useful wharf, and a dock for barges to come in, and the river opposite was considerably deepened, so as to permit large ships to lie with convenience, where they could not lie before; that upon the whole he thought their work of great use to the Warren, and of real public service.

The committee concluded that 'the labour done appears to be of solid advantage to the public, and may be estimated at rather more than one-third of the whole annual expense'.[45] The extension, on the suggestion of Treasury Secretary George Rose, of the hulks system to the naval yards at Plymouth and Portsmouth at the end of 1785 indicates that authorities continued to see the convicts' labour as being of real economic significance.

Figures drawn up by the Home Office in 1789 for the House of Commons Select Committee on Finance confirm this. Evan Nepean, Under-Secretary of the Home Office, estimated the value of the hulk convicts' labour at 10 pence per two thirds of a man for six days a week, or £8.15.3 per year, or approximately 38 per cent of the then annual cost of £23.2.11 of keeping a convict on the hulks.[46]

*

Taking his statements at face value, a reader cannot but be impressed by Campbell's solicitude for the welfare of those whom he termed 'poor creatures'. He used the *Censor* rather than a smaller vessel because he was 'sensible from experience that more room must produce salutary effects to these unhappy people'. In summer, he repeatedly declined to enlarge the complements 'for fear of crowding the ships at this hot season'. As numbers increased, he asked for more lighters, so that men would not have to work standing in the mud and water in cold weather. In winter, he reduced the hours of labour sharply and served dinner later, so that the convicts did not have to leave the ships again afterwards. When the cold was extreme, he suspended labour entirely.[47]

More than in the simple physical welfare of the convicts, however, Campbell was interested in their psychological and social well-being. One of his earliest insights was that, more often than not, those who died succumbed to psychic rather than to physical illness. 'Our greatest loss of people arises in a great degree from a depression of spirits', he reported to Eden in January 1778, and he subsequently reiterated this to the House of Commons committee. A year later Erskine told the new committee that 'those from the country jails were apt to be more dispirited than the *London* felons'.[48] Neither Campbell nor Erskine seems to have speculated on the reason for this difference, but Campbell separately remarked that friends might supply convicts with extra food and clothing, so it may be that the *anomie* among the country convicts was to a considerable extent caused by the loss of family and social networks. Campbell sought to counter this depression by having a Methodist preacher attend the men, but he also seems to have understood that the prospect of distant salvation did little to alleviate present despair.

Loss of hope arose directly from the nature of the punishment. There was a good deal of disapproval of hard labour as a substitute for transportation, on the grounds that it was comparable to slavery and therefore anathema to English values. Sir William Meredith told parliament in 1778 that the hulks system was 'totally repugnant to the general frame of our laws', and others shared this opinion.[49] The convicts themselves seem to have been among them. Campbell observed that 'on their first coming on board, the universal depression of spirits was astonishing, as they had a great dread of this punishment'. Interestingly, they seem to have preferred the thought of transportation to North America, where they would not be shackled and where they might have the opportunity to better themselves by their labour. Erskine told the 1779 Commons committee that the convicts 'had behaved well for some time, which he attributed to an expectation they had of some alteration in their punishment, in consequence of the present enquiry, as they said they had much rather be transported'.[50]

Campbell always endeavoured to hold out some hope to the convicts, but he made clear that it was conditional on a real change in their attitudes and behaviour. He was a careful observer of his charges, as this description from mid-1777 attests: 'It seems as if each convict was most desirous of showing his readiness and his obedience to discipline, being induced thereto by one only hope, viz., that of obtaining their liberty by good behaviour, which is the only means afforded them to get their liberty before the legal expiration of their time.'[51] In January 1778, discussing with Eden how best to implement the proposed new act, he suggested a minimum term of one or two years, with a maximum of six years, on the grounds that in this time 'with proper management great alterations may be made on the habits and minds of such prisoners'.

\*

There were two principal avenues by which a convict on the hulks could obtain his liberty. The first was a variation of the long-standing practice of entering the army or navy instead of being transported, of which I shall say more in a moment. The second was intriguingly modern. Hypothesizing that 'hopes of pardon … might have a good effect' on the prevailing depression among the inmates, in 1777 Campbell recommended that five well-behaved men be freed. Finding that the remaining convicts 'worked more cheerfully afterwards', he recommended another sixty men for pardon or early release. At the end of 1777 he told Eden:

I have ... looked over the names of the oldest prisoners in the hulks and luckily the commander of these vessels happened just then to come to me, who much assisted my memory touching their behaviour etc; and I submit whether the ten in the last report answering to the numbers 2, 4, 5, 7, 8, 9, 10, 14, 20 and 21 may not be fit objects for the representation you was pleased to suggest. The shortness of time since I had the honour of receiving your commands prevents my being so well satisfied as to their trades, connections and the probable means of their obtaining a future livelihood; but should you think it necessary for me to give you a further information in these respects it shall be done without loss of time.

Progressively, the first arrivals on the hulks became less despondent, as they 'look[ed] forward in hopes of recommendation of pardon'. By March 1779 Campbell had secured the early release of 100 inmates and had applied for remissions or pardons for another forty-odd 'under the age of eighteen, whom he deemed proper objects'.[52]

In recommending that a convict be pardoned or have the remainder of his sentence remitted, Campbell followed a set of principles. The prisoner concerned must have shown contrition and good behaviour over an extended period, and a genuine interest in reformation after release. This usually meant that it was the longer-serving convicts who obtained Campbell's favourable report. The candidate also needed to have prospects of being able to earn a living honestly. Here it was important to have statements of support from family, friends, parish officials and prospective employers. Campbell was also sensitive to claims on compassionate grounds. On leaving, the convict received a set of clothing and a bounty (usually 2 or 2½ guineas, the equivalent of about two months' wages) to help him on his way.[53]

In July 1778 Campbell reported to the Secretary of State that James Mills

has been during his confinement very orderly and quiet, [which] promises a reformation in his future conduct. There were convicted at the same assizes, viz. Stafford March 1777, another two, John Allen and John Slater for deer stealing, who have behaved themselves remarkably well and promise very fair to reform. I have many assurances from respectable people that they can have an immediate employment and get their living in an honest way. I therefore submit whether these may not with James Mills be proper objects of his Majesty's mercy.

The balance of their sentences was accordingly remitted. At the end of 1778 he told the Under-Secretary of State that a 'poor woman' had travelled from Cornwall to beg the release of her son William Pascoe, who had been sentenced together with his father. With the father now dead, the son was the woman's only family, and she needed him to support her. Observing that 'this young man stands no. 161 in the last report' and that 'he has behaved very well since his confinement', Campbell recommended his release. Pascoe was accordingly pardoned.[54]

Campbell was by no means an easy touch, however. In August 1778, he reported of one inmate, '[he] was received ... in February last. The shortness of his time on board does not admit of his being on the list with those of much longer standing who have behaved equally well, by which standard my recommendation is chiefly regulated'. In October 1779 he was particularly troubled by another request for clemency. He was, he told Eden, 'much at a loss what to say'. The convict had behaved well for the previous twelve months, and had often asked to be recommended for release. 'Had his offence been that of a common culprit', Campbell explained,

I believe ere this time he would have come in turn to my favourable mention ... But his crime and the eye of the public upon that crime, his ability to do mischief should his reformation be only external, about which I think you will have little doubt, may possibly raise a question in your mind whether if he is discharged it should not be under an express condition he should transport himself out of the kingdom, and his remission made out accordingly.[55]

In June 1780 Campbell recommended against Abram Barew's release because he suspected that Barew was continuing to forge drafts on the Bank of England. Barew remained a prisoner. In August Campbell declined to recommend the pardoning of one convict whom he thought was not as sick as his friends claimed, only to relent the next day when he learned that a brewer was willing to employ the man. Still, a fresh transgression was not always an absolute disqualification in Campbell's mind. At the end of 1780 an escaped convict named Thomas Hawley applied to the Secretary of State for a pardon. Campbell reported that Hawley, who had been sentenced to three years' hard labour, had arrived in September 1777 and had behaved well until he had run away in February 1779. As Hawley's term had now expired and as he had found employment, Campbell recommended that he be pardoned.[56]

Thereafter, Campbell maintained this enlightened and compassionate outlook. In November 1781 he recommended release for William Germaine, a 'poor creature at death's door from a consumption', who was 'unfit for labour and an object of compassion' and whose life might be saved if his sentence were remitted. In December 1781 he recommended clemency for William Waples, who had served more than two years of his three-year sentence, on the grounds that he had behaved 'very orderly' and had good prospects of earning an honest living, and his family was in distressed circumstances. The balance of Waples's sentence was remitted. In February 1782 Campbell recommended in favour of Thomas Jones, who had served two-and-a-half years of a seven-year sentence, who had behaved well, and whom the chaplain said had 'shown marks of reformation'. Jones was freed on condition that he enlist in the army. Four months later Campbell recommended the pardoning of a man convicted of grand larceny whose former master was ready to re-employ him.[57]

The records do not give us a clear picture of how successful this rehabilitation programme was. At first, Campbell was well pleased with it. He told the House of Commons committee in April 1779 that of the 100 convicts who had been pardoned, 'he had never heard but of six having been accused of fresh crimes', but no later figures are available. In 1785, the Commons committee commented pointedly on the failure of the hulks system to achieve reformation in comparison to the old system of transportation, but this does not necessarily mean Campbell's efforts failed.[58] Those whom he recommended for pardon or early release were always a minority, and they gained their freedom precisely because they showed a genuine interest in rehabilitation. The great majority of convicts left the hulks only when their sentences had expired, and it may well have been true that those in this second, much larger group congregated together after their release and continued their criminal ways, as the judges claimed.

\*

I mentioned earlier that another way a felon might be released from his sentence was by agreeing to serve in the army or the navy. While it is unclear how widespread this practice was before 1776, it did exist. In December 1770, for example, the King extended his mercy to Thomas Rutledge, convicted of stealing lead and sentenced to seven years' transportation, on condition of 'his entering and serving us as a sailor on board one of our ships-of-war'. And in early 1776, twenty-two transport convicts were similarly released on condition that they serve in land or sea forces 'out of the kingdom of Great Britain'.[59] Between 1776 and 1783, war – first with the American colonies, then with France from 1778 and with Spain from 1779 – created a lively demand for able-bodied men, and there were frequent draftings from the hulks and prisons. In February 1777 a small group from the hulks agreed 'to go to sea on a conditional pardon'. By 1778 Campbell had developed a standard letter to explain to local authorities the release of prisoners on these grounds; thereafter he continued to recommend this type of release for individuals as well as for groups. In November 1779, for example, he reported that George Rudrum, convicted at Norwich in 1777 of 'stealing goods and monies value £10.4.0 in a dwelling house', had 'behaved very well since his confinement, he is a stout young fellow very fit and willing to enter into the sea service'.

Thereafter the practice continued on a more regular basis. In July 1780 Campbell suggested to the Secretaries of State that the business be put on a regular footing, asking them to consider

> whether some mode ought not to be adopted so as to employ these poor creatures, who have undergone the punishment inflicted by the laws of their country, so as to keep them from returning to their former line of acquaintance and course of life. Many of them I am confident are very fit for and would make useful members of the community if employed in His Majesty's sea or land service. If the door is shut against them there what must be the consequence is easy to be conceived. It cannot be expected individuals will employ people of a description which is rejected in the different branches of His Majesty's service. What then is the alternative to those who have no friends or handicraft?

In October 1780 Campbell recommended John Russell and two others. About this time, he placed some worthy inmates on board privateers, including one he owned himself that cruised to Jamaica. In October 1781, Isaac Abraham and Francis William Hines were pardoned on condition that they serve at sea.[60]

These were rather sporadic enlistments. On at least two occasions, however, men went in significant numbers from the hulks into the armed forces. In March 1779, the army took 100 from the *Justitia* and *Censor*. 'Their general size [was] from 5 feet 7 inches and upwards, excepting a few, who have youth on their side', their recruiting officer reported. The youngest was aged seventeen; most were in their twenties, ten were in their thirties, and one was aged forty-four.[61]

In June 1781 Campbell sent another fifty-six men into the army, 'as they are willing to enlist, have most of them undergone a long confinement, and all have behaved orderly'.[62]

These men joined the two regiments of convicts then being raised for the defence of the Africa Company's fortified trading posts on the west coast of Africa, which in wartime were vulnerable to attack by the

French and Dutch. The total number enlisted in these curious regiments, the great majority of them convicts, was over 200, and what happened to them was to have strong repercussions for transportation after the end of the war. Two dozen died on the voyage out. Immediately after arrival at Cape Coast Castle in February 1782, they behaved so violently that 'their officers were afraid of their lives'. As the governor of the fort later remarked:

> from the very day these convicts were landed, their whole thoughts were turned upon rapine and plunder. The locks of the Company's warehouses, as well as those of individuals, were either picked or broke. The free Negroes' provisions and other property exposed to sale in the public market in town were stolen: nay, so abandoned were they that they even sold their muskets and ammunition, when against a Dutch fort, to the free Negroes for brandy.

He continued:

> from the immoderate use of spirits, (which being money in that country, it is impossible to keep them from) numbers of them died. Near thirty of them shortly after being landed, deserted to the principal Dutch settlement about nine miles from Cape Coast Castle, and the major part of those thirty fought against us, at the time we attacked and destroyed Fort Vredenburgh at Commenda. I saw one of them mortally wounded at the time we took possession of the fort, and who had just time to beg his life, before he breathed his last. Four- or five- and twenty of them, who were put on board a vessel bound to Commenda for the relief of our fort there, overpowered the crew, and ran away with the vessel. The far greatest part of the remainder soon died, not more than eight- and twenty or thirty of the whole (212 in number) having lived over a twelve-month from the day they were landed in Africa.[63]

As if all this were not enough, another band turned pirates, led by the commanding officer Captain Mackenzie. They captured and plundered two neutral vessels, one Austrian, the other Portuguese. Mackenzie also forged pay receipts for men who had died, including one man whom he had tied to a cannon and blasted.

The hulks on the Thames seem havens of tranquillity in comparison.

\*

Detailed investigation of British penal practice between 1776 and 1786, then, leads us to a number of conclusions. There can be no doubt that the revolt of the American colonists created a 'problem' for the British government, in that it made it impossible to continue transporting felons to the Atlantic colonies. For a number of years the North administration dealt with this problem by altering sentences in law and by instituting the hulks system. The numbers of felons held on the hulks increased steadily from 1776 to 1780, reaching a high point of about 510, then declined steadily, reaching a low point of about 180 in 1783–84. Then, with transportation re-instated as the fundamental punishment for felonies, and with the number of persons convicted increasing markedly, the number of convicts awaiting transportation rose very rapidly from mid-1784 onwards; even with a large expansion, the hulks system was unable to cope with these numbers. Contrary to popular belief, authorities did not at this time pack criminals remorselessly into the hulks. However, the jails around the kingdom did become crowded, causing local and county officials to complain bitterly to the central government.

It is most significant to understand that the decisions (taken successively by the Shelburne and Portland administrations) to resume transportation *preceded* the rapid expansion of convict numbers in the mid-1780s. In the period between July 1782 and March 1784, the number of people sentenced to transportation to Africa or America does not seem to have been significantly greater than before the Revolutionary War. Judge Frances Buller recorded that there were about forty felons sentenced to Africa in July 1782.[64] Campbell contracted to temporarily accommodate no more than 250 people who had been sentenced to transportation to America in January 1783, 200 in August 1783 and 200 in January 1784.[65] Since these figures do not include transports in other jails, or those sentenced to hard labour on the Thames, they do not offer a complete picture. Nonetheless, they appear to correlate with the average number of convictions for felonies before 1775, which was approximately 1000 per year.[66]

In viewing the hulks system itself as a distinctive penal practice, some interesting points emerge. There was considerable concern for the convicts' physical and psychological welfare, manifested in the careful regulation of numbers and in the provision of medical attention and a minister of religion. There was a strong interest in encouraging convicts to reform and to lead honest, industrious lives. There was equally an interest in obtaining some return to the nation for the cost of keeping them – as the solicitor-general asked parliament in March 1784, 'Why should they not be employed in such a manner as might defray the expense of their subsistence?'[67] Most often, as we have seen, they were employed on naval works – a point of considerable relevance to coming decisions.

# 4.

# The Atlantic World and Beyond: Proposals for Resuming Transportation, 1782–84

BERNARD BAILYN, THE PRE-EMINENT historian of the British colonization of North America, and others have argued persuasively that a distinctive civilization centred on the Atlantic Ocean had developed by the middle of the eighteenth century.

For decades now, at Harvard University, Bailyn has conducted a seminar on Atlantic history, the central premises of which have been:

1. That before the end of the eighteenth century, the Atlantic Ocean had become 'the heart of an economy, indeed of a civilization, diverse, complex, multiple ... yet essentially one';

2. That, given its multi-layered being – administrative, demographic, economic, social – it bound together Eastern as well as Western Europe, South as well as North America, the Caribbean islands and those adjacent to the western coasts of Africa, and Africa itself; and

3. That, indeed, the Atlantic Ocean was 'the inland sea of Western Civilization', 'the scene of a vast interaction rather than merely the transfer of Europeans onto American shores. Instead of a European discovery of a new world, we might better consider it as a sudden and harsh encounter between two old worlds that transformed both and integrated them into a single New World'.[1]

While large-scale migration and wide-ranging trading activities connected Britain to its North American colonies, it was principally the slave trade that connected Europe, West and Central Africa, the southern North American colonies, the West Indian islands, Spanish America and Brazil. Beginning in the mid-sixteenth century, this trade developed massively as Europe's demand for sugar became insatiable, and with it the need for ever more slaves to work the plantations.[2] It is estimated that in the eighteenth century European traders carried across the Atlantic some 6 million slaves from the principal areas of African supply (Senegal, the Gambia, Sierra Leone, the Gold Coast, the Bight of Benin, the Bight of Biafra, the Congo and Angola). British traders had the largest part in this forced migration, shipping some 2.5 million slaves, or 42 per cent of the total.

It is important to understand the extent to which Africans themselves dominated this trade, and so helped to shape the dynamics of the Atlantic world. In the eighteenth century Europeans, whatever their nationality, were never able to do more than establish trading posts (forts and 'factories') on the slaving coasts. These outposts were the points of interchange between European traders anxious to purchase slaves and African traders eager to sell them. It is also important to understand that, while the slave trade constituted by far the largest exchange on the West African coasts, it was not the only one. Africans willingly took muskets, spirits, metal tools and utensils, jewellery and brightly coloured cloths from the Europeans, who in turn sailed off with quantities of gold, ivory, gum, honey, bees' wax and timber.

\*

The British decision to resume convict transportation when the wars of 1776–83 were over demonstrates this Atlantic worldview in interesting ways. Lord North having resigned as Prime Minister after the failure of the war in America, the Earl of Shelburne formed a new administration in July 1782, with Lord Sydney as Secretary of State for Home Affairs, Viscount Keppel as First Lord of the Admiralty, and the young William Pitt as Chancellor of the Exchequer.

The major task of this administration was to negotiate peace with the Americans and with the French, Spanish and Dutch. This was no easy matter, as the Americans had beaten the British army in North America and the Royal Navy had been unable to achieve a decisive victory over the fleets massed against it. As well, the King sternly disapproved of any political settlement with the rebellious colonists, the Dutch were unwilling to surrender any of their territories and trading monopolies, particularly that of East Indian spices, and, as on many later occasions, the Spanish wanted Gibraltar back.

Shelburne pursued negotiations into 1783. He had a vision of a trading empire rather than a vast territorial one, and was willing to sacrifice some of the gains of war in order to open previously closed markets and sea routes to British merchants. In the end, however, he was unable to explain his vision adequately to parliament and the public, and therefore to justify his concessions to the enemies, and his administration fell from power at the end of February 1783. Before it did so, however, it also made a beginning at resuming transportation, and so began a discussion that would be taken up by subsequent administrations.

*

The coming of peace meant British politicians could again pay some extended attention to the business of punishment. And it is certainly true, as the traditionalist historians have pointed out, that from the middle of 1783, as the number of people convicted of felonies rose, government ministers received a barrage of complaints from municipal and country authorities, imploring them to relieve the pressure on local prisons. Between November 1783 and November 1784, for example, complaints were received from officials in Bristol, Northampton, Lancashire, Southampton, Worcester, Morpeth and Norwich, calling on the government to resume transportation.[3]

The administration's habitual response was that there was little it could do. In December 1784, writing to Lord Robert Spencer in Lord Sydney's name, Evan Nepean explained: 'It would make me very happy to give effectual relief to the jail at Oxford, but the great difficulty which has for some years past existed of carrying the sentence of transportation into execution has, I am sorry to say, been a means of crowding all the jails and places of confinement in and near this metropolis as well as the hulks in the River Thames.'[4]

Still, the complaints continued. At the end of December 1784, Mr Wallis asked that the transports in Dorchester jail be removed to the hulks. In February 1785, Henry Sedley demanded to know why Duncan Campbell had refused to take delivery of transport convicts. This same month, John Higgins told the Home Office that some prisoners in Lancaster Castle had been 'lingering here two years from the difficulty in contracting for their transportation'. On 12 April, Mr White, jailer at Winchester, advised that the number of transports being held there was 'very troublesome'. A week later, the sheriff at Shrewsbury said that his jail could not well accommodate the number of transports it was holding.[5]

In these years, there was no shortage of suggestions as to what to do with the excess of criminals. In July 1782, Robert Hurford said they should be sent to the Dey of Algiers and serve in his notorious galleys.[6] More than one person suggested they be sent into the fleet (that is, the navy), as this would satisfy the requirement that they be transported beyond the sea.[7] In 1785, Sir Watkin Lewes suggested that the convicts should be put to work in the Woolwich ropeyard.[8] More inventive, if more draconian, was the proposal from an anonymous pundit who argued that since the Lord had condemned sinners to languish in everlasting darkness, the convicts should be put to labour in the coal mines of Nova Scotia.[9]

*

In the early and mid-1780s, the ministers of the Shelburne, Portland and Pitt administrations also received a series of proposals for possible new sites of transportation within the Atlantic world. West Africa had been a minor place of transportation before the war, with some 746 convicts having been sent there between 1755 and 1776. Of these unfortunates, '334 had died; 271 had either been discharged, or had deserted, and of pany seems to have heeded this advice to some extent. In 1784, when Lord Sydney was once again pressing the merccept more transports, they agreed that men might be sent to st Castle, but not on the Company's ship.[17]

*

merica was also still seen as a potential destination. By the end 2, the Shelburne administration was considering how it might e transportation across the Atlantic. Late in December, Duncan bell and 'W.H.' [William Hamilton?] suggested terms for transing convicts 'to a port in North America', and for holding them on ip until this might be done.[18] It is most unclear if this in fact then urred; probably it didn't. However, there may have been a few smallale ventures about this time, of the sort that Nepean arranged in April 85, when he persuaded George Cartwright, a merchant who hunted seals and traded with the Indians in Labrador in northern Canada, to take with him four young convicts sentenced to seven years' transportation 'beyond the seas'.[19]

The first tangible efforts to resume transportation to North America came in mid-1783, when the Duke of Portland had replaced Shelburne as Prime Minister and Lord North had become Home Secretary. Rather than pursue a new initiative, North tried to revive the old system. Although the beginnings of his plan are now lost, North had clearly decided on it by the middle of the year, for on 11 July he informed the King that the merchant George Moore was willing to ship 150 convicts to Virginia and Maryland. The King replied the next day, 'the Americans cannot expect nor ever will receive any favour from me, but the permitting them to obtain men unworthy to remain in this island I shall certainly consent to'.[20]

North contracted with the London merchant George Moore to transport 143 convicts to Maryland, with the proviso that if this proved impossible he might land them in Nova Scotia.[21] These sailed in the *Swift* at the end of August, but the rogues rose while the ship was in the English Channel and about a quarter of them escaped into Sussex. The

many there was no account'.[10] Accordingly, the region had a fearsome reputation.

English judges had resumed sentencing felons to transportation to Africa from the middle of 1782, but there was no clear destination for them. Shelburne noted in a memorandum, which was presumably intended for his Cabinet colleagues, that 'convicts require to be sent to the coast of Africa. Something must be done immediately about them, for the judges have repeatedly remonstrated'.[11] One of the complaining judges was Francis Buller, who had come to the conclusion that the practice of sentencing felons to hard labour on the Thames was a failure, 'as offenders come from [the hulks] more hardened than they went, form themselves into gangs, are ripe for all kinds of iniquity, and engage in it immediately on their discharge'. Buller also thought that imprisonment in county jails was ineffective, since many of these were 'not fit to hold any considerable number of convicts. The prisoners are idle and dissolute and their morals no means improved; and where the number is great, there will be danger of pestilential disorders and the jails will be broken open'. At present, he said, 'prisoners are set at large after receiving slight punishment only', so that the country was 'swarm[ing] with rogues'. The only solution, he told the Prime Minister, was the resumption of transportation, and therefore he was recommending certain capitally convicted felons for the royal mercy on condition of their being transported to Africa.[12] This discussion marked the beginning of the idea of sending large numbers of convicts there.

At the end of September 1782, Sydney had Nepean ask the Africa Company to take in some convicts at Cape Coast Castle. Nepean told the merchants that a number of the men the Home Office proposed to send had been sentenced to serve in the army, and that there were also some women. When the merchants asked who was to provide for them, Nepean replied that the government would give them clothes before they sailed, but that the Company was to be responsible for them after landing. After considering the proposal, the merchants said that they thought 'the transporting such people to Africa would be extremely dangerous to the Company's possessions upon that coast; that it would render the British nation odious to the natives of the country; and be thereby a means of greatly injuring the African trade'. Nonetheless, they very reluctantly agreed to take a handful.[13]

Thirteen convicts were shipped on the *Den Keyser* in November and landed at Cape Coast Castle in January 1783. The Company advised the governor of this fort that he was to follow the Home Office's instructions concerning them.[14] It was a directive that Richard Miles was soon complaining very bitterly about, and his reasons for doing so are persuasive. 'I have paid a deal of attention to what I humbly conceive to be the views of government in sending those wretches to this country', he wrote,

> and the evident defect there is in the mode of transporting them. One motive is no doubt to save their lives, of which I conclude the major part have been forfeited to the laws of their own country; but the great consideration seems to be, *to get them out of Europe at all events*; without ever once adverting to the evil consequences that must attend this mode, a few of which I shall beg leave to lay before you.
>
> The governor and council [of Cape Coast Castle] are directed to receive a certain number of convicts. No provision whatever is made for them; neither are we directed to receive them as soldiers: from which it is natural to infer that government understands it is just simply landing these people in Africa, to let them shift for themselves, and get their bread in the best manner they can. In some other parts of the world they might by their industry maintain themselves, but here it is impossible. We have no employment for them but that of soldiers (to which I shall presently state my objections). The natives have none. How then are they to be maintained? They are landed as it were naked and diseased on the sandy shore. The more hardy of them probably will plunder for a living for a few days until the climate stops their progress, and then, shocking to humanity, loaded with the additional diseases incident to the country, these poor wretches are to be seen dying upon the rocks, or upon the sandy

> beach, under the scorching [...]
> support or the least relief affor[...]
>
> Miles went on to explain the da[...] men in the fort's guard, which consis[...] portion of convicts may I with safety ta[...]
>
> One-third you will allow is quite suffici[...] these would be much more likely to pois[...] other two-thirds, than of being themselves (b[...] brought to a sense of their duty. Punishments[...] more frequent among such men, than is consis[...] ings; and frequent punishments (more especially [...] productive of enervation. Some among the ten we ar[...] hardened in their iniquity as to be incorrigible. T[...] would have a very bad effect upon the others. Again, on[...] these very men to be our guardians by night against [...] from the enemy. Is there not every reason to apprehend th[...] of them would rather turn their arms against, than for us? H[...] not seen an instance of it in the two independent companies [...] out last year, and which chiefly consisted of these wretches? Up[...] the whole, I do assure you, Gentlemen, I would rather be confine[...] to twenty good men, than have any addition to them from such a[...] set, as we may suppose the convicts to consist of.[15]

Miles had an additional complaint. The *Den Keyser* had also landed some convicts at Gorée, further up the coast, and two of the women had made their way to Cape Coast Castle. He said that he and his colleagues would do what they could to help them, but added angrily: 'Good heavens, Gentlemen, only consider: women of our own colour landed here to be common prostitutes among the blacks. A knowledge of all the dreadful consequences of such a measure prompts me to say, that if their lives are forfeited to their country, it were humanity rather to let the forfeit be paid.' He begged the company not to send any more convicts.[16]

ship finally reached Baltimore on 23 December with 104 convicts, who were presented as indentured servants to a public markedly reluctant to purchase their labour. By March 1784, many who had been hired had absconded, while many others were ill or dead. Moore and his American partner suffered heavy losses.

*

Meanwhile, successive administrations had continued to investigate alternative sites within the Atlantic world, including other destinations in Africa. In July 1782, Justice Buller inquired about the suitability of one or another of the islands off the west African coast. He asked Duncan Campbell for information, who in turn asked William Hurford. Hurford thereupon asked traders who had resided in West Africa about the De Los Islands. These traders reported that, of the three smallest uninhabited islands, two were entirely without water, and this was only to be had on the third by sinking wells. Tamara, the largest and western-most island in the group, had about 100 inhabitants, who barely raised enough rice to survive; the terrain was rocky and the soil sparse. Factory Island in the east had about 150 inhabitants, who raised cassava and rice. While capable of some improvement, its soil was also thin. At different seasons, rains made all the islands unhealthy. Hurford's informants thought that to found a colony on any one of them 'would be madness in the extreme'.

However, they were enthusiastic about the prospects of doing so on Banana Island, about 150 kilometres south, off Cape Sierra Leone. Indeed, they spoke of this larger island with 'rapture'. The soil was 'deep, rich and grateful'. Here, sugarcane grew spontaneously; here were 'fine meadows' and cattle in the 'greatest abundance'; here was every kind of tropical fruit, and the European fig also flourished in 'great abundance'; the coast abounded with 'excellent fish'. It was 'the very healthiest spot in Africa'. Buller passed this information on to Shelburne, who interviewed Hurford, but there is no record of the idea being pursued further.[22]

In October, the Home Office asked Portugal if Britain might send its convicts to the island of St Matthews, further out in the Atlantic, so named because, sailing for the South Seas in 1525, García de Loaysa had supposedly discovered it on the saint's day. In the 1780s it was thought to be fertile, covered with large orange groves but 'abandoned and unoccupied'. In fact, this island was a phantom, one which curiously lingered on European maps until the end of the nineteenth century. Not realising that it did not exist, the Portuguese Court curtly rejected Britain's proposal, thereby missing an opportunity to get money for nothing.[23]

The British and French had begun detailed peace negotiations in September 1782. In October, Shelburne heard from Captain Edward Thompson, who had led an attack against the Dutch sugar region of Guyana, now in French possession. The planters there were 'miserably oppressed', Thompson said, with many having taken refuge in London. He suggested that the region might provide 'a grateful asylum to the Loyalists of America', or that it might 'equally serve for the transportation of convicts, where they may be made highly useful to the plantations'.[24]

Thompson returned to this idea two years later, in August 1784, by which time William Pitt was Prime Minister. Thompson told Pitt and the Home Secretary, Lord Sydney, that if the Dutch Guyanese settlements of Demerara, Essequibo and Berbice were to be colonized with American Loyalists and convicts, Britain might export its woollens and linens, pottery and metal manufactures there, and receive in return sugar, coffee, cotton, rum, chocolate, tobacco and indigo. They might send cattle, grain, rice and timber from these areas to the West Indies, and export molasses to Nova Scotia and Newfoundland in exchange for fish and timber. In short, with settlements in Central America, the nation would not feel the loss of 'Georgia, Carolina, Maryland or Virginia'.[25]

In February 1783 Daniel Houghton, who believed Britain had scarcely begun to exploit the trade potential of West Africa, urged Sydney to consider the likely advantages of a larger presence in the Gambia. Settlers there might trade with the inhabitants of the inland districts for ivory, gold, gum, drugs and slaves. These items were also to be had on the adjacent coasts, together with rice, cotton and honey.

Tobacco, indigo, sugarcane and vegetables might be cultivated 'to the greatest perfection', and also grapes. Cattle and sheep would thrive there, and poultry and fish were available in great abundance. To these advantages was added that of 'the affability and friendly intercourse' traders had with the natives. In short, there was 'no situation on the coast more desirable'.[26]

Indeed, in the course of 1783, a number of people submitted proposals for more extensive operations in West Africa. In March, Edward Morse, formerly its chief justice, began what would come to be an extended recital of the attractions of the province of Senegambia. The Gambia, he asserted, was 'the richest spot in Africa', its produce including slaves, gold, wax, ivory, rice, palm oil, dyes, indigo, cotton and drugs. If a colony were established there, all these items (slaves excepted) might be imported into Britain. The West Indian islands might also be supplied with timber, grain and 'other necessaries', and inland exploration would open up new avenues of commerce.[27]

In July 1783, parliament enacted legislation giving the Africa Company control of all British establishments in West Africa.[28] The Company thereupon advised the Home Office of the need to rebuild its fort on James Island in the mouth of the Gambia River, which had been destroyed by the Dutch in the late war, so as to stop incursions by rivals old (French traders) and new (Americans), and to extend the slave trade.[29]

During the next twelve months, the idea of transporting convicts in significant numbers to West Africa became entwined with that of expanding Britain's presence in the region. On 23 June 1784, Morse sent Sydney his analysis of 'The Advantages and Disadvantages to be expected from the Territory in the River Gambia being in the hands of the African Company or erected into a Colony'. Among the advantages he thought likely to arise from the creation of a formal colony were that many more ships would trade to West Africa, carrying out manufactured goods and returning to Britain with the products of the region, thereby also significantly increasing the nation's fleet of ships and seamen. Morse also thought that 'a considerable number of convicts may be sent there every year and employed to great advantage', and that these would find it easy to produce enough food for themselves.[30]

Then, at the beginning of August, Edward Thompson, now commodore of the small West Africa squadron, praised the virtues of São Tomé, the island off the West African coast held by Portugal. The Portuguese had first settled it at the end of the fifteenth century and founded sugar plantations, which they had later abandoned in favour of new ones in Brazil. Its 15,000 inhabitants raised only cattle, but, Thompson asserted, sugarcane, cocoa, coffee, grain, cotton, cinnamon and tropical fruits grew in profusion. He was sure that the Portuguese Court would sell it to Britain, and that once the convicts were established they would be useful 'as mechanics and husbandmen'. 'The benefits on every scale of commerce for our manufactures, as well as the returns of produce would yield every advantage to England', he concluded.[31]

These proposals to use convicts to increase Britain's presence in West Africa, and thereby to obtain greater economic returns from that vast region's resources, validate the notion that a strong concept of an Atlantic world existed at this time. Consider that which Lieutenant Clarke sent to Pitt in March 1785. Clarke described the Gold Coast as 'rich beyond conception, and capable of rewarding most profusely any undertakings'.[32] In his view, the fundamental impediment to realizing these possibilities was the African Company's continuing control of Britain's commerce in the region. He urged that these merchants be replaced by five commissioners, that the region be opened to free traders, and that a colony of 300 convicts be established to grow provisions for visiting ships as well as rice, indigo, cotton and tobacco for export. Clarke thought that a large trade with the interior districts might be developed, with rum and Indian cloths being offered in exchange for slaves, gold, ivory, wax, spices, drugs, saltpetre and other items. Some of these goods would be shipped to Britain, but a significant proportion of them might also be shipped across the Atlantic. As well as providing slaves and tobacco, 'the Gold Coast, were it attended to, would in a short time undersell the Americans in all their southern produce, and effectually supply the [West India] islands with lumber, staves and every kind of provisions'. Also, if Britain were to lose possession of the West Indies in a future war, its Gold Coast plantations might quickly become an alternative source of sugar and rum. And, since the inland inhabitants were eager to obtain 'fine muslins, chintzes and a variety of other India goods', the East India Company 'would find an immense market for their commodities'. Such would be the increase in commercial activity that the government would easily gather an extra £100,000 in taxes.

*

In this same period, some people proposed sites beyond the Atlantic world. In September 1782, John Bindley, a Middlesex magistrate, asked the Home Office 'whether some spot of this globe at present uninhabited and uncultivated might not be found, for the reception of those whose crimes and misconduct have made it impossible [for them] to earn their bread upon these islands'.[33]

In August 1783 James Matra, who had sailed on the *Endeavour* with Captain Cook, suggested to Lord North (who was then Home Secretary) that a colony might be established at Botany Bay, on the eastern coast of New South Wales. The area's climate and soil, he said, 'are so happily adapted to produce every various and valuable production of Europe, and of both the Indias, that with good management, and a few settlers, in twenty or thirty years they might cause a revolution in the whole system of European commerce, and secure to England a monopoly of some part of it, and a very large share in the whole'. Such a colony might produce spices, sugar, tea, coffee, silk, cotton, indigo and tobacco. By opening markets in Japan and Korea, it might also lead to the development of the China trade, of the fur trade between northwest America and Asia, and of trade in wool and manufactured goods. There was also the flax on the islands of New Zealand, and trees fit for large masts.

Indeed, Matra argued:

> The place which New South Wales holds on our globe might give it a very commanding influence in the policy of Europe. If a colony from Britain was established in that large tract of country, and if we

were at war with Holland or Spain, we might very powerfully annoy either state from our new settlement. We might with a safe and expeditious voyage, make naval incursions on Java and the other Dutch settlements, and we might with equal facility invade the coasts of Spanish America, and intercept the Manila ships, laden with the treasures of the West.

In time, a colony at Botany Bay might 'atone for the loss of our American colonies'.[34]

At this point, Matra was envisaging a colony made up not of convicts but of displaced Loyalists from North America, those unfortunates 'whom Great Britain is bound by every tie of honour and gratitude to protect and support'.

*

By the end of 1783, then, new sites for transportation were under active consideration, a process which William Pitt's administration continued. When he took office on 19 December, William Pitt, who was then only twenty-four years old, found himself in very difficult circumstances. He had only minority support in parliament, many of whose members bitterly resented the King's decision to sack the Fox–North coalition. This administration had taken office in April 1783. Although it was headed by the Duke of Portland as Prime Minister, its real leaders were Lord North (Home Secretary) and Charles James Fox (Foreign Secretary). It was therefore a very strange alliance, for its principals held very different political views and had been opponents during the American war. George III detested Fox, whom he thought encouraged his son, the Prince of Wales, in his profligate ways. When the administration introduced legislation into parliament which would have given it inordinate power over the East India Company, the King dismissed its ministers and asked William Pitt to form a new administration.

Repeatedly, Pitt found his administration out-voted in the House of Commons. But as the nation grew weary of the political turmoil and parliamentarians came to see that the young Prime Minister was both able and determined to put the nation on a better footing after the disastrous war, the tide slowly turned in Pitt's favour and he began to obtain a majority in the Commons.

(A few weeks before he did so, Pitt was involved in a very curious incident, one that again shows the incipient violence of London life. One night, as his carriage was passing Brooks's Club, a favourite haunt of Opposition politicians, a mob, mostly made up of chairmen, but including some club members, set upon it, smashing it to pieces with poles and attempting to do the same to the Prime Minister. With considerable difficulty Pitt's servants, other chairmen and members of a rival club, White's, got him to safety. Suspicion naturally abounded that the leaders of the Opposition had connived in this assault, but when confronted about it, Fox replied blandly that he had had no hand in it; indeed, he said, he had been in bed with his mistress, 'who was ready to prove it on oath'.[35])

By this time, Pitt's ministers had turned their attention to the question of resuming transportation. A bill 'to provide places for the temporary reception of criminals under sentence of death, and respited during His Majesty's pleasure, or under sentence or order of transportation, and also sick prisoners' was introduced into the House of Commons on 2 March.[36] After the usual consideration and debate, this passed the Commons on 18 March and the House of Lords on 23 March; it received royal assent the next day.

This act (24. Geo. III, c. 12) provided for the removal of transport convicts from the county jails to hulks and, if they could not be immediately transported, for their being put to labour on the waterways. Curiously, though, this could be done only with their consent, and with the proviso that they be given half the profit arising from their labour. Also, those who had not been sentenced explicitly to transportation to Africa could not be sent there. This act was intended as a temporary measure, so as to allow time for the preparation of a comprehensive new one to provide for the resumption of transportation.

It was in the context of the passage of this act that Sydney sought out James Matra and asked him whether New South Wales might not be 'a very proper region for the reception of criminals condemned to transportation'. Matra consequently added this idea enthusiastically to his proposal. Transportation to Botany Bay, he saw, would mean that the convicts would have to remain there and to work for their subsistence; 'they cannot fly from the country', and without items to steal they must either 'work or starve'. But Matra also saw positive benefits. If upon their arrival the convicts were given 'a few acres of ground ... in *absolute property*', and if they were not stigmatized for their former behaviour, it was 'highly probable that they will be useful, [and ... ] it is very possible they will be moral subjects of society'. As the cost of transporting them to New South Wales would be 'absolutely imperceptible, comparatively with what criminals have hitherto cost government', this would combine 'two objects of most desirable and beautiful union': 'economy to the public, and humanity to the individual'.[37]

The King disolved parliament on the 25 March 1784, ahead of a general election. Pitt was returned with a comfortable majority, and when the new session of parliament opened in April 1784 he began a legislative programme to effect much needed reforms and a diplomatic one to improve the nation's relations with the world. For example, he reformed taxation and created a 'sinking fund' to reduce the national debt. He made changes intended to improve administrative efficiency. He ordered an ambitious building programme for the Royal Navy. He set up a Board of Control to supervise the operations of the East India Company. And he set about negotiating new commercial arrangements with the United States, France, Spain and Russia.

The Pitt administration also produced a new act (24. Geo III, c. 56) to pave the way for the resumption of transportation. Passing through parliament in August, this provided for those convicted of transportable felonies, or those whose death sentence was remitted in favour of that of transportation, to be sentenced generally to 'transportation beyond the seas', with the Privy Council (King-in-Council) then fixing the place of transportation. This meant that, legislatively, the way was now clear for convicts to be sent anywhere in the world; the choice was no longer confined to places within the existing British empire.

This was a striking innovation. There evidently was some unease among parliamentarians at this last provision, on the grounds that it increased the power of the Crown. As the bill was passing, the attorney-general advised Lord Sydney that 'Lord Beauchamp intended to have objected in the House of Commons to the sending of transport convicts out of the King's dominions, but was absent when the bill came on'. In case any members of the House of Lords should raise this objection, he prepared a detailed paper to show 'that a law for this purpose existed in England from 1597 to 1714'.[38]

The passage of this act led to a fresh round of proposals for sites for a convict colony. As the bill was passing James Matra, blatantly trying to straddle the political fence, sent his New South Wales scheme to Fox.[39] Then, in September, the brothers-in-law Sir John Call and Sir George Young submitted detailed schemes for a Loyalist and convict colony in the southwest Pacific Ocean.

Drawing on the narratives of Cook's voyages, Call described New South Wales, New Zealand, New Caledonia and Norfolk Island. He wrote:

According to the object which may be in view for making an establishment, either the coast of New South Wales, or some other part of New Holland, which on a closer examination may be hereafter discovered, cannot fail to offer a convenient situation. But if New Zealand should be deemed a more promising island either for ports or fertility, there cannot be a doubt but situations may be found attended with every convenience that nature furnishes, and perfectly adapted to receive the improvements of art. Let the choice therefore fall on either, or both, for principal establishments, it is obvious that New Caledonia or Norfolk Island will afford useful auxiliaries.

Call mentioned many of the same benefits in navigation, trade and political influence that Matra had earlier pointed to. The reason for establishing one or more secondary settlement was to obtain naval materials – masts from New Caledonia, and masts and flax from Norfolk

Island: 'the timber, shrubs, vegetables and fish already found there need no embellishment to pronounce them excellent samples, but the most invaluable of all is the flax plant, which grows more luxuriant than in New Zealand'.[40]

There were also economic and political considerations. Sir George Young advised Pitt that a settlement at Botany Bay would allow the British to open a trade in manufactured goods with South America and that, in the event of another war with Spain, '*Here is* a port of shelter and refreshment for our ships should it be necessary to send any into the South Seas'. Settlers might cultivate exotic plants and spices to commercial advantage. There was the New Zealand flax, the uses of which 'are more extensive than any vegetable hitherto known', and the products of which (cables, cordage and canvas) would be cheaper than those of Russian fibre plants. He also pointed out how Russia 'may perhaps at some future period think it her interest to prohibit our trade with her for such articles'. The British might establish an international port at Botany Bay; the Loyalists would find a home there, and it would be a suitable place to send the convicts.[41]

Matra and Young now joined forces to promote the scheme. Matra spoke to his Loyalist friends, who indicated their willingness to move to the ends of the earth.[42] Young consulted captains who had sailed East Indiamen to China. They confirmed that, once past the Cape of Good Hope, these ships might proceed through the southern Indian Ocean and, rounding Van Diemen's Land, land the convicts at Botany Bay before proceeding 'to the northward round New Ireland etc, or through St George's Channel, and so on to the Island Formosa for Canton. With a little geographical investigation, this passage will be found more short, easy and a safer navigation, than the general route to the China ships, from Madras through the Straits of Malacca'. Young and Matra then persuaded the attorney-general to take up their cause.[43]

It is clear that Pitt's Cabinet did consider these proposals, for at the beginning of November Matra asked Nepean whether the ministers had come 'to a decided resolution to reject the plan, or if there be any chance of its being entered on, in the spring season?'[44] However, New South

Wales was not the only place the ministers were considering. At the end of August, Evan Nepean asked the Portuguese ambassador if his country might take the malefactors off Britain's hands, explaining:

> that England, after the separation of America, had nowhere where it could send its convicts, and that it would much appreciate it if Portugal were willing either to send them to or to receive them in some part of its dominions, making whatever use of them which might best serve its interests.
>
> That all England wanted was to save the life of the great numbers of wrongdoers who, for their crimes, should rightfully lose it. And that this death sentence having been commuted to transportation, Her Most Faithful Majesty would be able to put them to good use as galley-slaves or in any other manner, in the settling of remote parts of her vast dominions, or in the cultivation of land, mining, or any other forced labour, no matter how difficult or arduous. And that they could also be transported to the East as soldiers, just as [Portuguese] nationals were; and that the only condition would be that they should never serve in any war on the side of the enemies of Great Britain.

A week later, the ambassador forwarded to his Court details from Duncan Campbell, who indicated how the convicts had previously been shipped across the Atlantic and how much their labour had been sold for. It was in vain, however. In October, the Queen of Portugal said she could not agree to the idea.[45]

\*

Meanwhile, despite George Moore's earlier failure, the Pitt administration had sanctioned a further attempt to resume transportation to North America. On 2 April 1784, Moore's ship the *Mercury* left the Thames with 179 convicts – but this lot of rogues also rebelled, 'tak[ing] the ship from the captain and confin[ing] him and his people in chains after a very bloody resistance' and running it into Torbay on 13 April, where about 120 escaped before being quickly recaptured.[46] When at last the *Mercury* reached North America, authorities refused to accept the convicts who remained on board. In July, Moore's agent and the ship's master sailed down to Honduras with eighty-six of them, whose labour they tried to sell to the logwood cutters, only for the venture to turn out disastrously when the local magistrates refused to allow the sale. These magistrates and various others then plundered the ship.

The later deposition of Daniel Hill, Moore's agent, describing these events makes for some harrowing reading.[47] After calling at Jamaica, the ship reached Honduras in July with the convicts, twelve months' provisions and £2000 worth of goods. Hill and his colleagues asked two local magistrates where they might build a shelter for the convicts and a site at what was known as the 'Haulover' was pointed out. They set to building and landed the convicts. Then suddenly, in August, the magistrates and settlers declared that the convicts were not welcome and ordered that they be re-embarked. Anyone purchasing their labour, the magistrates announced, would be fined £100. Knowing that he could not legally return the convicts to England, Hill took twenty-two of them to the Northern River to cut timber, leaving the rest at the Haulover with his son in charge.

On his return to the Haulover, Hill was arrested as a consequence of a complaint by Henry Jones, one of the settlers at Northern River. Pleading that it was absolutely necessary that he return to Northern River, Hill obtained his release; but when he reached the timber-cutting site again, he found that Jones had persuaded the convicts to go to another, 'where he said he would show them plenty of wood, which they might cut for their own benefit; and offered immediately to conduct them to that place by which means the greater part of them were easily persuaded to follow his advice, and those that were refractory they forced along with them'. Instead of to Rio Hondo, however, Jones took the convicts to Key Chapel, a barren island where there was no timber growing, 'nor any thing else either for profit or subsistence'.

Hill then returned to Belize for the hearing of the charge against him, to find that a jury had concluded 'that Jones did very right in taking away the people and provisions, and that it was what they would have done themselves', and that the magistrates approved of this verdict.

The magistrates then persuaded Arnott, the *Mercury*'s captain, that he, rather than Hill, was in charge of the ship, convicts and cargo, prompting Arnott to bring a suit against Hill. The court found that while Arnott was in charge only of the ship and Hill of the convicts and cargo, both men were 'subject to the resolutions of the magistrates and inhabitants', and instructed Arnott and Hill to re-embark the convicts immediately.

Then, three days later, Hill said:

Arnott the master, with William Greaves his mate and part of the crew of the *Mercury*, came to my house at the Haulover, armed with blunderbusses and cutlasses, and put me by force into a boat, and carried me on board of the ship *Mercury*, where they detained me a prisoner for about six weeks; during which time all the convicts, as well as their provisions and the rest of the cargo, together even with my own wearing apparel and bedding, were made away with, the convicts being taken and employed by different inhabitants; particularly several of them by Mr McAulay [one of the magistrates], who kept them for a considerable time running wood for him; some by Mr Sullivan, some by Mr Davis, and one by Mr Potts. The goods were partly sold by the captain, and the money received by him; and about £900 worth taken by one Captain Tellet; but for none of them did I ever receive anything.

Hill tried to bring a suit to recover the stolen goods, but the magistrates told him that he must obtain a fresh power of attorney from Moore in London, a process that would take at least six months. He tried to bring other actions, but the magistrates declined to receive them, with McAulay telling him: 'Sir, you shall neither have law or justice while you stay in this country'. Hill replied that he was a British subject, entitled to the benefit of the law; whereupon McAulay responded that 'the people of Honduras had nothing to do with the King of Great Britain, that they were an independent people'.

Hill offered to show the magistrates the act of parliament authorizing the transportation of convicts to any place 'beyond the seas', whereupon the magistrates told him that 'no act of parliament was binding on the people of this country; and that they cared no more for an act of parliament than for a piece of brown paper'; and that he was 'a damned old rascal, and that if it was not for my years they would break my head'.

Hill wrote repeatedly to Moore for advice, only for the magistrates to withhold from him the merchant's replies. At last, Hill was able to get to Jamaica on a warship, and then returned to England. He said bitterly that he never received a 'sixpence' for the convicts and the cargo.

In 1785, while these events were playing out, Moore transported a further group of thirty convicts to Honduras. Leaving London towards the end of September, the *Fair American* reached its destination in December, but the settlers again refused to allow the convicts to be unloaded. After some weeks, Moore's agent landed them on the Mosquito Shore, where their fate is obscure but presumably unpleasant. Moore became bankrupt.

*

In October 1784, before the outcome of the first Honduras venture was known, Sydney observed to one correspondent: 'The more I consider the matter, the greater difficulty I see in disposing of those people, in any other place in the possession of His Majesty's subjects.'[48] This remark has underpinned the view that the British sent convicts to New South Wales because they could find no other place. This explanation has the virtue of simplicity, but also the vice of error, for it arises from a truncation of what Sydney actually wrote. Sydney's point was not that there was no other place to which the convicts might be sent, but that there was no other place in Britain's dominions, which left open the possibility of identifying a site not yet part of the empire.[49] The difference is significant. And in fact, the Pitt administration had already prepared for the solution Sydney hinted at with the Transportation Act of August 1784. Previously, parliamentary legislation had to specify the place of transportation; now, this could be decided by the King acting in conjunction with the Privy Council, and might be 'either within His Majesty's dominions, or elsewhere out of His Majesty's dominions'.[50] In searching for a place to which to transport convicts, the government could now look beyond the existing empire.

\*

At the turn of the year, the Home Office received two separate but similar proposals to establish a convict settlement in West Africa. The first came from John Roberts, who had been governor of Cape Coast Castle, on the Gold Coast, between 1778 and 1782. Although fundamentally opposed to the idea, Roberts clearly knew what Lord Sydney was inclining to, and he offered his scheme in the belief that 'Africa is positively the part of the world [the convicts] are destined for'.[51]

Roberts suggested that 200 convicts be sent annually to Cape Coast Castle. There, they would be under the general authority of the governor, who would have the help of a criminal court and the power to release well-behaved prisoners from irons and, in the longer term, to emancipate them. They would be accommodated in purpose-built prisons, which would be arranged to form an interior square and which would each hold ten men. In the middle of the square would be an open shed, where they would eat. A 'pay-master' would dispense their weekly ration each Monday. There would also be a hospital capable of housing fifty men. The convicts would be guarded in their barracks and directed in their labour by 'bomboys' or 'drivers', one to each gang of ten. These would be armed and have the power to administer corporal punishment. Roberts conceded that many of the convicts would soon die; indeed, *'several hundreds might be sent* before *200* could be found to stand the climate'. However, he asserted that the hardy survivors 'would in time be useful to the state'. These white slaves would be set to cultivating cotton in the castle's extensive (but long neglected) garden:

> There is not an island in the West Indies that produces better cotton, than we every day see growing spontaneously in Africa. The Company's garden at Cape Coast in not less than five or six miles

in extent, although not three-quarters of a mile of it is cultivated by their officers and servants for the purpose of raising vegetables. I would have the convicts clear the whole spot; the labour it is true would be hard, and very trying to European constitutions, but this set of people are now got so numerous, that it seems absolutely necessary for humanity to give way in some measure to the good of our country. The ground once cleared, should be laid out in small cotton fields, or plantations, one to each gang. It might be three or four years before the good effects of such a plan would appear; but there cannot be a doubt that by that time they would be able not only to remit cotton sufficient to maintain themselves, but to pay all expenses government may be put to in establishing it.

While Roberts evidently presented this proposal to the African Committee, it is lodged among Home Office papers. How closely the Pitt administration attended to it is uncertain. It was quickly supplanted by an alternative scheme to send the convicts to Lemain, an island about 400 miles up the River Gambia (a plan which I describe below). However, the Home Office officials clearly kept Roberts's plan in reserve, for when Sydney advised the committee of the Lemain scheme, its secretary replied:

In consequence of what Lord Sydney mentioned on Saturday I ordered the African Committee to be summoned for this day, when they accordingly met, but as no letter came from his Lordship I presume he has dropped the intention of sending an additional number of convicts to the forts on the Gold Coast in case matters are not arranged for their reception at the island of Lemain at their first arrival there. I hope that plan is dropped so far as regards their being ordered to the Gold Coast eventually, as I believe [it] would be impossible to lodge them there without the most imminent danger to the forts in their present situation.[52]

The second proposal came from a group of African Company merchants headed by John Barnes, who suggested to the Home Office that convicts might be send to Lemain, which they represented as fertile and capable of accommodating 4000 persons.[53]

This was an exceedingly strange scheme. The island was to be purchased from local rulers and the convicts sent there were to be under no authority other than that they themselves might choose to create:

> [They are to] be left entirely to themselves, and before they leave the river [i.e., the Thames], be directed to elect a chief and at least four more, as a council, out of their own body, and to invest such chief with powers to appoint any subordinate officers that might be necessary for the regulation of their affairs, and to have charge of the provisions and property provided for their use, and also to try and punish any of them for crimes.

The slave traders conceded that many of the convicts would die in the beginning, but that the survivors would gradually become inured to the region's climate and diseases. These would find it impossible to escape through the country, and a guard-ship would prevent their doing so downriver. Like Roberts, Barnes predicted Britain would eventually derive significant benefits from such a colony. As it became established, it would offer more resources and become healthier, so that 'a regular succession of convicts might be sent out annually'. As for the initial cost, Barnes wrote:

> The amount [needed], admitting it to be £10,000, is really no more than the absolute and certain expense to government for the support and confinement of the same number of convicts in the River Thames for eight months. And it must at the same time be considered that the sending out a like number the second year will not, in all probability, exceed one half of that sum; the third still less, and in a short time the expense will be reduced solely to that of their conveyance thither.

As well as food, he went on, the convicts might cultivate cotton, tobacco and indigo. Once they were established as planters, they might 'take those to be sent out hereafter into their service'. And 'as they grow rich they naturally grow honest, and from the commodities which might be collected from the natives, it is more than probable that it would in a short series of years be of considerable advantage to this country. Gold is often found in the interior parts, as well as other articles of value'.

\*

By December 1784, then, the Pitt administration had three distinct proposals for convict colonies outside the existing British empire, two within the Atlantic world, in the Gambia and on the Gold Coast, the third in the great world beyond, on the coast of New South Wales in the southwest Pacific Ocean.

On 24 and 25 December, in the context of a wide-ranging appraisal of Britain's strategic needs in the East (which I describe in Chapter 6), Pitt and Sydney asked Earl Howe, the First Lord of the Admiralty, for his opinion of Matra's proposals. Howe replied: 'The length of the navigation, subject to all the retardments of an India voyage, do not, I must confess, encourage me to hope for a return of the many advantages in commerce or war, which Mr Matra has in contemplation'.[54]

Nonetheless, the administration remained interested. In an agenda for a Cabinet meeting just after Christmas, Nepean outlined 'Matra's Plan':

The erecting a settlement upon the coast of New South Wales, which is intended as an asylum for some of the American Loyalists, who are now ready to depart, and also as a place for the transportation of young offenders, whose crimes have not been of the most heinous nature;

And 'Barnes's Plan':

The transportation of convicts to the island Lemain in the River Gambia, and furnishing them with provisions, tools and implements for husbandry and for erecting habitations.[55]

The Cabinet ministers took their decision on 27 December. Two days later, Nepean wrote privately to the mayor of Plymouth, whom he knew: 'It is at last determined that [the convicts at Plymouth] shall forthwith be removed, with some others who are now in the jails in and about London, to the coast of Africa'.[56] By the end of 1784, then, the worst offenders among the convicts were destined for a most precarious future, unsupervised and unprotected, on the island of Lemain in the River Gambia.

# 5.

# The Lemain Fiasco of 1785

In telling John Nichol, the mayor of Plymouth, of the decision to send the convicts to Lemain, Evan Nepean cautioned:

> You are certainly the best judge, whether any person brought before you for a petit larceny should suffer so severe a sentence as that of transportation thither, which you know in the routine of punishment is considered as next in degree to that of death ... If you follow my advice you will sentence the convicts generally to 'transportation beyond the seas', for should the present plan, from obstacles that may hereafter appear, be laid aside, some other must shortly be adopted, and upon that general sentence you can have no further trouble.[1]

The trouble that Nepean anticipated appeared immediately, when the African trader Richard Bradley told him that he doubted that the convicts would be able to maintain themselves on Lemain and warned that 'the wretched state they would in that case be reduced to I am very certain would much hurt the humanity of Lord Sydney, and ... would excite great complaints amongst the dissatisfied people here'.[2]

Then, on 3 January 1785, Sydney had a 'long conference' with Edward Thompson 'about the state of the public jails and the disposal of the convicts', during which he told Thompson of the Lemain decision. William Pitt joined them. Thompson told the Prime Minister and the Home

Secretary that 'there was an inhuman appearance in the style of the business, and it would never be received by the people of England. It was in one word an African grave, and they went there devoted to death'. The ministers, Thompson recorded, 'stared, surprised at the boldness of my assertion', and replied that 'it was immediately necessary to clear the prisons'. Thompson suggested that he should locate a site in Sierra Leone, which he thought was 'a better place', where a colony might be 'cherished'. A week later, he repeated his advice about São Tomé and suggested that, despite Portugal's earlier refusal, this island might still be obtained were one of that Court's ministers given a 'proper present'.[3]

Thompson continued to discuss alternatives to the Gambia with administration figures in the next weeks. Eighteenth months earlier, he had suggested to Lord Keppel, the First Lord of the Admiralty, that he should explore the southwest coast of Africa between 20°S and 30°S latitude, 'where there was a fertile country defended north from the Portuguese and south from the Dutch by high, barren, inaccessible mountains – and between these extremes there were fine harbours'. The bay at Cape das Voltas, he had said, would 'answer in point of harbour, climate, and fertile country', and he proposed a settlement there 'for our Indiamen to call at and refit and come up with [the] SE trade [wind] in war to avoid the enemy, without returning the beaten road from the Cape, and the necessity of putting into the Rio de Janeiro'. According to Thompson, Keppel and the Prime Minister, Portland, had 'minutely attended' to the idea, but they thought 'in so infant a peace it would be dangerous to alarm our new friends by exploring, and they therefore proposed to postpone it until the succeeding year, when vessels should sail under my directions'.[4]

Nor was this the first time that the Das Voltas Bay region had been thought of as a possible place of refreshment for ships plying the India route. In January 1782, Alexander Dalrymple had urged the East India Company to survey the southern Atlantic Ocean for places of refreshment. On the outward route, these might include the islands of Trinidada, Ascensão and Tristan da Cunha; and on the homeward one, 'the *west coast* of *Africa* between the north extremity of the *Dutch districts* and the south extremity of the Portuguese territory on the *coast* of *Angola*'. Twenty months later, the Company did send the *Swallow* off on this mission, telling its commander that he was to examine 'proper places on this side of the Cape of Good Hope not in [the] possession of, or frequented by, Europeans, at which the Company's ships may be supplied with water and refreshments'; and with the particular instruction that 'the voyage must ... be kept as secret as possible'. However, the voyage was aborted.[5]

Now, with the prospect of being able to utilize the convicts' labour, Thompson revived this idea. In the context of a broad discussion of the nation's strategic position in the East, he mentioned it to Charles Jenkinson on 20 February. Then, he wrote up a detailed proposal on 9 March, in which he pointed out that the Das Voltas Bay area was fertile, animals were abundant and the inhabitants friendly. He listed the site's advantages:

> 7. The superior advantage the Dutch, Portuguese and French have reaped over us in their Indian navigation and commerce, has arisen from their having more convenient ports of refreshment in their passages, for while we are compelled to Rio de Janeiro and to St Helena, where little provision is to be obtained, they enjoy with every advantage the Cape of Good Hope and the fertile kingdom of Angola, where the Portuguese and French put in, and by this means the latter have escaped our cruisers in war.
>
> 8. The bay and river of *de Voltas*, called *Angra das Voltas*, or the port, would therefore be an excellent reception for our Indiamen on their return; and the passage may be made coastways, from Guinea and St Thomas's outwards.

And he cautioned:

> 11. I could wish secrecy was observed in this matter and plan, for the moment it is divulged and committed to the public, the French will embrace the advantage and possess themselves of this country, as they have done of the Andamans in the Bay of Bengal.

Thompson presented this formal proposal to Sydney on 21 March.[6]

Despite these warnings and suggestions, the administration continued with the plan to transport convicts to Lemain. Evan Nepean arranged for the merchant Richard Bradley to go out to Africa to negotiate the lease of the island, and he asked one of the naval officers who had served on the Africa station whether he might be interested in overseeing the venture.[7]

Nepean also had John Barnes and his friends expand and refine their proposals, which became four: a description of Lemain; the terms on which they would carry the convicts out; the terms (many and convoluted) on which Barnes would keep a guardship downstream from the island, so as to prevent the convicts escaping; and the terms on which Richard Heatley was prepared to act as the government's agent in the Gambia.[8]

On 9 February, the Home Office informed the Treasury that 150 convicts were to be sent to Africa, and forwarded the merchants' proposals for appraisal. Three days later, it advised that the number would in fact be 200. The Treasury duly passed the various tenders on to the Navy Board for comment, which recommended acceptance of that for transportation, even though it was 'high', but found that for maintaining the guardship 'very extravagant', and recommended against it.[9]

At the beginning of March, the Recorder of London drew up two lists of the convicts whose place of transportation was to be changed to Africa, which Sydney sent to the Privy Council on 3 March. Orders-in-Council were issued on 11 March substituting this destination for the 'America' or 'beyond the seas' in the sentences of the convicts selected.[10]

By this time, however, having realized that it was now too late to land the convicts in Africa before the onset of the wet season, with all its unhealthiness, the administration had decided to defer implementation of the scheme for six months. On 4 March, Nepean asked Duncan Campbell to supply a ship 'for the reception and security of 250 convicts' until September. The administration quickly accepted his terms; Sydney advised the Treasury of the need on 20 March and Campbell started putting convicts on board the *Ceres* from the beginning of April.[11]

It was as well that the Home Office did defer the scheme, for news of the plan and of the issuing of the Orders-in-Council leaked out and the Opposition attacked in parliament. On 16 March, Edmund Burke sorrowfully told the House of Commons that the convicts destined for Africa had now been given sentences 'infinitively more severe' than those 'inflicted in the utmost rigour and severity of the laws'. He castigated the imposition of a worse punishment in the guise of extending the royal mercy. He also criticized the cost of transportation at a time when 'frugality and economy' were essential in national affairs. He then turned the full vigour of his renowned rhetoric on the Prime Minister. He wished to know, he said:

> what was to be done with these unhappy wretches; and to what part of the world it was intended, by the Minister, they should be sent. He hoped it was not to Gambia, which though represented as a wholesome place, was the capital seat of plague, pestilence, and famine. The gates of Hell were there open night and day to receive the victims of the law; but not those victims which either the letter or the spirit of the law, had doomed to a punishment attended with certain death. This demanded the attention of the legislature. They should in their punishments remember, that the consequences of transportation were not meant to be deprivation of life; and yet in Gambia it might truly be said that there 'all life dies, and all death lives'.

Burke then demanded to know whether the administration had signed a contract for this transportation, to which Pitt answered 'No' – which was literally true, but also a prevarication.[12]

The Opposition returned to the attack on 11 April. Lord Beauchamp pointed out that there had as yet been no report to the House of Commons on how the administration intended to dispose of the transport convicts, even though such a report had previously been ordered, and hinted darkly at a hostile motion. Pitt pleaded 'a very great hurry of public business' and asked Beauchamp the likely tenor of his motion.

Beauchamp repeated his opposition to transporting convicts outside the King's dominions, but would not otherwise be drawn.[13]

Burke then once again drew attention to the miserable fate awaiting any wretches unfortunate enough to be sent to Africa, and repeated that doing so was scarcely an example of humanity: 'the merciful gallows of England would rid them of their lives in a far less dreadful manner, than the climate or the savages of Africa would taken them'. When Pitt interjected that he was 'assuming facts without any better authority than report', Burke replied that he understood that there were seventy-five convicts aboard a ship that 'might sail before morning, and the wind would soon carry them out of the reach of the interposition of parliament'. He then sarcastically compared the full state of the 'House' of Newgate with the few members present in the House of Commons.[14]

The next day, the administration presented the Orders-in-Council of 11 March to parliament, and on 20 April the Commons set up a committee to enquire into the workings of the transportation act of the previous August. With Beauchamp as its chairman, and Burke and Fox among its many members, this was scarcely a group friendly to the administration.

The Beauchamp Committee's hearings divided into two stages.[15] In the first, from 26 April to 3 May, its members heard testimony about the state of the jails and hulks, and the suitability or otherwise of West Africa as a place of transportation.

On 26 April, Thomas Bailey, a magistrate, told of the recent difficulties in carrying out sentences of transportation. The next day, Evan Nepean testified about the administration's intentions. This was not an easy task. He explained that the African Company had refused to take any more convicts at its settlement, and that therefore 'a plan has been suggested, for the transportation of convicts to the island of *Lemain*, about 400 miles up the River Gambia'. He said that this site had been chosen partly in the absence of suggestions of others. Asked 'Whether the plan respecting the island of Lemain is finally determined on', he replied that it was 'under the contemplation of government, and preferred [to] every other plan, though not finally resolved on'. He added that it would have been put into effect were the season for sailing not so far advanced and described the scheme in detail.

Nepean was followed by John Boon, a surgeon who had lived in Senegal for three years, who told of how 'putrid fevers' and 'fluxes' were very prevalent among Europeans in the area. Someone who labours in the field, he said, 'could not live a month, unless he had an able surgeon with him'. Moreover, 'no reliance could be placed on the faith of the natives', who 'would rob any settlers that might be sent there of their tools, and of everything they could lay their hands upon, particularly iron'.

The committee then heard from John Barnes, who announced that the Lemain idea was originally his, and that he and Home Office officials had worked out its details in conversation. Barnes testified to the healthiness and fertility of the area, to the friendliness of the natives and to the usefulness of the scheme proposed, concluding that Britain was likely to receive distinct benefits from it.

John Call and the Recorder of London testified on 28 April. Call said that he had visited both Senegal and Gambia in 1750, and that Europeans there 'almost generally laboured under fluxes or fevers'. He thought that convicts sent from England were likely to arrive debilitated and unfit for work, that conflicts with the natives would certainly follow; and that the inevitable mortality among the crew of the guardship would diminish its effectiveness. The Recorder described the workings of the new transportation act, with its provisions for fixing the place of transportation by Order-in-Council.

Sir George Young, Mr Sturt, Edward Thompson, Henry Smeathman and John Barnes appeared on 2 May. Young cited his four tours of duty on the Africa station, and said that it would be impossible to restrain 'a colony of convicts without order or government'; if the convicts were armed, he warned, they would 'probably kill and rob the natives, or if unarmed, the natives would rob and kill them'. The Gambians were 'very peaceable, if well treated, but very revengeful, if insulted', while 'death would be the consequence of [European labourers] continuing an hour exposed to the sun'.

Sturt, who had accompanied the convict regiments to Cape Coast Castle in 1782, told of the soldiers' bad behaviour and desertion. Thompson reported that the area was generally unhealthy and that the natives were likely to kill the convicts. If they didn't, fevers and the climate would. Moreover, he said, a convict settlement needed more control than a guardship stationed downstream could provide. Smeathman, who had lived in Sierra Leone for four years, described the natives there as 'exceedingly vindictive'. Barnes offered what opposing views he could, but by this point the overall tenor of the testimony had become clear. Jonathan Nevan and Thomas Nesbitt added to it the next day, when Richard Akerman also gave details of the crowded state of Newgate prison.

Beauchamp then prepared a report of this stage of the committee's hearings, which he presented to the Commons on 9 May.[16] The administration can scarcely have been happy with it. The committee had heard from a stream of witnesses, administration supporters among them, who had tellingly exposed the weaknesses and callousness of the Lemain scheme, publicly confirming the severe criticism Edward Thompson had made of it at the beginning of the year. With the tabling of this preliminary report, it became impossible for the administration to proceed with the scheme.

*

The Beauchamp Committee began the second stage of its hearings on 6 May, when James Matra testified about the suitability of Botany Bay.[17] While the minutes of this day's hearings have not survived, Matra evidently presented members with his fully-fledged scheme for a Loyalist colonization of New South Wales. It is also possible that they were given details of Sir George Young's scheme, which he had had printed on 21 April, obviously in preparation for the committee's hearings; however, there is now no indication that Young appeared to testify about it. (It may be that his brother-in-law John Call, who was a member of the committee, instead distributed copies of the printed version.)[18]

Matra appeared again on 9 May. Committee members opened their questioning with an enquiry about numbers:

> Supposing colonization to be out of the question and that the only object was the inquiry of this Committee, viz., to send criminals out of the kingdom, that a guardship and some marines being sent to control them 300 or 400 might not be sent in proper transports and established in a situation where by hard labour, [and] if furnished with proper tools and seeds, they might be able to provide convenient residence and future subsistence for themselves and those appointed to govern and direct them?

Matra replied that 500 convicts might be safely sent, provided the guardship remained.

Although the scope of its enquiry was limited, it is interesting that the committee did not rule out a free colonization of New South Wales. Could both sorts of settlement co-exist, at sufficient distance from each other that there need be no intercourse between them, a member asked. Matra was certain that they could. He thought that the initial colonizing expedition should leave England not later than the beginning of August and that, given necessary stops for provisions at the Cape of Good Hope and other places, the voyage would take a minimum of six months. He described how on Cook's first voyage they had been on the coast of New South Wales between April and July and had found the climate 'perfectly agreeable to [the] European constitution'. He said that the inhabitants of New Caledonia and Tahiti were 'of a quiet nature' and as happy 'as human nature generally are'. As Tahitian women preferred European men, he added, they might be brought to the new settlement 'in any number'. A committee member then raised a point that was later to be of considerable significance: 'Do you think government would run any risk in attempting this plan without further examination than you or anybody you know could give them of that country?' 'I think they would not', Matra replied. He added that rather than see the idea dropped he would, if the administration wished, 'undertake it not on the footing of a contractor, but as an officer under the government, to be the conductor and governor'. On being asked whether he meant 'as a sober regular colony or as a colony of convicts', he replied, 'Either or both'.

If the decision were for a colony of 500 convicts, Matra continued, he would need a force of 200 marines and a guardship (a 40-gun ship 'of the old build' would be most suitable). The colony would need to be under military law, and ministers of religion should be sent. He concluded by saying that he had not calculated the likely costs of transporting convicts to New South Wales, but that the seeds and livestock needed might be purchased at the Cape of Good Hope, Madagascar and the Moluccas.

Sir Joseph Banks appeared before the committee the next day (10 May). The members told the now-famous naturalist that they would be glad to know 'whether in your voyage with Captain Cook it occurred to you that there were any places in the new discovered islands to which persons of such description [i.e. convicts] might be sent in a situation where they might be able by labour to support themselves?' Banks replied that he had 'no doubt that the soil of many parts of the eastern coast of New South Wales between the latitudes of 30°S and 40°S is sufficiently fertile to support a considerable number of Europeans who would cultivate it in the ordinary modes used in England', and that Botany Bay was 'in every respect adapted to the purpose'.

Banks confessed himself ignorant of the Aborigines' language and form of government, so that he could not advise about negotiating the cession of an area, but he said that fish were plentiful on the coast, and that there were no wild beasts. The timber appeared 'fit for all the purposes of house-building and ship-building'. He thought European cattle would thrive there, as would grains and legumes. Women for the 500 convicts might be brought from the Pacific islands. He concluded by saying that 'from the fertility of the soil, the timid disposition of the inhabitants and the climate being so analogous to that of Europe, I give this place the preference to all [others] that I have seen'.

Charles Coggan, the East India Company's chief shipping official, and Duncan Campbell appeared before the committee on 12 May. Coggan gave members some idea of the likely costs of transporting to

New South Wales, by providing those of sending troops out to India. His figures showed this to be on average £25 per man, but he pointed out that this sum did not include the cost of a surgeon's services on the voyage, of food and accommodation, and of some other minor expenditures.

Campbell followed Coggan. He briefly described how he had transported convicts to North America, and his trading activities there. He explained that, on average, he had received £13 for the sale of each convict's labour; and that he had had the advantage of a homeward trade in tobacco. He thought that he would have required a minimum of £12 per person, if he had been unable to obtain a return cargo and been 'obliged to come back in ballast'.

A committee member friendly to the administration (who may have been John Call) then asked Campbell a series of questions prepared by the Home Office:[19]

> If you were to carry convicts a voyage of probably six months to a place where no kind of trade is carried on, how much per man would you contract for?
>
> I think the ship ought not to be of less tonnage than 700 or 800 for this purpose. It ought to carry out 300 convicts exclusive of crew. Then if she goes alone I apprehend 70 or 80 men would be enough to man her. I must reckon on a 15 months' voyage; provisions for the ship's company for that time; for convicts for the outward voyage, for 7 months. I think it could not be contracted for less than £30 a man.
>
> If the ship carried only 200 what could it be done for then?
>
> About £40 a man.
>
> In the calculation do you include the expense of a surgeon and medicine?
>
> Yes, all expenses and a profit to the undertaker of the plan.

The committee received a follow-up letter from Campbell 'relative to the expense of transporting convicts into the southern ocean beyond the Cape of Good Hope' when it next met on 23 May.[20] Its members had some more questions for Matra:

> Do you conceive that cattle, sheep, poultry, hogs and other live stock may be obtained more easily and expeditiously both for consumption as well as propagation from countries much nearer to New South Wales than the Cape of Good Hope?
>
> I do, from Savu and the other Molucca islands. I believe any quantity may be obtained, at a very easy expense and at a very short space of time, and from the Friendly and Society islands hogs and poultry may be obtained.
>
> Don't you think that grain of some kinds, vegetables and fruit may be also obtained from these and other islands in the neighbourhood?
>
> At the Moluccas there is the greatest abundance of all kinds of grain that grow in the east. There is a Dutch agent resident in each of the islands, who gives permission to trade and of whom the permission may be purchased.
>
> Though Mr Campbell seems to think that a ship that should take on board 300 convicts would not be able to take stores, provision and water, can you suggest any other mode by which that difficulty may be obviated?
>
> If the ship be burden of about 800 tons she will certainly carry stores and provisions sufficient for the voyage, and sufficient to bring her crew back, especially if she is under convoy of a frigate, and in case it is meant to retain them there under any kind of government, then undoubtedly a storeship would be necessary.
>
> When you [were] examined upon a former occasion touching the propriety of sending convicts to New South Wales did you give any information of that country being taken possession of by Captain Cook in the name of His Britannic Majesty?
>
> I don't recollect that any such question was put to me, but Captain Cook regularly took possession not only of the different parts of the coast, but also of the strait which separates it from

New Guinea, and there are no accounts known to the public of any European powers having visited them previous to our discovery, nor is there the least trace to be found among the natives of any European manufactures or utensils.

Have you any doubt that the Dutch will supply us with those necessaries from the Moluccas for the purpose of such settlement?

I don't imagine there would be any difficulty at first, as there is but a single agent. I think we might even [have traded] without assistance when we were there in the *Endeavour*. We found no difficulty, and I imagine that if he acted properly we might get as much at the first supply as would be necessary.

Anyone witness to the committee's enquiry to this point would have been in no doubt that its members would recommend Botany Bay as the new site of transportation. All the testimony they had heard in this second phase had related to this region, and that testimony had provided the basis for a well-founded scheme. Yet this did not happen; instead, the committee opted for another site in Africa. Some aspects of this abrupt change of mind remain obscure, but enough details are extant to provide a fascinating glimpse of behind-the-scenes manoeuvring.

At the end of June, when the committee's final report had been written but not yet presented, Lord Beauchamp observed darkly in parliament that 'he, as chairman of the committee, should have stated some place [as the site for transportation]; but a particular circumstance occurred during the sitting of the committee, that rendered it improper for him to mention it at the time'.[21]

What had happened was that the Pitt administration had abandoned the Lemain proposal in favour of Das Voltas Bay, that site on the southwest African coast recommended by Edward Thompson. In a tantalizingly incomplete memorandum, which, while also undated, must have been written about the time of the committee's presenting its first report to parliament (9 May), Evan Nepean suggested this alternative:

As so much noise has been made and so many objections started to the sending the convicts to the island of Lemain, on account of its very unhealthy situation, it may be advisable to change the place of their destination. The southern coast of Africa at or near Angra das Voltas between the latitudes ... is not subject to the same objections, the climate being nearly the same as that of Lisbon, and although the interior part is very little known or indeed even the coast, it has been ascertained by ships that have touched at places upon that coast that the natives are not inclined to act with hostility, and that they are amply ...[22]

While Nepean does not state the other attractions of the Das Voltas Bay region, as he is so obviously paraphrasing Thompson's proposal, we may know that these were strategic and commercial.

Events in the next weeks show that the administration adopted Nepean's suggestion, and Africa remained its preferred destination for the convicts. As Lord Sydney remarked to Lord George Cavendish, a member of the committee, on 20 May, 'transportation to Africa is the sentence of many of these convicts, and the wish of many others, who are sensible that no climate is worse than that of a jail'. He added: 'But there are those who are disposed to make transportation to that part of the world impracticable'.[23] It was in keeping with this outlook that, on 13 May, the administration issued new Orders-in-Council nominating Africa as the place of transportation for an additional number of convicts.[24]

Signs of the administration's change of plans soon appeared. When the Beauchamp Committee met on 25 May, John Call brought 'a paper containing information with regard to the western part of the southern coast of Africa, accompanied with some observations of his own'. The copying of sentences and paragraphs from these documents into the committee's final report shows that they were Thompson's Das Voltas Bay proposal of 9 March 1785, and Call's New South Wales proposal of September 1784.[25]

The committee members asked Beauchamp to seek further information about the southwest coast of Africa from the Home Office and from published narratives of exploration, and to form 'such a report as he conceives they may be warranted to make relative to the coast of New South Wales or the west coast of Africa between the latitude of 20°S and 30°S'.

Beauchamp had this report ready by 21 June, and he presented it to parliament on 28 July.[26] After an initial complaint about lack of co-operation from Lord Sydney, the report began by deploring the problems afflicting jails and hulks, asserting that:

> the extraordinary fullness of the jails makes a separation of offenders impracticable, and that by constant intercourse they corrupt and confirm each other in every practice of villainy; that the hulks, however necessary they may have been as a temporary expedient, have singularly contributed to these mischievous effects; that they form distinct societies for the more complete instruction of all newcomers; who, after the expiration of their sentences, return into the mass of the community, not reformed in their principles, but confirmed in every vicious habit; that when they regain their liberty, no parish will receive them, and no person set them to work; that being shunned by their former acquaintances, and baffled in every attempt to gain their bread, the danger of starving almost irresistibly leads them to a renewal of their former crimes.

In the committee member's view, these evils arose from the discontinuation of transportation to North America, which they saw as having 'answered every good purpose which could be expected from it':

> it tended directly to reclaim the objects on which it was inflicted, and to render them good citizens; that the climate being temperate, and the means of gaining a livelihood easy, it was safe to entrust country magistrates with the discretionary power of inflicting it; that the operation of it was thus universally diffused over the whole island, as well as this metropolis; that it tended to break, in their infancy, those gangs and combinations which have since proved so injurious to the community ...

Transportation to North America had also, the committee noted, been comparatively cheap.

The report pointed out that the committee members had not considered the idea of sending convicts to labour under foreign governments, as the negotiations that would be required were the legal responsibility of the administration of the day. It then set forth the criteria the members considered necessary for a new site of transportation:

> That the climate and situation ought to be healthy; as, although many of them have forfeited their lives by their original sentences, it is implied, by His Majesty's conditional pardon, that their transportation shall not expose them to any imminent danger of their lives; that unless they are removed to a considerable distance, from whence the means of returning may be rendered difficult, the end of their transportation will be defeated; that, subject to this caution, a coast situation is preferable to an inland one, for the convenience of supplying the settlers until they are able to provide for their own subsistence, as likewise to furnish them an asylum, if any natives should be disposed to annoy them.

The report then stated the committee members' strong opposition to the common premise of Banks's 1779 proposal, Call's proposal, and Barnes's scheme:

> it was their decided opinion, that the idea of composing an entire colony of male and female convicts, without any other government or control but what they may from necessity be led to establish for themselves, can answer no good or rational purpose; that such an experiment has never been made in the history of mankind; that the outcasts of an old society will not serve as the sole foundation of a new one, which cannot exist without justice, without order, and without subordination, to which the objects in question must of necessity be strangers; that confusion and bloodshed would probably soon take place among them; and that no spot, however distant,

can be pointed out by the Committee, in which the mischiefs of realizing so dangerous a project might not be felt on the trade and navigation of these kingdoms.

The report then enunciated the principles that committee members had had in mind in pursuing their enquiry, the most important of which were that the new site should not offer temptations to further crime, but rather hold out the means of social redemption; that the convicts' labour should there be 'employed to the most useful purposes', by which they meant the obtaining of strategic and commercial advantages; and that these advantages should repay the nation the cost of establishing a colony there.

Accordingly, the committee had considered:

First, those parts of Africa which already belong to the Crown of Great Britain, or which may probably be acquired for the purpose in question; secondly, the provinces as well as islands which are subject to His Majesty in America; and lastly, such other parts of the globe as have been already, or which may be, taken possession of for the object under consideration (if policy warrants the measure) without violating the territorial rights of any European potentate or state.

The report gave details only of the committee's findings on Africa. They though that grave disadvantages would attend transportation to either the Gambia or Guinea, but that the area about the Das Voltas River was promising. No other Europeans had settled or claimed it; the local inhabitants were evidently peaceful; and it was highly probable that these would cheerfully lease as much land as was required. The site was coastal; it was fertile and had abundant water; there were great herds of horses, cattle and sheep; and the climate was healthy. There was copper in the nearby mountains (of strategic significance now that warships were being sheathed with this metal), and a 'fine bay and harbour for the shelter of shipping'. A settlement here might become a very useful port of supply for ships returning from the East, since (copying Thompson):

the superior advantage which the Portuguese, Dutch and French have reaped over us in their Indian navigation and commerce has arisen from their having more convenient ports of refreshment in their passages; for while we are confined to Rio de Janeiro and Saint Helena, where little provision is to be obtained, they enjoy with every advantage the Cape of Good Hope and the fertile kingdom of Angola, by which means the French Indiamen have often escaped the British cruisers in war; that the bay and river of Das Voltas would be an excellent place for the homeward-bound Indiamen; and that the passage may be made coastways from Guinea and Saint Thomas's outwards.

As well, it was only about ten days' sail from Das Voltas Bay to the coast of Brazil, where whales abounded. A settlement at Das Voltas Bay might also 'promote the purposes of future commerce or of future hostility in the South Seas' – that is, along the western coasts of the Spanish colonies in the Americas.

The committee members thought that the site would be suitable for the Loyalists as well as the convicts, but added that if the administration established a convict colony, the settlers should be properly equipped for their tasks with food, tools, seeds, etc. They recommended that the colony be policed by marines and a prudent officer put in charge, with the 'most absolute control over the settlers', and recommended Edward Thompson 'as the fittest person for the service'. They qualified all this by noting that they proposed this venture 'so far only as the commercial and political benefits of a settlement on the southwest coast of *Africa* may be deemed of sufficient consequence to warrant the expense inseparable from such an undertaking'.

Yet at the same time as they issued this caution, the committee members appealed to the nation's imperial inclinations, pointing out (copying Call):

That all the discoveries as well as great commercial establishments now existing in distant parts of the globe, have been owing to the enterprise and persevering exertions of individuals, who at great personal risks, frequent losses, and in some cases total ruin, have opened the way to the greatest national advantages; that the first settlements in North America were undertaken under every circumstance of an inhospitable climate and an ungrateful soil, as well as the fiercest attacks from the natives; yet, in the space of two hundred years, a new world has sprung up, under many untoward circumstances to which the undertaking in question does not appear to be exposed.

In recommending Das Voltas Bay, the Beauchamp Committee gave the Pitt administration what it wanted, and the government quickly moved to implement the scheme. On 22 August, Sydney formally asked the Admiralty to direct Edward Thompson to investigate the area, 'in order to fix upon a proper spot for making a settlement upon that coast, if such a measure should hereafter be judged expedient'.[27] Thompson had been expecting these instructions for some time. Late in the previous year, he had begun to gather officers skilled in survey work and had asked Admiral Howe for a suitable ship, so that he might accurately chart parts of Africa's western coast.[28] Howe now approved the idea; he added the smaller *Nautilus* to Thompson's command, and the Navy Board proceeded to fit the little squadron out. In secret instructions, the Admiralty told Thompson that, after inspecting the various forts in West Africa, he was to send off the *Nautilus*:

> directing her commander to use every means in his power to obtain the best survey or intelligence that he possibly can respecting the navigation at the entrance of and in the said river or bay, as well as upon the coast contiguous thereto and to examine, as minutely as circumstances will admit, the face and produce of the country, the character and disposition of the inhabitants; and, in general, to use his utmost diligence in gaining every sort of information that may be requisite to be acquired previous to [a colonization].[29]

Sir Joseph Banks arranged for Anton Hove, a Pole with training in languages, botany and medicine, to sail on the expedition, and drew up detailed instructions for him. Banks advised him that his general mission was to find out if the country was 'fertile or barren'. If it were inhabited, he was to 'take especial notice of the lands cultivated by the natives, what is the nature of the soil, in what manner and with what kinds of implements they practice their tillage; whether they use any kind of manure to increase its fertility, and, if they do, of what kind; and whether their crops are rank and strong, or poor and weak; [and] to collect specimens of every plant, root or fruit which is cultivated'.

He was, moreover, to 'attend to the general appearances of the country – whether mountainous, hilly or plain; rocky, stony, gravelly, sandy or morassy; whether heathy, like the moors of England, [or] shrubby, grassy or covered with wood'. He was to investigate with an eye to locating land that might be able to be cultivated; and he was to collect specimens of all other plants for the King's garden at Kew.[30]

The expedition sailed at the end of September. As it did so, the administration received two proposals for a settlement on the southeast coast of Africa, about 500 miles to the east of Cape Town. On its voyage back from India, bad weather had forced to *Pigot* to take refuge at Krome River, about 150 miles to the east of Plettenberg Bay. A Dutch farmer had fed the ship's company from his abundant harvests and herds for several weeks. While they waited to resume their voyage, two of the military officers on the ship had looked about them with a careful eye and then written lengthy reports for the East India Company.

Henry Pemberton said that the bay into which they came offered shelter for many ships, and abounded with fish. The surrounding country was:

free from brush or underwood, a most luxuriant soil, with regular hills and dales containing the most beautiful sheep walks which extend many miles up the country, and only wants the hand of the ploughman and gardener to produce everything that grows in Europe, or indeed in the world. It is free from all kinds of wild beasts, excepting wolves, which are not numerous or troublesome, abounds with all kinds of cattle and game, the largest and fattest sheep and oxen we ever saw, and in the greatest number besides. Deer, goats and hogs, excellent horses of a small kind and tractable, all kinds of grain, excellent wheat and barley, European and tropical fruits, and vegetables, potatoes, cabbages, etc etc, with milk, butter, fowls etc, all equal in their several kinds to the best in Europe. The climate [is] as mild as the south of France, neither experiencing extreme heat nor cold, and productive of the choicest vines.

He pointed out that, from the English Channel to the coasts of India, the British did not possess 'a single port capable of affording shelter and protection or refreshment to their ships', and that therefore one on the southeast coast of Africa would be 'an object of national importance'. He also stated that the area was a suitable one to which to send the convicts because, surrounded by the Kaffir tribes, they would not be able to escape, while its temperate climate and ready means of obtaining food meant that they would not die in droves.[31]

Colonel William Dalrymple wrote to his wife ahead of his arrival home, telling her to draw up a proposal in his name and send it to William Devaynes, the deputy chairman of the East India Company, who should give it to Pitt. Dalrymple reiterated Pemberton's glowing praise of the area:

It is the finest soil I ever saw, with a divine climate ... It requires no clearing, as in America; only ploughing and sowing wheat, corns, cabbages, potatoes, etc, etc, and abounding with cattle, game of all sorts, and plenty of fish; producing also oranges and a tolerable wine from the grape.

'We should in a few years derive every advantage from a settlement here that the Dutch have from the Cape', he asserted, 'and in time of war, and returning home, would refresh here: with this additional advantage, that the French would not be so likely to capture our ships, as they could not know whether they would touch at St Helena or at the settlement.' 'We are at a loss where to send our convicts', Dalrymple continued, 'to send them to this country would indeed be a paradise to them, and settlers would crowd here'.[32]

Devaynes duly passed this proposal on to Henry Dundas and Pitt, saying that it deserved to be considered seriously, and that he believed that if it were to be pursued, this should be done *'secret and out of hand'*; he had therefore not told the East India Company's Court of Directors of it.

Pitt and his colleagues did consider these proposals. Pitt asked his cousin W.W. Grenville's opinion at the beginning of October, pointing out that such a settlement would 'answer in some respects the purposes of the Cape, and ... serve also as a receptacle for convicts'.[33] But – presumably because Das Voltas Bay was their first choice, and because Thompson had already sailed – the administration does not seem to have pursued this idea further at this time.

# 6.

## *Thinking about the Whole Globe*

IN THE PERIOD 1782–85, up until the Pitt administration's decision that Das Voltas Bay would be the new site for convict transportation, the thinking of ministers about penal practice had been conventional and had proceeded within accustomed parameters. They had attempted to resume transportation to Nova Scotia, Virginia and Maryland, Honduras and the west coast of Africa, and had considered various islands. These prospects all represented variations on the old practice of exporting a domestic problem to somewhere else in the Atlantic world, and of obtaining an economic benefit by doing so.

The Das Voltas Bay decision represented a striking departure from this thinking. First, because for the first time the proposed solution to the convict problem bore on Britain's imperial endeavours in the larger world beyond the Atlantic one – in the Indian and Pacific oceans, and along the coasts that bordered these vast realms. And second, because the government itself would be the employer of the convicts.

*

What premises underpinned this change in thinking?

As always with broad assertions about a new outlook, it is difficult to fix a precise beginning. However, so as to avoid taking readers back to Drake, and before him to Magellan and Columbus, let me begin this part of my story in the early eighteenth century.

From the time of the War of Spanish Succession (1702–13), British administrations had progressively enlarged the role of the Royal Navy. After capturing Gibraltar (1704) and Minorca (1708), and after augmenting existing dockyard facilities or creating new ones at these bases, the British turned to deploying a squadron permanently in the Mediterranean. In the 1720s and 1730s they built extensive facilities at Port Royal, Jamaica, and English Harbour, Antigua, which then became bases for the West India squadron. In 1739, at the commencement of the war with Spain, they sent Edward Vernon with a squadron to ravage the enemy's Caribbean settlements. In the middle of the 1740s, they established a permanent squadron in North America. Between 1745 and 1749 they kept a squadron in the East Indies based on Trincomalee, in Dutch Ceylon.

Daniel Baugh has succinctly delineated the general nature of this expansion:

The growth of the British navy in the eighteenth century was to a large extent the direct result of its radically enlarged strategic commitments in foreign waters. Between 1689 and 1714 England assumed a role in Continental conflicts which, whether she liked it or not, she could not renounce, and as a natural consequence of this role the Mediterranean turned into a major theatre of operations for the British navy. Simultaneously colonies and foreign trade prospered, and Whig governments were neither able nor inclined to deny colonists and merchants the protection they demanded from piracy, privateering, and raids of plunder. Moreover, naval strength had to be found, not only to defend the empire, but also to support a policy of expanding its boundaries by conquest. All of these things had been necessary at one time or another before. But where a cruiser had sufficed in the seventeenth century, it was now often necessary to employ a squadron; what had been a squadron's task now seemed impossible without a fleet; and what had been accomplished by an expedition now required a permanently stationed force.[1]

During the Seven Years' War (1756–63), the British developed a distinctive strategy, first of paying allies to engage enemies on the continent of Europe, rather than committing their own troops there; and second, of using their naval strength to attack those enemies in their shipping and overseas colonies. In the end, this strategy saw the British emerge triumphant from the conflict with their naval dominance confirmed, and with the French having lost colonies in North America, the West Indies and India, while the Spanish had suffered the ignominy of the capture of their two great hubs of empire, Havana and Manila. The success the British had in Europe, in North American waters, in the West Indies, off West Africa and around India, together with the accompanying land actions in French and Spanish colonies, meant that the Seven Years' War was a great watershed in European imperial rivalry. And in developing this strategy, British planners had been required, really for the first time, to think on a very broad scale – as the Duke of Newcastle remarked in 1758, 'Ministers in this country, where every part of the world affects us, some way or another, should consider *the Whole Globe*'.[2]

As the British expanded the scope of their maritime operations in the Seven Years' War, the problems of building and maintaining a sufficient number of ships and of their operating ever more widely became more apparent. Throughout the war there were delays in obtaining new ships. There was a shortage of masts in 1757, and the next year one of frame timbers. In the warm waters of the West and East Indies, barnacles and seaweed enveloped hulls, and the marine borer *Teredo navalis* ate them away. The disadvantages of inadequate bases in the East Indies became clear, as the squadron there was repeatedly rendered ineffectual by the lack of dockyard facilities, of naval stores (masts, spars, canvas, cordage, pitch) and of harbours to give protection from the northeast monsoon. Bitter indeed were the complaints about these deficiencies from desperate commanders charged with repulsing the French in the seas about India. And, always, there were the problems of finding men to crew the ships, and of keeping them healthy in a climate where 'living a fortnight or three Weeks on [salt meat] will throw half a ship's company down in the scurvy'. At the turn of 1762, Admiral Cornish took his squadron out from Bombay round to Madras. He lost 600 men to scurvy during the passage, and on arrival sent another 1400 to hospital.[3]

Still, the Seven Years' War was a naval triumph for Britain. Spain lost ten line-of-battle ships and twelve frigates – a fifth of its navy – at Havana, and France's navy was similarly crippled. Immediately on the return of peace, both these nations looked to rebuild their fleets in preparation for yet another war in which they might redress their losses and humble their inveterate enemy; but the process went slowly, and it was only in the mid-1770s that they were once more in a position to contemplate renewed naval conflict.[4]

\*

When these enemies did take the side of the rebellious Americans (France in 1778 and Spain in 1779), they found circumstances much more favourable than during the Seven Years' War. As there was no conflict on the Continent, they were free to pursue naval war undistracted. They had modernized their navies since the last war, so that for a time, combined, they in fact out-matched the British. And when Britain declared war on Holland in 1780 in an attempt to stop Dutch ships supplying its enemies with naval stores, France and Spain obtained the use of Dutch colonial bases in addition to their own. Meanwhile, Britain was distracted by a fratricidal conflict in North America, which required that it maintain an army there, with the attendant problems of supply, including of food.

In September 1779, the Earl of Sandwich, then First Lord of the Admiralty, summed up the situation:

> It will be asked why, when we have as great if not a greater force than ever we had, the enemy are superior to us. To this it is to be answered that England till this time was never engaged in a sea war with the House of Bourbon thoroughly united, their naval force unbroken, and having no other war or object to draw off their attention and

resources. We unfortunately have an additional war upon our hands, which essentially drains our finances and employs a very considerable part of our army and navy; we have no one friend or ally to assist us, on the contrary, all those who ought to be our allies, except Portugal, act against us in supplying our enemies with the means of equipping their fleets.[5]

Gradually, the British did manage to bring more ships into commission, so that by the end of the war they were matching their enemies' squadrons; but it was lack of money in France's and Spain's treasuries, rather than decisive defeats, that forced these nations to negotiate for peace in 1782.

*

In particular, the wars of 1776–83 showed the British just how vulnerable they were in the East when opposed by well-resourced naval enemies.

To service the very long route between Europe and India the Dutch had the incomparable Cape of Good Hope, which formed a fulcrum of the southern oceans' wind and current systems. The colony's two bays provided anchorage for most of the year, and while the dockyard facilities at Simon's Bay were not extensive enough to permit either careening or rebuilding, they were adequate for other repairs. Cape Town's fortifications were sound, its climate healthy and its agriculture abundant. On the southeast coast of India, the Dutch had Negapatam, which gave reasonable anchorage for half of the year and some food; and on the northeast coast of Ceylon, Trincomalee, the only port in European possession that faced the Bay of Bengal and offered safe anchorage year round. Trincomalee had a fine natural harbour, but its hinterland was unproductive jungle, and the Dutch had not developed its naval potential much, nor fortified it extensively. In the East Indies, they had a network of minor bases and major ones at Malacca and Batavia (Jakarta). Batavia was notoriously unhealthy, but it stood at the junction of busy sea routes and offered sheltered anchorage, efficient dockyards and abundant food and naval supplies.

France possessed a major base at Mauritius (also called Ile de France) and a lesser one at Bourbon (now Réunion). Although authorities made concerted efforts to improve the situation in the 1770s, Mauritius was not self-sufficient in food, with quantities having to be imported from the Cape of Good Hope and Java (and to a lesser extent from Madagascar). As well, the climate was unhealthy, the weather unpredictable, and reefs and prevailing winds made the approach to the island hazardous. However, it had a good harbour, with adequate dockyards that the French kept well supplied. Bourbon was of limited use, for it too had the disadvantages of sparse agriculture, hazardous approaches and unhealthy climate, and lacked a good harbour. However, both islands lay adjacent to outward as well as homeward shipping routes, and while their distance from India detracted a little from their usefulness, they together constituted a satisfactory springboard for war or trade. On the coasts of India, the French had only minor anchorages at Mahé, Pondicherry and Karikal.

While the old papal division of the non-European world between Spain and Portugal meant that Spanish ships did not operate in the Indian Ocean, in the western Pacific Ocean the Spanish had Manila, the centre of an extensive and productive realm of islands.

Between Europe and India, by contrast, Britain possessed only St Helena to assist its shipping. This small island had no harbour, only an open roadstead. It was not self-sufficient in food and authorities had to import supplies from the Cape. As the winds prevailed from the southeast, it was not easily approached from Europe, and ships sojourning there were very vulnerable to attack by cruisers sailing out of Mauritius or the Cape. In India, the British were better served at Bombay (Mumbai), which had a good harbour, dockyards, an established shipbuilding industry and an extensive hinterland to supply food. They were less well placed on the eastern coasts, however, for though Madras (Chennai) and Calcutta (Kolkota) were also fed by extensive hinterlands, these places offered poor dockyard facilities and inadequate shelter to large ships during the northeast monsoon.

All the maritime powers encountered severe problems in keeping the naval arsenals at these bases adequately equipped. The Cape of Good Hope was deficient in timber, so the Dutch sent building and naval varieties of wood from Europe, as well as other stores. They made more use of local materials at Batavia, but also brought out European ones. The French supplied their dockyards at Mauritius almost entirely from Europe, sending out timber, masts and spars, cables and cordage, and canvas. The British sent the same items to Bombay, despite the fact that the Indian artificers they employed otherwise used teak and other regional materials. The Dutch, French and British all obtained saltpetre (used in gunpowder) in India.

As a consequence of this habit of being supplied from Europe, these bases were often severely limited in their ability to meet the calls on them. A yard's having supplies depended first on the goods' availability in Europe, then on navy officials having obtained adequate quantities, then on their having shipped them out with foresight. It depended, too, on store ships surviving tempests and shoals and reaching their destination. The safe arrival of a cargo, however, did not in itself guarantee that stores would be available. Sails mildewed in the tropical heat; masts and spars rotted in the warm ponds; a cyclone might see a carefully compiled supply reduced at once, with no prospect of its being rapidly replaced. In peacetime, the Europeans partly countered these problems by drawing on each other's resources; in war, the difficulties of supply often had a marked effect.

This was so in the naval war in the East between 1778 and 1783. After the declaration of war on Holland, the British sent an expedition to capture Cape Town, but this failed. In May 1781, Admiral Hughes, the commodore of the East India squadron, resumed patrols in the Bay of Bengal. He and land forces captured Negapatam in November, and then Trincomalee in January 1782. Upon his return to Madras, Hughes learned that his French counterpart, the Bailli de Suffren, had arrived. The squadrons met in full battle four times this year (17 February, 12 April, 6 July and 3 September), fierce encounters with no decisive result, and both commodores were left desperately searching for materials to repair their damaged ships.

In 1783, both having been reinforced, the squadrons met again on 20 June. Hughes had eighteen line-of-battle ships, Suffren fifteen. The British ships were faster, but as thousands of the British sailors were afflicted by scurvy the French were better manned. The outcome was again inconclusive, the damage to ships again heavy. Hughes described returning to Bombay in December 1783 with 'the nine sail of His Majesy's line-of-battle ships … not a serviceable lower mast on board any of them, nor a fish for a mast or a spar for a topmast to be found but at Bombay'. He reported again in September 1784 that the 'line-of-battle ships in these seas are in the greatest want of cables, no supply of that article or any naval stores having been sent to India for these eighteen months past'.[6]

\*

Distant though the Indian theatre of war was from Europe, Britain's strategic needs were soon of concern to William Pitt and his principal advisers.

The first months of the young Prime Minister's tenure of office were difficult, and not only because he faced a hostile House of Commons. Taken all in all, his Cabinet ministers were a mediocre group. Later in life, Pitt's cousin W.W. Grenville made a scathing assessment of them, to which historians have added. Earl Howe, the First Lord of the Admiralty, was perhaps the finest fighting officer of the day, but his character was otherwise 'cold and repulsive', his thinking about civil matters was 'clouded and confused', and he took little part either in the 'councils of the government' or 'the general business of the country'. Earl Gower, the Lord President of the Privy Council, was a sociable man who 'lent his prestige rather than his efforts' to the administration. Lord Camden, who became Lord President in 1784 when Gower moved to Lord Privy Seal, was 'experienced and shrewd, but indecisive and rather tired'. The Duke of Richmond, the Master-General of the Ordnance, had considerable intellectual ability but was 'capricious in his disposition', 'uncertain' in his opinions and 'visionary' in his thinking. Lord Thurlow, the Lord Chancellor, was a notable lawyer but an 'irresolute and timid' statesman who 'shunn[ed] with studied ingenuity the labour and the hazard of decision'. Thurlow disliked Pitt and was in turn disliked and distrusted by the Prime Minister. Lord Sydney and Lord Carmarthen, the Home and Foreign Secretaries, 'were unequal to the most ordinary business of their own offices'.[7]

Grenville was certainly right on this last point: Sydney was manifestly not up to his work. For example, the India Act made him the formal chairman of the Board of Control, but within four weeks he told Pitt that he was 'ready to abandon it to the ambition of those who like the department'. 'Lord Sydney never attends [an India Board meeting], nor reads or signs a paper', Dundas told the governor-general of India in July 1787. Even more telling is the observation by William Smith, who personally experienced Sydney's inertia in 1786 and felt for his loyal and diligent Under-Secretary: 'Poor Nepean! He knows not what to say, and is willing to conceal Mr Pitt's contempt of the Secretary of State'. He added: '[Pitt] is really the Minister at least over that Office [i.e., the Home Office], which dare not it seems show any resentment'.[8] I have spent decades reading through the papers of the ministers of the first Pitt administration, and noted only one consideration that roused Sydney from his prevailing torpor: the prospect of obtaining preferment from the King for members of his family.

And poor Nepean, indeed! To him fell the major burden of directing the work of the Home Office and of composing its extensive memoranda. There are exceedingly few of these papers in Sydney's hand, in sharp contrast to the many written by Pitt, Dundas and Mulgrave, for example, in the records of other departments. If he had ever spoken candidly about it, I think Nepean too would probably have said that he held his political master in contempt.

Pitt eventually dropped these unhelpful ministers when political circumstances allowed, but the first did not go until mid-1788. In the early years of his administration, he was forced to adopt another strategy for overcoming their deficiencies. This was to let them direct the ceremonial and mundane business of their offices, but to instruct or bypass them in matters involving the national interest.

As First Lord of the Treasury and Chancellor of the Exchequer, Pitt watched over the nation's financial affairs. From the beginning of his tenure, he also supervised foreign affairs, especially those which involved Holland and France, frequently drafting despatches for the Foreign Secretary to sign and sometimes even having the Under-Secretary send them off without the minister's having seen them. He also oversaw much colonial business.

But if Pitt became 'essentially the government in all its departments',[9] he did not determine the reforms intended to strengthen Britain's position both at home and abroad alone. Rather, he sought the help of a small group of men outside the Cabinet who were masters of their business, and in whom he had confidence – Henry Dundas, W.W. Grenville, Constantine Phipps (Lord Mulgrave) and Charles Jenkinson (Lord Hawkesbury). He discussed matters privately with these men and he put them on the administrative bodies he set up to develop detailed policies. On particulars he sought the advice of the trusted and efficient department heads, whom he also used to implement policies – George Rose and Thomas Steele at the Treasury, Evan Nepean at the Home Office, William Fraser at the Foreign Office, Philip Stephens at the Admiralty, Sir Charles Middleton at the Navy Board.

Pitt's procedures meant that he and his close colleagues conducted much of their initial planning in conversation, of which there is often no detailed record. Let me give one example of how they dealt with business. At the beginning of 1786, East India Company authorities in Bengal sent Colonel Charles Cathcart off to Mauritius to negotiate with the French governor-general a settlement of some disputes arising from differing interpretations of the 1783 peace treaty. Having done so, Cathcart reached England in mid-August and gave the Secret Court of Directors details of the agreement he and the governor-general had reached. The directors sent Cathcart's information to the India Board and Pitt, Dundas and Mulgrave read the various papers formally on 26 August. They then gathered privately at Dundas's Wimbledon house to consider the convention clause by clause. 'Mr Pitt and Lord Mulgrave are here', Dundas told Hawkesbury on 16 September, and he advised William Eden twelve days later, 'I only drew the first sketch, but Mr Pitt and Lord Mulgrave lived with me on the subject for a week at Wimbledon'. On 16 September, Pitt gave Carmarthen the 'heads of a despatch' to send to Eden if he 'concurred', adding: 'I have sent to Fraser a letter to Eden to accompany this despatch if you send it.' Cathcart duly forwarded these papers.[10]

The fact that so much was done in conversation can make it difficult for the historian. After Pitt's death, a would-be biographer asked Henry Dundas for relevant papers. Dundas replied:

I don't recollect amidst the many years in which we lived almost unremittingly together that I ever had a walk or a ride with [Mr Pitt] that a very considerable part of the time was not occupied in discussions of a public concern, and for the same reason it is that most of the useful knowledge I possess of his sentiments either as to men or measures does not exist in any written documents, but rests upon my memory and recollection, and must die with myself.[11]

*

Still, despite the inevitable gaps it is possible to reconstruct a good deal of these politicians' thinking.

As events and a later extended elaboration by Dundas make clear, from the mid-1780s Pitt and Dundas envisaged the development of a global trading network, the centrepiece of which would be a triangular exchange across the Pacific Ocean. One of the perennial problems facing the East India Company was that the Chinese would take little but silver for their goods. This meant that the Company's ships usually sailed from Europe with empty hulls. Silver bullion, moreover, was often very expensive to buy and at times impossible to obtain, as during the wars of 1776–83.

If British ships could carry manufactured goods to Spain's American colonies, these might be sold for silver, which might then be used to purchase Chinese teas, silks and porcelains for sale in Europe and Spanish America. At this time, there seemed also to be a demand in northern Asia for sea-otter pelts from the northwest Pacific coast; if merchants could sell these and other wares (woollen clothing, pots and pans) to Korea and Japan, they might again obtain bullion for trade with China and expand their economy at the same time. The British were also eager to extend their trade in cotton goods with China. To achieve these things, they needed to revise the terms of the East India Company's charter, which gave it a monopoly of all British trade between the Cape of Good Hope and Cape Horn, and to extinguish the South Sea Company's charter, which gave it the right to trade with Spain's American colonies. Then, they needed to negotiate trade agreements with China, France and Spain. As we shall shortly see, the Prime Minister began to set steadily all these things in train.

If they were to succeed in realizing this grand scheme, Pitt and his colleagues also needed to strengthen Britain's resources in the Indian and Pacific oceans and on the very long sea routes to and from them. They now turned their minds to this matter, and did so with five particular points in view.

The first was the crucial importance of the Cape of Good Hope to ships going to and coming from India – as the chairmen of the East India Company had pointed out in 1781:

> that the power possessing the Cape of Good Hope has the key to and from the East Indies, appears to us self-evident and unquestionable. Indeed we must consider the Cape of Good Hope as the Gibraltar of India ... No fleet can possibly sail to or return from India without touching at some proper place for refreshment, and, in time of war, it must be equally necessary for protection ... Not only the Company's possessions in India, but also the immense trade between Britain and that part of the world will be hazarded and in extreme danger, if the Dutch and French are permitted to hold possession of the Cape of Good Hope.[12]

Second, possession of Bombay was similarly important to operations in the seas about India – as Admiral Hughes pointed out at the conclusion of the war:

the safety of Bombay is of the utmost importance to the safety of the whole [British establishment in India], for at no other port or place in our possession could the ships of the squadron be even properly refitted, much less repaired. At Bombay, as the only place of refit, are deposited all the masts and other stores for the ships, and it not only furnishes a great number of expert native artificers, but its docks are of the utmost consequence. In short, without Bombay or some other as convenient harbour in our possession, no squadron of force could be kept up in this country.[13]

Third, there were intelligence reports that the French were pursuing a treaty of defensive alliance with the Dutch, and, following a scheme of Admiral Suffren, were forming a settlement at Acheen (Ache), on the northern tip of Sumatra. Suffren considered that possession of Acheen and Trincomalee together would give France 'the quiet dominion of Hindustan'. So did the members of the Pitt administration, with the Foreign Secretary observing that French possession of 'Trincomalee on the western and Acheen on the eastern side of the Bay of Bengal would indeed render the safety of the British interests in that part of the world to the most alarming degree precarious'.[14]

Fourth, if British ships were to ply between Asia and South and North America, they would need resources in the Pacific Ocean.

And fifth, the administration believed that India would be the principal theatre in any future war. As Henry Dundas put it in November 1784, 'our force now, and hereafter, must be regulated by the intelligence we have of the force kept up by our European rivals, at the Mauritius, Pondicherry, Ceylon or other places in India. Taking it for granted that India is the quarter to be first attacked, we must never lose sight of keeping such a force there, as will be sufficient to baffle all surprise'.[15]

*

At Christmas 1784, with the Cabinet about to decide on what to do with the convicts, Pitt asked the First Lord of the Admiralty's opinion of a series of proposals (probably nine) for strengthening Britain's position in and about the Indian Ocean. These included a scheme to build a new harbour near Calcutta, the taking possession of the Nicobar Islands, and Matra's (and perhaps Young's) proposals for the colonization of New South Wales. Howe replied that the idea of building the harbour was 'a wild scheme'; that the Nicobar Islands in the eastern Bay of Bengal were 'much the most eligible station for ships of war, were commercial purposes less in contemplation for fixing at Acheen', but that 'it would require a long time before magazines could be formed for keeping a squadron on that side of India, all the year'; and that the length of the voyage to New South Wales, 'subject to all the retardments of an India voyage', did not encourage him 'to hope for a return of the many advantages in commerce or war, which Mr M. Matra has in contemplation'.[16]

Howe's unenthusiastic responses by no means put an end to the Pitt administration's consideration of these options, however. Mulgrave, who had held a very unusual appointment during the war, serving as one of the Lords Commissioners of the Admiralty at the same time as commanding a ship of the Channel squadron, was very knowledgeable about maritime affairs. (He is said to have had the finest naval library in England.) His particular role on the India Board was to pursue naval strategy concerning India, and a series of moves from 1785 onwards were the direct results of his efforts.

On 9 April 1785, meeting in secret session, the India Board instructed the East India Company's Bengal presidency to survey the Nicobar Islands with a view to occupying them, noting that in the hands of an enemy 'their situation would give the greatest alarm to our possessions, and the most effectual check to our operations in a future war'.[17] The manuscript copy of the Beauchamp Committee's second report, with its recommendation for a settlement at Das Voltas Bay to 'promote the purposes of future commerce, or of future hostility in the South Seas', is dated in Pitt's hand 'June 1785', and in another hand '21 June 1785'.[18] On 27 June, the India Board told the Bombay presidency to survey and occupy Diego Garcia, in the western Indian Ocean, and to advise 'the best manner of settling it, [so as] to make it a place of refreshment for ships'.[19]

By the end of June 1785, then, the Pitt administration was moving decisively to secure the shipping routes from the Atlantic into the Indian and Pacific oceans.

\*

In 1782, as war was drawing to a close, British governance structures had been revised. The Secretaryship of State for American Colonies was abolished, and the old Northern and Southern departments reorganized into the Foreign and Home offices, the latter becoming responsible for (among many other things, of course) convicts and colonies.

Partly because he was Home Secretary at the time, and partly because he signed the letter to the Treasury formally announcing the decision to use convicts in the colonization of Botany Bay, historians have been wont to see Lord Sydney as the prime mover in that decision. Manning Clark declared that 'one factor alone had convinced [Lord Sydney] of the need for a definite decision: the several jails and places for the confinement of felons were so crowded ...', and he was followed by a legion of historians repeating the same view.[20] However, it is a misguided legion, for this was another matter that a reforming Prime Minister took out of an incompetent Secretary of State's hands. Let me tell you how it really was.

It is evident that Sydney had some role in developing the Lemain scheme; just how significant this role was, however, is another matter. John Barnes told the Beauchamp Committee that 'I did propose to government some time ago a plan for transporting [the convicts] to Lemain in the Gambia, not a regularly formed plan, but from different conversations with Lord Sydney and at the Secretary of State's Office such a plan may have been formed'.[21] Sydney personally informed Edward Thompson of the plan. But there is also evidence to suggest that it was in fact Evan Nepean who put the proposal together from the advice offered by the slave traders. Be this as it may, Sydney was closely associated with it; and when opposition to it swelled, Pitt was left to defend what was indefensible on humanitarian grounds, to his own embarrassment in parliament. When the Beauchamp Committee roundly condemned the scheme, his embarrassment was increased.

Although we can now see only some points in the process, there is sufficient evidence for us to understand that, from this point, Pitt took over the business of finding a place to which to send the convicts. First, by December 1786, the mounting of the First Fleet had progressed as far as convicts being embarked. Thinking that he might be questioned about it when parliament resumed, Pitt became anxious to have a clear idea of the cost of the venture. He therefore had Evan Nepean find this out. Nepean wrote to Middleton at the Navy Board on 12 December, explaining that he was 'desired by Mr Pitt to request that he will order a statement to be made of the expenses which it is supposed will be incurred under the direction of the Navy Board for the providing of provisions, clothing, implements, etc for the convicts, and sending them out to Botany Bay, including the expenses incurred for the detachment of marines'. He added that he had also requested details from Philip Stephens at the Admiralty and Augustus Rogers at the Ordnance Board. All three sets of estimates reached Pitt by the end of December.[22] That is, instead of Lord Sydney, the minister responsible for convicts and colonies, acting to ascertain the costs of the coming Botany Bay venture, the Prime Minister, William Pitt, was the one who did so.

The second indication of Pitt's central role is rather tangential, but nonetheless offers additional insight. During the same period, Pitt was pursuing the plan to bring breadfruit plants from the Pacific Ocean to the West Indies. This was a complex business. The breadfruit would provide food to maintain a larger number of slaves, who would produce greater amounts of cotton for Britain's burgeoning manufacturing industry. With the cultivation and manufacture of these species of cotton favoured by the Chinese, more cloth might be sold to them, provided Britain could obtain freer access to the Chinese market.

The *Bounty* voyage, the first of the breadfruit missions, is beyond famous, and the second – which succeeded in transferring the breadfruit after the *Bounty* was lost – is quite widely known. What is much less well known is that in 1787, on behalf of the Board of Trade, Sir Joseph Banks sent Anton Hove to India to collect cotton seed, and that, also in 1787, acting as the India Board, Pitt, Dundas and Mulgrave sent

Colonel Cathcart to China to negotiate a new trade agreement – an initiative that came to nought when Cathcart died *en route*. Initially, the breadfruit scheme involved Botany Bay: after unloading, one of the First Fleet transports was to sail on to one or other of the Pacific islands. In line with this idea, Governor Phillip reminded the Home Office in March 1787 that his instructions should include the provisos that 'I send one of the ships to Charlotte Sound, in the island of New Zealand for the flax plant, and to the Friendly Islands for the breadfruit; and as women will be there procured, that I put an officer on board such transport'.[23] Banks later recorded that he was 'employed by Mr William Pitt to arrange for him a plan for bringing the breadfruit from the South Sea islands to our western dependencies', and that he gave the 'original plan' of the voyage to Pitt, together with 'the instructions intended for Governor Phillip which were to guide him in framing instructions for the master of the vessel originally intended to have been despatched from Botany Bay'.[24] But then, partly at Phillip's suggestion, Banks decided that the ship would be much better fitted out for the task in England. So, under the command of William Bligh, the *Bounty* sailed for the breadfruit separately, after the First Fleet had left. But in initially tying the breadfruit voyage to the Botany Bay venture, Banks was following Pitt's wishes.

Though tantalizingly brief, the third indication of Pitt's role is the most significant. As they waited for the results of the *Nautilus* survey, the Home Office prepared for the resumption of transportation. In May and June, Nepean obtained estimates of costs from merchants. When he asked the Treasury to scrutinize these, he stated: 'It seemed to me to be Mr Pitt's intention at all events that if Cape Voltas was not found to correspond with our expectations for the settlement of the convicts, that some other spot should be fixed upon to the southward of the Line, and as that is his determination ...'[25]

This statement by Nepean has never received due attention from historians of Australian colonization, yet it is illuminating for two reasons. The first is that it shows clearly that Pitt had taken the business away from Sydney. The second point is that in any event the site for the new convict settlement was to be *to the southward of the equator.* That is, it was to be the point of departure and resort for British merchant ships and warships plying between the Atlantic world and the greater one beyond. Far from being merely a dumping ground for convicts, the new colony was to play a crucial role in the expansion of British trade.

*

It is true that there is no written statement from the mid-1780s by Pitt or his colleagues overtly linking the various elements of their far-reaching plan. But the fact that they did not write the plan down does not mean they did not have it. Consider the analogy of a wagon wheel. The rim equates to those places in the far reaches of the world to which these planners turned their attention – the West Indies; the southwestern and southeastern coasts of Africa; the islands of the western Indian Ocean and the Bay of Bengal; China, Korea, Japan, Kamchatka; the northwest American coast; the western coasts of Spanish America; the islands of Polynesia; New South Wales and New Zealand. The spokes that were to link these distant places to the imperial hub were, variously, sea-going merchants interested in carrying goods between one place and another; control of sea routes; possession of islands, harbours and bases where ships might refresh; the transfer of breadfruit and other exotic foods from one hemisphere to another; cotton and flax; convicts; slaves; the industrialization of cloth manufacture; and negotiated access to new markets.

All these things we know because we have written evidence for them, since administrative procedures had to be followed in order to effect them. For example, the India Board couldn't send Colonel Cathcart to China to negotiate agreements without giving him formal instructions and arranging his travel. Pitt, Dundas, Mulgrave and Hawkesbury's plan to expand British commerce into northern Asia involved obtaining from the Chinese the use of a base further north than Canton. In instructing Cathcart for his mission, the India Board told him that he was to assure Chinese officials that Britain wanted only 'a place of security as a depot for our goods' – 'a small tract of ground, or detached island, in some more convenient situation than Canton'. If the merchants who would reside there enjoyed the 'protection of the Chinese government', the site would not need to be fortified. This modest request was possible because Britain's 'views are purely commercial, having not even a wish for territory'. If the Chinese should mention 'our present dominion in India', Cathcart was to point out that it had 'arisen almost without our seeking it'. If permission were granted for a new base, Cathcart was to 'endeavour to obtain free permission of ingress and regress for ships of all nations'.[26]

At this time, the phrase *ships of all nations* was shorthand for 'free' trade, having gained wide currency following the publication of Adam Smith's *The Wealth of Nations* in 1776. In analyzing Europe's trade with the East, for example, Smith commented:

> During the greater part of the sixteenth century, the Portuguese endeavoured to manage the trade to the East Indies ... by claiming the sole right of sailing in the Indian seas, on account of the merit of having first found out the road to them ... But since the fall of the power of Portugal, no European nation has claimed the exclusive right of sailing in the Indian seas, of which the principal ports are now open to the ships of all European nations.[27]

It was Smith's strong view that if the mercantilist trading system, which gave exclusive rights to national trading companies, were replaced by one of 'free ports', then ships of all nations might enter them, to the infinite benefit of economic activity.[28] These ideas were very influential. In 1786, for example, the Board of Trade discussed the establishment of 'free ports' to which 'ships of all nations' might resort, and this duly happened in Jamaica, Dominica, New Providence and Grenada in 1787.[29]

*

It is not, then, that we lack documentation for the various spokes. What we lack, rather, is a description from its builders of the central hub from which the individual spokes extended, a hub constructed by, variously, strategic, commercial, diplomatic and philosophical considerations. We may, however, gain insights into the nature of this hub from actions taken and from the remarks of people who were closely involved in shaping it.

In the mid-1780s, the Pitt administration began the process of opening the areas of the charter companies' monopolies to independent traders. After reports that the Russians, who were already involved in the north Pacific fur trade, were commencing extensive whaling operations, the Board of Trade held hearings which resulted in Britain's Southern whalers receiving permission to go east of the Cape of Good Hope into the Indian Ocean south of 26°S latitude as far as 15°E longitude, and round Cape Horn into the Pacific Ocean no further than 500 leagues (c. 1500 miles or 2400 kilometres) west of the South American coast.[30]

In October 1786, reflecting on the Botany Bay scheme, in which he had had the greatest organizational hand, Nepean wrote:

> some of the timber is reported to be fit for naval purposes, particularly masts, which the fleet employed occasionally in the East Indies frequently stands in need of, and which it cannot be supplied with but from Europe. But above all, the cultivation of the flax plant seems to be the most considerable object.[31]

And in 1787, at Mulgrave's urging, the members of the India Board planned a comprehensive survey of shoals, islands and coastlines of the Indian Ocean. They did so because they considered that

> it is of the greatest importance to ascertain the most proper stations for the shelter, refitting, refreshment or protection of squadrons and ships-of-war, as well as convoys and East India ships during the different seasons under various circumstances in the East Indies, in case of a future war; as well as the places most worthy of attention either for offensive or defensive operations in the extensive possessions of this country in that part of the world.[32]

The political turmoil caused by the King's illness delayed the beginning of this survey for eighteen months, but when it was at last undertaken it produced much valuable information.

When he outlined his plans for a massive transfer of plants between the Eastern and Western hemispheres (including, but not limited to, the breadfruit), Sir Joseph Banks also left an insight into the central plan. Writing as he was overseeing preparations for the *Bounty* voyage, Banks stressed the potential for economic expansion in the East:

If we consider but for a moment that the greatest part of the merchandizes imported from India have hitherto been manufactured goods of a nature which interferes with our manufactures at home; that our cotton manufactures are increasing with a rapidity which renders it politic to give effectual encouragement and that a profit of 100 per cent is to be got with certainty upon the importation of the raw materials of cottons and probably on many things besides. How is it possible for us to encourage even sufficiently everything which tends to the cultivation of raw materials? In India labourers are abundant, their labour incredibly cheap. Raw materials of many sorts: dyeing drugs, medicines, spices, etc sure of a ready market and of producing a most beneficial influence upon the commerce of the mother country. Why then should not raw materials of every kind furnished by the inter-tropical climates except perhaps sugar be sent to us from the East Indies cheaper than they can be from the West where the immense price of labour performed by slaves purchased at extravagant rates more than compensates for the difference of distance and consequent enhancement of freight and charges in bringing the produce home.

If we look towards the Chinese market we shall see a still more flattering prospect. The immense population of that enormous empire ensures a consumption for very large quantities of all those things which necessity, fashion or prejudice have brought into vogue among them and the vegetable productions which their junks fetch from countries situated very near the confines of the

[East India] Company's territories we know by experience to be numerous.

That drugs the natural produce of this island [i.e., Britain] as chamomile, valerian, peppermint, penny royal, etc, though plentifully to be found in the fields and woods, are carried to market by those who cultivate them for that purpose cheaper and better than by those who collect them wild is well known; and the same will certainly be the case in India where labour and land are so much cheaper than in England. Why should not we then, if proper means are taken to discover and obtain the plants which produce the articles they want and if by means of the garden the cultivation of them is set on foot, why should we not, I say, be able to undersell the Chinese in these articles at their own markets and diminish at least if not annihilate the immense debit of silver which we are annually obliged to furnish from Europe?[33]

*

Events during the Nootka Sound alarm and in its aftermath show the interrelation of these things.

In 1789, the Spanish naval officer Estéban José Martínez seized a number of British trading vessels at Nootka Sound on Vancouver Island. When news of this action reached Britain early the next year, the India Board and the Home Office organized for one frigate to sail out from England to New South Wales, to be joined there by the *Sirius*, and for both to link up with a third warship sent from India. Mulgrave's input into this scheme was again central. However, when Lieutenant John Meares arrived home claiming that the Nootka had requested British protection and that he had taken formal possession of territory for Britain, the Pitt administration decided instead to bring Spain to heel by a massive show of force in European waters. As Pitt had continued the building programme begun towards the end of the wars of 1776–83, the Royal Navy was in very good condition; and when dozens of British warships exercised off its coasts, Spain capitulated.[34]

The convention that the two nations then negotiated opened the way for British traders to sail much more widely in the Pacific Ocean; and the Board of Trade set about giving them permission to do so. Calling them to hearings in January 1791, it examined the whalers at length about the possibility of extending their operations. One of the Board's questions was:

Do you conceive that it would be for the interests of the merchants concerned in the Southern Whale fishery to send a ship across the Line into the Pacific Ocean, upon the joint venture of fishing etc, and to trade with the natives on the western coast of North America?

Another was:

In case permission was granted you to carry on your trade and fishery in all the seas and on all the coasts of the west and east of South and North America ... would it operate as any detriment to the said trade or fishery, if the owners, masters, or others concerned therein, were bound by bond not to carry on any illicit trade, contrary to law or treaty?[35]

The whalers answered that they did indeed want permission to operate north of the equator in the Pacific Ocean, and that they also wished to go east of the Cape of Good Hope, south of 15°N latitude and as far as 'the eastern side of New South Wales, so as to include our settlements on that island'. They added that they 'would not request this extension of limits, if they did not know that whales were in great plenty within the limits they have requested, and that the French and American whalers will have that fishery to themselves, without [i.e., unless] the English whalers have the same privilege'.[36]

In fact, wishing to see more extensive trade, the politicians had a much greater range in view – as Grenville wrote to a colleague, 'Our general idea ... is to enable any persons to carry on that trade under certain licences, to which are to be annexed as conditions such regulations as are, *bona fide*, necessary to secure the East India Company's monopoly of the tea trade to these kingdoms, the only one of the objects under the charters I have mentioned that is of real importance'.[37] Further, what they wanted was for independent traders to be able to enter the Pacific either via the Cape of Good Hope or Cape Horn, and to touch at

any part of the western coast of the continent of America, not occupied by Spain . . . or [at] any part of the Pacific Ocean, for the purpose of trade and fishery; and to sail from thence to any of the ports of China, or to any part of the coast of Asia north of China, or to any islands to the east of the longitude of Canton, for the purpose of selling there any articles the produce of such trade or fishery.[38]

The members of the Board of Trade persuaded the chairmen of the East India Company to agree to these changes, only to have the Company twice renege.

Instead, the Company proposed that the whalers should not trade in Asia north of Canton; that they should be able to off-load goods they obtained on or off the western coasts of the Americas only at Canton; that those proceeding east of the Cape of Good Hope would need to be licensed; and that they might operate in the Pacific Ocean south of the Tropic of Capricorn (23½°S latitude) and only to the east of 140°E longitude; and that only the Company should trade from Asia to the Americas.[39]

The politicians were furious. Hawkesbury asked, rhetorically, whether it was right that British subjects should be able to enjoy freedom of navigation and trade only with the permission of a private company. And he pointed out that the Company's proposal to restrict the private traders who wished to operate south of Canton to the waters bounded by 23½°S latitude and 140°E longitude would 'exclude these ships from the Philippine Islands and from the principal part even of New Holland ... [And it] will also exclude them from another part of New Holland, from New Guinea, as well as from the Moluccas, with respect to which the chairmen thought it was not our business to lay these ships under any restrictions.'[40]

In the end, the conflicting parties reached a compromise, whereby the whalers might operate in the south and north Pacific Ocean to the east of 135°E longitude and would not need licences if they sailed via Cape Horn. However, they were required to give any trade goods other than whale products they acquired to the East India Company at Canton, for transhipment to Europe.

*

Together, these comments and actions provide insights into the grand scheme Pitt, Dundas and their colleagues pursued from the mid-1780s, a scheme which involved securing a more reliable supply of naval materials for British ships in Indian waters; a base on the southwestern edge of the Pacific to facilitate war or trade; a trading base in northern China; the transfer of useful plants from one hemisphere to another; the manufacture in England of cotton goods for export to China; and increased freedom for independent traders, so that they might operate successfully in the East.

What does all this mean for Botany Bay and our understanding of its origins? In Pitt, Dundas and Mulgrave (and Middleton, Hawkesbury and Banks) we have a group of exceptionally far-sighted men. This is best illustrated by another spoke in the wheel of their scheme, one I've not yet mentioned. By the 1780s, it had become clear that the forests of Europe would not go on supplying naval timbers forever. As more ships were built, and as these grew ever larger, oaks – which supplied frame timber and planks for hulls – were cut in greater numbers. As it takes a good one hundred years and more for an oak tree to reach maturity, this rate of ship building was not sustainable. Pitt, Dundas, Mulgrave and Middleton began discussing the possibility of building warships from Indian teak in the mid-1780s,[41] and at the beginning of 1788 they drew up what we would call a 'White Paper' on the subject. 'Few of our naval stores except those of metal are produced in Great Britain', they pointed out:

We have our hemp, our masts, deals, plank and part of our iron from abroad at a very considerable expense, independent of freight. We have at present an interest in India. We want to make it useful to us in such a way that will not impoverish the country; and we are willing to spare as much as possible of our own oak timber for fifty or sixty years to come. Whatever helps therefore India can afford, whatever supplies we can prudently draw from it, we should readily accept, and freely use. Nor should any article be sent out from England for the equipment of India guardships, that can be procured on the spot, or in the adjoining settlements.[42]

The India Board pursued this scheme for over twenty years.[43]

How probable is it that such men, otherwise so capable in their thinking and so alert to Britain's commercial interests, were indifferent to the potential value of convict labour? It is inconceivable that economic considerations should not have influenced their approach to dealing with the convict problem. And having developed the Das Voltas Bay scheme in 1785, with its clear strategic and commercial rationales, is it likely that, upon learning that the site was not suitable, these planners lapsed into hopeless incompetence? Can they really have suffered 'a fit of absence of mind' and decided simply to dump the convicts as far away as possible?

In defending the administration's hard line with Spain over Nootka Sound, Dundas told the House of Commons that 'we were not contending for a few miles, but a large world', by which he meant networks of transoceanic trade linking Europe, the Americas and Asia.[44] The 'dumping of convicts' view fails as an explanation of the Botany Bay decision, for it does not comprehend the Pitt administration's intention that New South Wales should also play a role in this 'large world'.

Had he been present the day Dundas spoke in parliament, Arthur Phillip would have understood his remark that the Pitt administration had been 'contending … for a large world'. In mid-1788, as the First Fleet transports were leaving New South Wales, he wrote a series of letters home. As he had then received no new despatches from England, what he said can only reflect understandings he had been given before sailing in May 1787. Phillip told Sydney how in January he had had the 'satisfaction' of finding Port Jackson to be 'the finest harbour in the world, in which a thousand sail-of-the-line may ride in the most perfect security'. After describing the initial problems the settlers had encountered, he told Shelburne (now the Marquess of Lansdowne), 'I think that perseverance will answer every purpose proposed by government, and that this country will hereafter be a most valuable acquisition to Great Britain, from its situation.' And he sent a chart of Sydney Harbour to Middleton, which he said 'will show that hereafter, when this colony is the seat of empire, there is room for ships of all nations'.[45] The *finest harbour in the world ... from its situation ... the seat of empire ... ships of all nations*: these were signifiers of a scheme comprehending very much more than the dumping of convicts.

# 7.

# *Voices Prophesizing War*

As the *Nautilus* sailed to investigate the suitability of Das Voltas Bay, on the southwest coast of Africa, as a site for a convict colony, the political situation in Europe turned sharply against Britain, as France prepared for another war. At stake were Britain's dominance of the seas, generally but particularly around India, and its commercial supremacy in the sub-continent. France had lost a great deal of valuable overseas territory to Britain in the Seven Years' War, and had not had victories decisive enough in that of 1778–83 to regain it. This rankled, and even as the French ministers negotiated an end to hostilities in 1782–83, at least some of them were already preparing for another contest that would restore the nation's pride, humble its enemy and increase its wealth.

In September 1783, when the ink on the peace treaty was scarcely dry, the Secret Committee of the East India Company forwarded to the Bengal Council copies of Marquis de Bussy's scheme for joining with Indian rulers to overthrow the British there, and of the French Crown's instructions for his 1781–83 expedition. In doing so, the Secret Committee warned that while the peace treaty might mean these plans were now in abeyance, they could easily be taken up again in the future.[1]

There is a superabundance of evidence that in the mid-1780s French ambitions and British anxieties centred on India. At the very beginning of 1784, Lord Carmarthen, the Foreign Secretary, told Anthony Storer, one of the officials at the embassy in Paris, that it was a matter of urgency to have details of 'the sailing of ships of force, under the usual disguise of being *armés en flûte* [i.e., with guns de-mounted and carried in the hold], for the East Indies, the French West India islands, the coast of Africa, but more particularly for the first of these destinations'. Storer was therefore 'to obtain any information, which by any means you can acquire of a nature to be depended upon, as to the ships of force which may have sailed from Brest, or any other ports of France, in the course of the last three months'. The Foreign Secretary added that 'this enquiry is of so much importance that any reasonable expense to obtain accurate and authentic accounts will be allowed'.[2]

In April, the British heard that the French King had given three warships *armés en flûte* to merchants trading to the East. This information prompted Pitt to emphasize to the Foreign Secretary the importance of knowing what naval forces the French and the Dutch intended to maintain in Indian waters.[3] Twelve months later, when the French had reconstituted their East India Company, such reports became more ominous. In June 1785 Daniel Hailes, another of the Paris embassy officials, passed on a spy's report that a 64-gun ship *armé en flûte* had sailed for Bourbon, carrying naval stores and 300 troops. The next month he advised that the French were planning to send out two more such ships. In August, he reported that 'the property of the ship-of-war *Dauphin* is transferred by the King to the East India Company, under whose direction she is to make a voyage to China'. He warned: 'Should any of the 64-gun ships intended to be laid up, as it is said, be hereafter converted to the service of the Company, I shall be apt to think that that establishment is meant to mask designs much more hostile than commercial'. Four months later, he reported that the French navy was supplying all the Company's ships.[4]

The sailing of these old warships to the East was not the only ominous sign of French intentions. In mid-1784, British authorities received intelligence reports that the French intended to order Admiral de Suffren back to India. Carmarthen asked Hailes to investigate, remarking that 'sending an officer of his abilities and high rank in a time of peace would certainly give rise to suspicions of something more being meant'.[5] Then, in July, the Duke of Dorset, the British ambassador at Paris, reported that France had successfully negotiated with Sweden to establish a naval depot at Gothenburg, which was to be stocked from the Baltic regions.[6]

Such reports would gain in significance if there were unusual activity in French dockyards. In September 1784, Hailes sent details of naval works at Cherbourg, which seemed designed to increase France's ability to command the English Channel. In October, Dorset wrote that three new two-deck ships had been launched at Toulon, and that others were under construction. Carmarthen then instructed Dorset to obtain 'the fullest and most accurate intelligence of the present state of the French marine, of the particular force now fit for, or preparations for service, both at Brest and Toulon, as well as what ships of war may have sailed from either of those ports since June last, and as far as possible the respective destinations of such ships'. Again, the Foreign Secretary said that 'no expense can be reckoned ill-bestowed which may be laid out in the procuring such useful information as this must be if really authentic'.[7]

By this time, however, the inner council of government had acted to obtain 'authentic' information in another way. On 14 October, Captain Arthur Phillip, who spoke French fluently, asked the Admiralty for a year's leave, so that he might go to Grenoble to settle some 'private affairs'. This reason was a blind to cover one of national significance. One month later, Evan Nepean recorded paying Phillip £150 'to enable him to undertake a journey to Toulon and other ports of France for the purpose of ascertaining the naval force, and stores in the arsenals'. Phillip reported to Nepean at intervals thereafter. In January 1785 he advised that the French were paying the 'greatest attention' to their navy. They were fitting fourteen line-of-battle ships at Toulon, and eleven frigates and storeships. They were recruiting additional shipwrights and importing naval timber from Albania.[8]

There was other evidence of France's intentions. In April 1784, Hailes reported that the French were investigating setting up 'a communication with India by the way of Alexandria, Suez and the Red Sea'.

Dorset also reported this in July. Twelve month later, he wrote that 'there is much reason to believe that the French Cabinet have serious designs of making an establishment in Egypt whenever a favourable conjunction shall offer itself'. In December 1785, Sir Robert Keith, the ambassador at Vienna, relayed Joseph II's information that 'France is firmly determined to strike a bold stroke by making herself mistress of all Egypt'. The Emperor asserted that he knew this 'with certainty from more quarters than one', adding: 'Monsieur Toff himself told me at Paris that he had travelled through all Egypt by order of his Court to explore that country in a military light, and to lay down a plan for the conquest of it'.[9]

The British knew only too well that possession of Egypt might be the means to a much greater end. As one commentator put it to the India Board:

> France in possession of Egypt would possess the master key to all the trading nations of the earth. Enlightened as the times are in the general arts of navigation and commerce, she might make it the emporium of the world. She might make it the awe of the Eastern world by the facility she would command of transporting her forces thither by surprise in any number and at any time – and England would hold her possessions in India at the mercy of France.[10]

Accordingly, the Board moved to set up its own courier service via Suez and the Red Sea.[11]

*

Such reports could not but give the British grave cause for alarm, for they confirmed the ministry's central assumption, namely that in the next war, France's principal aim would be to expel the British from India. As Dundas had told Sydney in November 1784:

> Our force now, and hereafter, must be regulated by the intelligence we have of the force kept up by our European rivals, at the Mauritius,

Pondicherry, Ceylon, or other places in India. Taking it for granted that India is the quarter to be first attacked, we must never lose sight of keeping such a force there as will be sufficient to baffle all surprise. In that shape, I believe, the attack will first be made.[12]

The next month, the British received the report that the French were pursuing Suffren's scheme for a settlement at Acheen, on the northern tip of Sumatra. As mentioned, the French admiral considered that possession of Acheen and Trincomalee together would allow France to control Eastern trade.[13] Carmarthen wrote urgently and confidentially to both Dorset and Hailes on 23 December, asking for details (which they were to forward by a specially hired 'packet', i.e., express boat) and observing that Acheen's situation made it 'of the utmost importance to British interests should it ever fall into the hands of France or Holland'.[14] Dorset replied five days later that all seemed tranquil. Hailes responded on 15 January 1785 that he had been unable to confirm this report.[15] Before the administration had this advice, however, Pitt had commenced that far-reaching review of Britain's strategic needs in the East described earlier.

*

Other circumstances, too, conspired to confirm these beliefs. The 1783 peace treaties had left for future negotiation the question of what naval establishments Britain, France and Holland would maintain in the Indian Ocean. In February 1784, Carmarthen asked Dorset to obtain from the Comte de Vergennes, the French Foreign Minister, 'the most explicit declaration ... of the number of ships they mean to keep in those parts'. With each side chiding the other for being dilatory, and with each suspecting the other of duplicity, discussions were protracted. The British repeated their request in July. At the beginning of October, Carmarthen again asked for information, saying that 'as the time is drawing near when the Navy estimate will be prepared, it will be necessary to know what force the French propose keeping up in India in order that we may be enabled to ascertain the number of ships to be employed by us in that quarter of the world'. One month later he suggested that it would be in both nations' interest not to maintain a line-of-battle ship in the East, to which – surprisingly, on the face of things – Vergennes readily agreed.[16]

There was a reason why the French Foreign Minister might be accommodating on this point. The issue was not simply what naval force the French intended to maintain in the Indian Ocean. As the Dutch had lately been the allies of the French, there was also the question of what Holland's force there would be. At first the British enquired about this via the embassy in Paris, but, having no satisfaction, at the beginning of 1785, the Foreign Secretary told Sir James Harris, the ambassador to The Hague, that details were needed 'in order that we may know what number of ships it may be necessary for the King's service either to leave, or to send out, in proportion to the marine establishment of France and Holland in that quarter of the globe'. Again, however, the Dutch were slow in providing details – a tardiness Harris attributed to the French influence over them, an influence that caused him to warn: 'Our wealth and power in India is their great and constant object of jealousy; and they never will miss an opportunity of attempting to wrest it out of our hands'.[17]

*

In Europe, the central diplomatic strategy pursued by the French was to persuade the Dutch to abandon the neutral stance they had maintained until the British had declared war on them in 1780, and to become professed allies. It took the French more than two years to conclude the treaty that achieved this.

This was mostly because, in the aftermath of the war, Dutch politics were even more confused than British politics. Resentful of the humiliating peace terms the British had insisted on, the merchant-based Patriot party, which controlled the States General (parliament), sought to gain ascendancy over the hereditary ruler (the Stadholder) and his aristocratic followers.

Backing intrigue with money, the French supported the Patriots and proposed that the nations reach a formal agreement. Hailes reported in June 1784 that the treaty was to be one of defensive alliance but not of commerce and that, 'though believed to be in great forwardness, none of the particular stipulations are known'. In July, Carmarthen advised Dorset that, 'so far as any progress has been made in the projected alliance between France and Holland, the most serious consequences to this country (in regard to our oriental possessions) are to be guarded against, the mutual guarantee of foreign possessions being plainly concerted with a view to future hostilities with us in that quarter of the world'. Soon afterwards, Carmarthen obtained a draft of the proposed treaty, and on 26 August Dorset reported that 'the French Cabinet now presses very much the conclusion of the Treaty of Alliance with the Dutch, according to the plan proposed'. The difficulty of Holland's being in conflict with Austria, France's partner in another treaty, over navigation rights in the Scheldt, then delayed the French concluding the negotiations.[18]

Deeply disturbed by the rising French influence in Holland, the British counter-moved. Having been given a large allocation of secret-service money, in August 1785 Harris sought 'to discover if it was possible, not only to separate the interests of the Dutch East India Company [the Vereenigde Oost-Indische Compagnie, or VOC] from those of France, but to unite them with those of Great Britain'. He assured representatives of the VOC, which was then in severe financial difficulties, that Britain had no plans for commercial expansion in the East Indies that would harm their activities. He underlined this point by tentatively suggesting that Britain might choose not to exercise its right, given in the peace treaty, to navigate freely through the eastern archipelago.[19]

In September Harris made a friendly contact with the Zealand directors of the VOC and soon after developed a close understanding with Mr Boers, its solicitor. The directors suggested that one way for Britain to increase its influence over their company would be to arrange for the English East India Company to make them a large loan, for which they would offer three ships loaded with tea as security. If the VOC's financial position did not soon improve, they said, they would be forced to accept the terms which the Patriots were making a condition of financial help. Harris and Carmarthen were in favour of the English company's providing the funds, but Pitt ruled against it, unless the Dutch could offer something more advantageous in return.[20]

Despite Harris's efforts, this diplomatic struggle in Holland went badly for Britain in the autumn of 1785. With advice from the French, the Austrians and the Dutch settled their dispute. This cleared the way for the French to advance the treaty negotiations, which they did vigorously. In early September Harris told Carmarthen he was attempting to fling 'delays and difficulties in the way of the French alliance'; but only a week later he had to report 'a manifest intention to make us feel the close intimacy which subsists between the Republic [Holland] and the Court of Versailles'. On 8 November he wrote that 'all appearances' indicated that the nations would 'inevitably and expeditiously' conclude a treaty and that he saw little hope of 'saving' Holland. The next day French and Dutch representatives signed preliminary articles, which the States General then accepted. The nations exchanged acts of ratification at Versailles on 21 December 1785.[21]

*

In September and October 1785, as negotiations for this treaty neared conclusion, one of the French emissaries, the Comte de Grimoard, urged upon both Vergennes and Castries, the French Minister of Marine, his idea that the nations should make a secret treaty to strengthen their position in Asia. This idea found immediate favour with Castries, who very much wished to see the British humbled. He considered that, by themselves, the French would always find it difficult to defeat their enemy, but that they might do so with the help of the Dutch, particularly if they were able to use the Dutch bases in Africa and the East.[22]

Castries saw that three steps would be necessary to achieve this aim. First, the VOC must hand over control of its colonies' naval and military affairs to an independent officer. Second, this general commanding officer must be French. And third, the Company must increase its forces in the East. He considered that if the two nations agreed either that each should maintain six warships and 6000 troops, or that Holland should contribute the twelve ships and France the 12,000 men at the eastern bases, they would have a force sufficient to overwhelm the British at Bombay, Madras and Calcutta.

It is here that we see France's cunning. By the treaty of peace, Britain and France had agreed to maintain only a token naval force in the Indian Ocean. However, as Holland had made no such commitment, it might station a strong squadron there. If it were to do so, Britain would be in a difficult situation. If Britain kept the agreement with France, and the French then took charge of the Dutch forces, it would be heavily outnumbered. But if it broke the agreement with France, the French would be justified in increasing their forces and the imbalance would remain. In February 1786, Carmarthen advised Dorset to tell the French that the French and Dutch squadrons in the East should together not exceed the strength that the British and French had agreed to. A week later, he instructed Harris to tell the Dutch the same thing. It was a futile hope. In April, Vergennes advised that it was impossible that the French and Dutch squadrons should be counted as one. The British had been outmanoeuvred.[23]

Even then, the British did not know how close the French were to pulling off this plan. The French did indeed ask the Dutch to make a French officer effectively the governor-general of their colonies in the East and the commander of their armed forces. The person they had in mind was the Marquis de Bouillé, but to their irritation a Dutch aristocrat thought that he was the man for the job.

The Rhinegrave de Salm was very keen to see the British brought low and driven out of India. His plan had many facets.[24] He proposed that Holland should conclude treaties for the mutual defence of eastern possessions with France and Spain, and perhaps also with Portugal. (As Portugal was Britain's longest – and sometimes only – ally in Europe, this last move would have isolated Britain even more and denied its ships the use of Rio de Janeiro in wartime.) Holland and France should increase their forces in the East, and he should assume command of the

VOC's. France should send a representative to India to confirm old treaties or negotiate new ones with rulers hostile to Britain. These should then make war on the British settlements, so as to destroy the East India Company's military power and ruin its trade. If France and Holland were to achieve all this, Salm thought, Britain would have the unenviable choice of giving up its claim to control Indian politics and commerce, or of losing its position anyway in an all-out war.

In the middle of the diplomatic struggle between Britain and France for control of Holland, a copy of a French memorandum fell off the back of a cart into British hands. In it, the central issues were stated with stark clarity. 'Our politics and our views', the author wrote, 'are and must be principally directed against our maritime rival [i.e., Britain]. [We] must prepare the way, at the first occasion for a rupture, for decisive blows on the coasts of India in concert with the United Provinces.'[25]

*

In the mid-1780s, then, in the aftermath of the war of 1776–83, those who governed both Britain and France believed that a new war was inevitable, and that this time it would centre on India.

In 1786, the British received ominous signs that hostilities were imminent. At the beginning of February, Sir James Harris warned from The Hague:

> The intentions of France in forming a connection with this country are too evident to admit of a doubt. The Patriots are in the plenitude of power and concur heartily with the Court of Versailles in all its operations and designs. If the direction of the East India Company falls into their hands (and I very much fear it will) you may be assured that all its force, wealth and resources (without any regard being paid to its commercial interests) will be employed against us in India the moment France chooses to give the signal.[26]

Then, in letters that reached the India Board in the spring, John Macpherson, temporarily governor of Bengal, warned of the arrival of a warship with 450 soldiers at Pondicherry, and of French interest in the Andaman Islands. Three months later, Hailes advised that he had now learned that 'a certain government' – either the French or the Dutch – had asked the Austrians to cede their outposts in the Bay of Bengal. Now that they had obtained effective control of Trincomalee, gaining control of additional settlements, particularly any in the Nicobar Islands, would enable the French to close the eastern Indian Ocean to British shipping. As Hailes observed, 'the situation of the Nicobar Islands, commanding the entrance into the Straits of Malacca, and if joined with Trincomalee, [is] likely to render truly formidable the French and Dutch power in the Bay of Bengal'.[27] The Foreign Office sent this information to Pitt and the Admiralty and India boards.

Then, in mid-June, the Board received Macpherson's reports of incidents in Bengal that boded very ill. On the face of things, the problems had arisen from differing interpretations of the relevant article of the peace treaty, by which Britain had agreed to give France back the trading posts and territories it had possessed prior to 1749, and that France should enjoy 'certain, free and independent commerce' on the eastern and western coasts of India and in Bengal.[28] But this was a vague and faulty stipulation. Before 1783, the British had had a monopoly of the saltpetre and opium trades in Bengal. Europeans pursuing other commerce had had to submit to British control, to pay customs duties and to permit their cargoes to be inspected. Now, the French claimed that the treaty clause meant that they were no longer subject to these restrictions, and also that their ships might sail up the Ganges River unhindered.

Asserting these supposed rights, in November 1785 the French agent in India sent a cargo vessel into the Ganges for the upriver outpost at Chandernagore. When the captain attempted to pass the British fort at Budge Budge without stopping, the fort's commander, who had reports that the ship was carrying a cargo of saltpetre, fired cannon balls across its bow. The master stopped and allowed the British to search the ship, and they did not in fact find the suspected cargo. Two weeks later, the captain of the French frigate *Espérance*, which was leaky and in urgent need of repair, also attempted to pass the fort without stopping. Again,

British cannonfire brought it to a halt. The delay proved too much for the decrepit ship, which sank.

The Bengal Council of the East India Company reported these events in a series of letters that reached the India Board in mid-June 1786.[29] In doing so, the Council members stressed how weak Britain's naval position in the East was. 'The French have ships at Mauritius', they pointed out; 'they have cruisers in the Gulf of Persia, and they sometimes have frigates on the Coromandel coast. The Dutch too have a fleet in India, while the English are without any, or at least will be so on the expected departure of the ships now commanded by Captain Hughes.' In the absence of a British squadron, they asserted, two enemy warships would be sufficient to stop them supplying Madras and Bombay; and since these centres were dependent on Calcutta 'for the means of carrying on war, we shall be involved in the most serious dilemma if at the commencement of hostilities there shall not be a British marine force in India equal to that of our enemies'. They then reiterated the point that had greatly concerned the British ministers for the previous two years:

By the Indian Seas we should certainly understand the seas east of the Cape of Good Hope, and every precaution should be taken that no large French ships *armés en flûte* should visit these seas, for they may soon be fitted out at Mauritius as ships-of-the-line, and unless the engagements between France and Holland are fully known to our ministers, and provided against, the squadron of the States General may on any sudden rupture between us and the Dutch or between us and the French, act against us.[30]

To the authorities at home, as well as to those in India, the provocative gestures in the Ganges seemed intended to create a pretext for war. And no sooner had they learned of them, the British had even more unwelcome news. On 1 August 1786, Sir James Harris wrote that he understood that the French ambassador to Holland had received 'some very important instructions, relative to the future plans of the French in the Dutch East Indies', and that there would soon be a major development.

Harris said he gathered that the French intended to send troops to the Dutch bases in the East. Three days later, he reported again:

The Court of Versailles is to represent, ministerially, to the Republic the defenceless state of the Dutch settlement in India; and to insinuate that if Their High Mightinesses expect France to fulfil the article of the late treaty by which she guarantees to them their possessions in that part of the globe, it is absolutely necessary to put their military establishment there upon a more respectable footing – that is to say (according to a plan given in some time ago), to raise it to 14,000 European troops.

The States [General], on receiving the representation, are to send it to the East India directors. These are to repeat what they have already said, 'that the exhausted state of their finances puts it out of their power to increase their expenses, and that they cannot supply a fund for more than 9,000 men'.

To this the States [General] (supposing the power of the pensionaries equal to the work) are to reply, 'that they will furnish the money'; and France is to lend the 5,000 men deficient in the complement, which are to be carried out by the Rhinegrave de Salm, who is to take upon himself the supreme command of all the Dutch forces in Asia.

Both these reports reached the Foreign Office on 7 August and were passed on to Pitt. In a letter of 8 August, which arrived four days later, Harris said that 'the crisis which ... is to determine the political existence of this Republic is drawing nearer and nearer every hour'.[31]

Then, Colonel Cathcart reached London from Mauritius on 15 August. He brought the convention he had negotiated with the French governor-general and other relevant papers, which he gave to the Secret Committee of the Court of Directors, which passed them to the Secret India Board, whence they went to the Foreign Secretary and then to the King. Cathcart also brought information about France's naval capacity in the East, which he gave to Sydney. Sydney sent an account of their interview to the King at 3.25 p.m. on 16 August, and George III replied three hours later that 'France certainly under the name of *flûtes* can soon collect a considerable naval force in the East Indies'.[32]

*

British authorities were thus confronted with a complex jigsaw of international politics in the aftermath of the wars of 1776–83, and there were two more important pieces to be dealt with. The first was that in mid-1785, the French mounted an ambitious expedition to complete whatever exploration Cook had left unfinished in the Pacific Ocean. This expedition was, as Cook's were, a monument to Enlightenment science; but, inevitably, it also had political and strategic implications, with the French Court instructing the commander, the Comte de Lapérouse, to report on the commercial potential of the lands in and about the great ocean, and on the purpose of any settlement the British might have formed in its southern half.[33]

The French government spared no expense to equip Lapérouse's expedition for its scientific work, but Britain's diplomats and spies in France reported that the voyage had a secret purpose. Dorset wrote in early May 1785 that he had heard on some authority that Lapérouse had

> orders to visit New Zealand with a view to examine into the quality of the timber of that country, which is supposed by the account given of it in Captain Cook's *Voyage* may be an object worthy of attention. This plan is recommended by Monsieur de Suffren, who says that ships may with little difficulty go from the Mauritius to that country. It is believed that the French have a design of establishing some kind of settlement there if it shall be found practicable.

A month later, he reported further that 'sixty criminals from the prison of Bicêtre were last Monday conveyed under a strong guard and with great secrecy to Brest, where they are to be embarked on board Monsieur de Lapérouse's ships, and it is imagined they are to be left to take possession of that lately discovered country'. Lord Dalrymple also sent this intelligence, advising that the convicts were to be landed in New Zealand, a move that left 'little room to doubt of their being a design to make a settlement in that country'.[34] Comprising two ships, the expedition sailed in August 1785.

Consider, then, the situation that British planners thought they faced in August 1786. Including that at the Cape of Good Hope, the French would have at least five bases adjacent to the shipping routes to the western and eastern Indian Ocean, bases which would be stocked with naval materials from New Zealand; and they had a significant number of warships and former warships which might rapidly be converted back to their original purpose at Mauritius. This network of bases and these ships would allow them to dominate at sea and therefore also on land, as foreign troops and munitions reached the coasts of India only by sea. It was a grim prospect indeed; and once established in New Zealand, the French might also dominate the eastern route into the Pacific Ocean.

\*

The other remaining piece of the jigsaw concerned Britain's troubled relationship with Russia.

In mid-1785, in an effort to contain the French, who were then consolidating their alliance with the Dutch, the Pitt administration pursued a surprising, and risky, course. Believing that 'France ever must be considered as our natural and inveterate rival at best, if not our declared and open enemy', the Foreign Secretary instructed Alleyne Fitz-Herbert, the minister at the Russian Court, very discreetly to sound out the Empress Catherine about forming a triple alliance with Austria, as a means of preventing France from increasing its influence further in Europe.[35]

Nothing seems to have come of this approach and by the end of the year the Pitt administration had in turn become anxious about certain Russian activities. On 20 December, Carmarthen asked the ambassadors to European countries (except France) to ascertain:

1. Whether the Court of Russia has taken, or is taking, any measures

for the encouragement of a Southern whale fishery, and particularly whether the Empress has granted any, and what bounties for that purpose.

2. Whether any ships have sailed, or are intended to sail, from any of the ports of Russia, for the purpose before-mentioned, and what success such ships as have already sailed, on this fishery, may have had.

3. Whether the Court of Russia is giving any encouragement to the consumption of whale, or other animal oil, with the Russian dominions.

4. Whether that Court is negotiating with the United States of America for the admission of whale or other animal oil, produced by the fisheries carried on by the people belonging to the said States into the dominions of Russia.

The unstated background to these queries was that Britain and Russia needed to negotiate a new commercial treaty, as that concluded in 1766 was due to expire in June 1786. Russian expansion into the southern oceans and a trading alliance with the United States would increase the existing pressure on Britain arising from a large trade imbalance in favour of Russia, one caused particularly by Britain's heavy dependence on Russian hemp.

In 1968, downplaying the significance of the naval stores motive in the Botany Bay decision, Geoffrey Bolton asserted that 'diplomatically ... 1786 was by no stretch of the imagination a crisis year in Anglo–Russian relations', and that 'it is very doubtful whether the trade in flax and hemp was affected by the commercial treaty'.[36] In fact, the very opposite was true. Towards the end of 1785, Fitz-Herbert presented the Russian Vice-Chancellor with a draft treaty very largely based on the previous one. The Russian Court was slow in responding. Fitz-Herbert wrote of a 'species of lethagy', but subsequent events strongly suggest that the delay was deliberate. In January 1786, Fitz-Herbert conveyed in 'civil, but pointed language' Britain's unease at the delay.[37]

When it came, Russia's response concerned the British greatly. Many of the articles taken over from the earlier treaty were now worded in a 'new and exceptionable ... manner'; and some of the newer ones were very objectionable. One of these was that the bulk of the trade should be conducted only in Russian ships. Another was that the tariff differential should be widened – i.e., that Russian merchants should pay lower duties than previously, and British merchants higher ones. A third was that Britain should not insist on searching Russian ships in time of war (and the criteria for determining what was a Russian ship and a Russian sailor were also widened). As Carmarthen observed, some of the new articles were 'contrary to the rules of maritime law, stipulated in former treaties, and others directly contrary to the laws of this country'. In particular, the British thought that that concerning Russian ships and sailors was likely to be 'productive of the most dangerous and fatal consequences in time of war'.[38]

Negotiations became protracted. In the hiatus, the Russian Court agreed to extend the provisions of the previous treaty for six more months; but the business gave the Pitt administration much trouble. Various officials produced very detailed analyses of the Russian proposals, with the Board of Trade repeatedly asking Fitz-Herbert for further information.

As the business dragged on, the Russians gave the British a demonstration of just how vulnerable Britain's dependence on Russian hemp made it. As spring burgeoned in Europe, and evidently with the encouragement of the Empress, Russian hemp merchants formed a cartel to withhold supplies from British buyers, so as to drive up the price – very much in the same way as the Middle Eastern oil-producing countries did in the mid-1970s. They also had merchants buy up supplies on the London markets. As it happened, the Navy Board was holding sufficient quantities of hemp to meet its immediate needs, but private shipping merchants and hemp manufacturers were very badly affected, with the price per ton rising from £23 to £32. The owners of thirty-four ships who had contracted to bring hemp from St Petersburg at the old price were facing heavy losses, and hemp manufacturers had no materials to continue their business.[39]

By August, the situation had become acute. Indeed, on the very day that the Cabinet ministers decided to colonize New South Wales, one of the London newspapers published a long account of the situation by an observer recently returned from Europe:

> Upon coming to town on Friday last, and paying a visit to a rope-maker in Sun Tavern Fields, I found him very busy discharging his workmen, who all appearing in the utmost distress, I naturally enquired the cause, and received the following very melancholy answer.
>
> That a monopoly in the article of hemp took place in April last; and that the engrossers had advanced the price six or seven shillings per hundredweight. Their agents abroad had purchased considerable quantities, and had influenced the sellers to demand very high prices for the rest. These agents had again disposed of great part to foreigners, purposely to reduce the quantity that might otherwise have been sent to this market, so that the regular trader, not supposing it were possible men in credit would form engagements so contrary to the general rule of trade, ... had not taken measures to counteract any such proceedings, the transactions abroad, if not amenable to the laws of this country, are to those of Russia. The buying Russian products, and selling them again in the country, is confiscation of the whole property. Thus by art and injustice, both here and abroad, our poor labouring subjects are deprived of the means of supporting themselves and families; for it is an incontrovertible fact that the manufacturer cannot purchase under a monopoly more hemp than he has fixed the price for when manufactured. The consumption is hereby greatly reduced; and many hundred labouring men, during the course of the ensuing winter, will be left without employment.[40]

The Pitt administration made the consideration of Russia's proposed terms of the new treaty the first item when the reconstituted Board of Trade commenced hearings on 24 August. The Board interviewed

Edward Forster and Godfrey Thornton, two members of the Company of Merchants trading to Russia, who said that 'of hemp, little comes from any other country. Of flax, a small quantity comes from the Prussian dominions, the rest from Russia'; and that the other maritime powers were mostly supplied from Russia too. When asked what would be the effect if Britain had to purchase supplies of Russian hemp in another country, the pair replied that it 'probably would not receive so good a price, or be so well paid'; and they also pointed out that, whereas British merchants gave extended credit for the goods they exported to Russia, Russian merchants were paid in cash for the goods they sent to Britain.[41]

One of the changes the Empress was proposing was a reduction in customs duty levied on goods sent to Britain in Russian ships, and the merchants confirmed the Board's suspicion that this would sharply lessen the number of British ships involved in the trade, and therefore the trade itself. Accordingly, the Board of Trade asked the Customs and Admiralty boards for details of 'all iron, hemp, flax, flax in yarn, pitch, tar, turpentine, tallow, timber, masts, yards and bowsprits, sail cloth and cordage imported into this kingdom from the year 1763'. The Navy Board responded with details of prices the next March.[42]

It was in the context of this wide-ranging consideration that Pitt asked Sir Charles Middleton for advice about the naval stores situation. Middleton replied on 29 August that

the consumption of hemp in the year 1779 on the part of the Navy was about 9000 tons, but when at the highest in 1781 – 12,000 [tons], including about 2,000 tons of Riga. But I am of opinion 10,000 tons will be a sufficient quantity under a proper management of the fleet in any future war.

The annual consumption at present is about 3,000 tons, and the quantity in store about 2,800, exclusive of 4,600 contracted for and to be delivered in this and early in the next year. Great Britain consumes very near 2/3 of what grows at St Petersburg.

It does not occur to me that any inconvenience can attend a neutrality but in the article of naval stores. In that article neither

France nor Spain can be supplied in time of war but by the consent or inactivity of Great Britain. And if permitted by neutral vessels, it will exceedingly strengthen the operation of their fleets against this country. It is incredible how much they suffered in the two former wars from our command of the Baltic trade.

Middleton wrote further a week later that 'it is for hemp only that we are dependent on Russia. Masts can be procured from Nova Scotia and iron in plenty from the ores of this country. But as it is impracticable to carry on a naval war without hemp, it is materially necessary to promote the growth of it in this country and Ireland'.[43]

On 21 September, James Mitchell, another merchant, told Hawkesbury the Russians had achieved their monopoly by controlling supplies at home and buying up those available in London. He suggested that a short-term solution to the problem of idle ropeyards would be for the Navy Board to release some of its reserve, but added:

As to future means, I leave to your Lordship's wisdom and commercial knowledge. To me the prospect is dark, and the evil without remedy, whilst St Petersburg shall remain the almost only market of that necessary commodity for the completion of a maritime equipment. We must depend on Russia, unless we cultivate our own plains, or promote the growth of hemp in some other quarter of the globe, to rival that emporium of commerce in naval stores.[44]

The crisis subsequently faded, when an overabundant harvest forced Russian merchants to open the market again and the two nations at last concluded a new agreement. But the whole business had provided a powerful insight into the importance of Russian hemp to Britain's maritime endeavour, and how vulnerable it was because of this dependence.

*

In mid-August 1786, then, to Pitt, his Cabinet ministers and his principal advisers, war with France over India seemed both inevitable and imminent. What's more, they now understood that Britain's bitter rivalry with France extended into the Pacific Ocean. Russia, too, had turned antagonistic. It was at this time that the Pitt administration decided to establish a colony at Botany Bay. It is simply fantastical to suppose that there was no connection between these politicans' perceptions of the international situation and this decision.

And, indeed, there is quite explicit documentary evidence that they were connected. First, the proposals for the colonization of New South Wales were considered in the strategic review of Britain's situation in the East that Pitt undertook at Christmas 1784.[45] Second, when the administration sought the East India Company's agreement to the venture (which it was required to do by the Company's charter), it pointed out, ominously, that this move would 'be a means of preventing the emigration of our European neighbours to that quarter, which might be attended with infinite prejudice to the Company's affairs'.[46] And third, when the First Fleet was preparing to depart, Arthur Phillip was instructed to occupy Norfolk Island so as to 'secure the same to us, and prevent its being occupied by the subjects of any other European power'.[47]

The historians who have proffered the traditional explanation for the Botany Bay decision have ignored this clear evidence, and have thereby mistakenly represented it as quite unconnected to events in the world at large. Just as did Pitt and Dundas's scheme for trans-Pacific trade, the political and commercial situation in Europe and the strategic situation in the eastern seas bore directly on the decision.

A convict colony in New South Wales would certainly solve an irritating domestic problem. Much more importantly, however, it would increase Britain's ability to combat France, Holland and Spain in the Indian and Pacific oceans; and it would assist British traders in the coming competition with the Americans and Russians for the resources of these distant regions of the world.

# 8.

## *An Overseas Convict Colony: Investment and Return*

As Gary Sturgess has acutely pointed out, the binary concepts of investment and return on investment are central to any real understanding of the reasons for the establishment of an overseas convict colony.[1]

If undertaken as a state venture, building such a colony from scratch would cause the government much time, trouble and expense. Not only would there be the cost of transporting the convicts themselves, there would also be those of carrying out and paying the officials and guards; of building materials and agricultural equipment; of medicines; of food (even if some native supplies might be found); and of domestic animals. The further away from Britain the colony was, the higher these costs would be. Moreover, they would remain high until the colony achieved self-sufficiency or at least approached it. And in the first years, before agriculture, trade or other activities had developed, there would be no return cargoes.

In the eighteenth century, as now, governments usually did not spend large amounts of money on ventures that would need years of support unless they thought the nation would receive benefits in return. It is significant that all the proposals made for government-sponsored overseas convict colonies in the 1770s and 1780s involved the notion of return on investment. This was present, for example, in William Eden's

1771 suggestion that 'the more enormous offenders ... might be compelled to dangerous expeditions; or be sent to establish new colonies, factories, and settlements on the coasts of Africa, and on small islands for the benefit of navigation'.[2] And it was present in the proposals – no matter how fantastical they now seem – for convict colonies in the Gambia or elsewhere in West Africa, which were represented as likely to lead to much more extensive trade, which in turn would generate greater revenue for the state.[3] It was present, too, in the proposals for a convict colony on the southeast coast of Africa. As Pitt himself observed in asking Grenville's opinion, such a settlement would 'answer in some respects the purposes of the Cape, and ... serve also as a receptacle for convicts'.[4]

This notion was also prominent in the decision for Das Voltas Bay. Edward Thompson told Pitt and Sydney that 'the superior advantage the Dutch, Portugueze and French have reaped over us in their Indian navigation and commerce, has arisen from their having more convenient ports of refreshment in their passages'; and that 'the bay and river of Das Voltas, ... or the port, would ... be an excellent reception for our *Indiamen* on their return'.[5] In recommending Das Voltas Bay as a site for a convict colony, the members of the Beauchamp Committee cautioned that they did

> so far only as the commercial and political benefits of a settlement on the southwest coast of Africa may be deemed of sufficient consequence to warrant the expense inseparable from such an undertaking, at the same time that it restores energy to the execution of the law, and contributes to the interior police of this kingdom.[6]

\*

So, on the one hand, the establishment of an overseas convict colony needed to deal with the crime problem in Britain, and, on the other, to produce commercial and 'political' – i.e., strategic – benefits. What, then, were the returns that the Pitt administration might reasonably have expected from a convict colony at Botany Bay?

First, there was the solution it offered to the convict problem. As Evan Nepean put it, from 'the fertility and the salubrity of the climate, connected with the remoteness of its situation (from whence it is hardly possible for persons to return without permission)', it seemed a country 'peculiarly adapted to answer the views of government, with respect to the providing a remedy for the evils likely to result by the late alarming and numerous increase of felons in this country, and more particularly in the metropolis'.[7] And if properly planned, such a colony would be able to absorb new drafts of convicts year after year, with the costs of sending them out diminishing as it became established.

These benefits are the only ones traditionalist historians have offered to explain the Botany Bay decision. However, they pertain only to the domestic side of the investment/return equation. What of possible external – that is, commercial and strategic – returns on the investment? As the evidence I present in the following chapters makes clear, the Pitt administration envisaged benefits in the areas of naval materials, access to the Pacific Ocean, and desirable products.

The most immediately realizable of these external benefits would be a maritime one: a convict colony in New South Wales would help to improve Britain's naval stores situation. In order to establish this point, it is necessary that I examine this situation in detail. In the second half of the eighteenth century, the Royal Navy experienced repeated shortages of masts and spars, cables, cordage and canvas. Just as I have counted the numbers of convicts on the hulks, so too have I counted the numbers of masts and spars and amounts of timber and hemp in the Royal Navy's dockyards in the 1780s. They tell an interesting story.

The merchant and military ships of the European maritime powers grew progressively larger in the course of the eighteenth century. The increase was not only in number, but also in size. Ships built after 1755 were typically 40 per cent larger than those built in the first half of the century. Britain's merchant marine, for example, increased in capacity from some 473,000 tons in 1755 to 588,000 tons in 1774 to 752,000 tons in 1786. Although the records are very imperfect, roughly the same degree of increase seems to have occurred in the merchant marines of

France and Spain. Between 1775 and 1790 the volume of shipping above 500 tons displacement in the Royal Navy rose from 327,300 tons to 458,900 tons. In the French navy this volume rose from 190,000 tons to 314,300 tons. Altogether, in this period European warship tonnage increased by approximately 46 per cent.

The consequence of this expansion was an ever-increasing demand for timber and fibre. After all, in an age before iron hulls and steam power, a large, ocean-going ship could not be built without frame, hull and deck timbers, nor sailed without masts and spars, cables, cordage and canvas. Blainey was perfectly right: in the eighteenth century, these materials were as important to military and commercial powers as steel and oil are today.[8] And the demand for them inevitably increased sharply in wartime, thus exacerbating the underlying problems of supply.

This was the general situation. Let me now give details only for the 1770s and 1780s.

Responding at the end of 1781 to criticism of his performance as First Lord of the Admiralty, Lord Sandwich commented that when he had taken office in 1771, he 'came to the management of a fleet that had been exceedingly neglected for some years past, [and] was greatly out of repair; that there was scarcely any timber in any of the dockyards, and a total despondency at the Navy Office as to means of procuring it, it being generally understood that the timber of England was exhausted'.[9]

There was no doubt some embellishment here for political purposes, but there was also a good deal of truth. Many of the ships of the great fleet assembled during the Seven Years' War were in disrepair by its end, and they had not thereafter been properly maintained. As Sandwich's ally Admiral Palliser pointed out, 'the bad condition of those ships ... is best shown by the small number of them that remained at the beginning of 1778'.[10]

It was not that Sandwich had done nothing to rectify the situation; in fact, he had done a considerable amount. He had broken a cartel of timber merchants, thus freeing up supplies, which he had had the Navy Board purchase. In 1771, the Admiralty and Navy boards and parliament had adopted a policy of maintaining approximately three years' supply of naval timbers in the dockyards – that is, 66,000 loads, where a 'load' was approximately one ton, the usual product of a substantial oak tree.

For a time, authorities were able to meet this goal. At the end of 1778, there were some 72,000 loads in the dockyards. But thereafter, due to wartime demands and the building programme that continued through the 1780s, there was a sharp decline in the amount of timber held. In 1784, there were 29,157 loads of English timber and 274 loads of foreign timber in store; in 1785, 21,186 loads of English and 216 of foreign; in 1786, 15,880 loads of English and none of foreign.[11]

In the early 1770s, British authorities also sought to build up reserves of masts, spars and bowsprits. But the pine and fir forests of the Baltic countries had been harvested for centuries for the benefit of the maritime powers of Western Europe, and increasingly they were unable to offer 'sticks' (as masts and spars were then commonly called) of large dimensions. Between 1764 and 1770, the British obtained 'great masts' (of 38 down to 30 inches diameter) for the largest warships from New England, but the American war disrupted this supply. By November 1777, the Deptford yard had no sticks larger than 30 inches. In the course of the war, the number of smaller masts and bowsprits held in the dockyards also declined very sharply. Moreover, those that did arrive were often defective, with knots, other faults and excessive sap.

In this emergency, the Navy Board turned to 'making masts' – that is, shaping smaller sticks and binding them with iron or rope about a central spindle. Depending on its size, a 'made' mast might require six to eight small sticks. In the wars of 1776–83, the Navy Board was forced to make masts not only for line-of-battle ships, but also for vessels as small as 20-gun frigates and sloops. In the period 1780–83, the Deptford yard made eighty masts and bowsprits.[12] This method was labour-intensive and time-consuming and, being less flexible and less reliable, made masts were much less satisfactory than single-stick ones. Sir John Jervis voiced the heartfelt plea of the service in 1783 when, as one justification for peace, he cited 'the want of sticks of a proper size for masts, which occasions most tedious process in making them'.[13]

The situation was similar when it came to hemp products, which European producers – particularly Russia – supplied to Britain's enemies as well. Early in 1782, James Durno, the consul at Memel, sent home a plan for 'engrossing for His Majesty's navy, masts and hemp, the produce of those parts, which are at present supplied to France and Spain'. 'Nothing less than purchasing all the naval stores that are brought into the Baltic' could prevent the evil, he thought. The Foreign Office passed this suggestion on to the Admiralty, which consulted the Navy Board, whose members considered that it would be both very expensive and also impractical, given the problems of storage. As Sir Charles Middleton later remembered, about this time 'the idea prevailed in the Cabinet of purchasing all the hemp that could be procured at St Petersburg and Riga, but finding it impracticable, it was given up'.[14]

In the wars of 1776–83, the consequences of the shortages of naval materials were even more apparent on tropical colonial stations, which were also beset by the problems of distance from the major sources of supply; the destructive forces of cyclones and shoals; seaweeds and barnacles, which weighted down hulls, and marine borers, which ate into them; and warm air and water, which hastened the deterioration of masts, cables, rigging and sails.

The situation in India is indicative. After sailing from England to take command of the India squadron in March 1779, Sir Edward Hughes wrote home in April 1780, 'should the storeship not be arrived we must be very much distressed by the want of canvas, running rigging, cables, sticks for topmasts and spars of all sorts, as there is not one to be got in Bengal, or on either of the coasts [i.e., Coromandel and Malabar]'.[15] The *York* did arrive with its precious cargo three months later. The next year, after he had taken his ships round to Bombay for repairs, Hughes wrote that without the storeship 'it would have been impossible to have refitted the squadron for sea, as there was not anywhere in India, so much as a spar fit to make a jib boom for a 64-gun ship, nor any timber to be had of a size to make an anchor stock for a line-of-battle ship'. He pointed out that he now needed another cargo of stores, and complained that sails 'never arrive in condition for service, always rotten, and not answering the proper dimensions'.[16]

Throughout 1782, Hughes contended with his French counterpart Suffren for naval supremacy in Indian seas. In January, having reached the Bay of Bengal first, he was able to capture Trincomalee, thus giving his ships a secure anchorage, though the area otherwise offered very few resources.

As described in Chapter 6, the French and British engaged four times this year in the Bay of Bengal.[17] These were fierce contests, and Hughes reported after the clash on 6 July that, with their masts, spars, rigging and sails shattered, the majority of his ships were 'greatly disabled and in general ungovernable'.[18] He retired to Negapatam roadstead, but finding few resources there sailed on to Madras, with spars 'only secured sufficient to prevent them falling in the short passage'. At Madras he also found replacement naval stores just about non-existent. He wrote, 'our distress for anchors, cables, cordage and spars of all sizes is still very great, no naval stores having been imported at this place since the arrival of the *York* storeship in July 1780'; and warned that the squadron was in 'great straits'.[19] Because of this shortage of spares and stores, Hughes could not effect repairs quickly enough to put to sea again before Suffren, who occupied Trincomalee. After the battle on the 3 September the British ships were once more in desperate need of repair. Again finding it impossible to obtain materials at Madras, Hughes was forced to abandon his eastern position and retire to Bombay. [20]

*

In the war of 1776–83, then, the British experienced severe shortages of naval materials, particularly of large sticks for great masts and bowsprits, and of cables, cordage and canvas. This continued to be the case in the next years.

Partly because of the innate problems of supply, and partly because of Pitt's continuing the extensive building programme that had commenced in the later years of war (which included two ships of 98 guns, fifteen of 74, one of 64, two of 44, three of 36, three of 32 and nine of 28), in the mid-1780s the Navy Board was far from achieving its aim of maintaining three years' supply of ship's timber in its yards. As mentioned, in 1786 the reserve was a mere 16,000 loads rather than the 66,000 it should have been. It was only in 1790 that holdings again approached the desired reserve figure.

At this time, the Navy Board also found it impossible to obtain New England sticks of a size for great masts. In 1788, when the Board set new targets for peacetime reserves, its holdings in its yards were: of masts between 30 and 38 inches diameter, only two of the twenty-seven required; of bowsprits between 30 and 38 inches, twenty-nine of a total of forty-nine (but only two of these were larger than 33 inches). In general, the stocks of smaller sticks approached and in some cases exceeded the reserves stipulated; however, as the officials noted, since these had been 'a long time in store, it is supposed that the greatest part are in a defective state'.[21]

The situation was similar with larger Riga sticks, with those greater than 20 inches in diameter continuing in short supply. In April 1786, for example, the Chatham officers asked the Navy Board for sticks of 21 to 24 inches to make masts for the *Bellerophon*, for the Board to reply that 'sticks of large sizes are become very scarce, and there being a great stock of masts of smaller sizes, we shall send [you] by the coach in a day or two models for making masts for a 74-gun ship, ... [and direct you] to maturely consider each method and give us [your] opinion which [you] think advisable to adopt'.[22]

As described in Chapter 7, there was also a crisis in the supply of hemp and flax at this time. Indeed, in the middle of 1786 it seemed that Sir George Young's prophesy – that Russia may at 'some future period think it her interest to prohibit our trade with her for [hemp and flax]' – was coming true.[23]

The situation remained similar on the colonial stations. Hughes reported from India in September 1784, for example:

the line-of-battle ships in these seas are in the greatest want of cables, no supply of that article or any naval stores having been sent to India for these eighteen months past, and what cables are brought out for sale on the Company's ships are few and too small for 64-gun ships, and unless a supply of cables arrives at Bombay before March next, the line-of-battle ships must be reduced to the use of coir cables.[24]

Clearly, then, new sources of trees suitable for great masts and large spars, and of hemp and flax for canvas, cables and cordage, would be very beneficial to Britain's maritime endeavours generally, but particularly where India was concerned.

It was here that the islands of the southwestern Pacific Ocean, with their towering pines and New Zealand flax, might play an important role. As Sir George Young and Sir John Call pointed out in asking for permission to colonize Norfolk Island, '[this enterprise] will prove of great utility, by furnishing a supply of those valuable articles of *cordage* and *masts* for your shipping in India, which are now obtained at a most enormous expense; and from their scarcity have often reduced the maritime force employed in the East Indies to great inconvenience, and even distress.'[25]

True, it might well be expensive to harvest these materials at places so distant as New Caledonia, Norfolk Island and New Zealand; however, a convict labour force would lessen the cost. And in any case, cost was not necessarily the final consideration – as the East India Company instructed its officials in Bengal in 1791:

We are desirous of obtaining the best information you may be able to afford touching the present state of the growth of hemp and flax in any of the districts within your government. In respect to the former, if considered only commercially we are aware that no successful [competition] can be set up against the Russians; but as a plentiful supply of these articles from every possible quarter is of the highest importance to the well-being of the British nation we recommend this object to your very serious notice.[26]

\*

The second benefit to be expected from a convict colony in New South Wales was also a maritime one: it would serve as a base for ships proceeding into the Pacific Ocean.

In 1786, the worsening political situation in Europe and India, the scheme to establish a trans-Pacific trading empire, and the existing threat of competition from the French and the emerging one from the Russians and Americans for this ocean's resources meant that it was necessary for Britain to create new maritime resources on the route to it.

'New resources' comprehended not only a harbour and naval materials, but also food, wood, water and personnel. Being adjacent to the route taken by Cook in his second and third voyages, and evidently fertile enough, Botany Bay appeared a suitable site. A population of convicts become yoemen farmers might raise domestic animals and cultivate grains, fruits and vegetables, and also supply replacement seamen.

Such a colony might therefore become most useful for commercial and military purposes, as James Matra had pointed out in 1783:

> The place which New South Wales holds on our globe might give it a very commanding influence in the policy of Europe. If a colony from Britain was established in that large tract of country, and if we were at war with Holland or Spain, we might very powerfully annoy either state from our new settlement.
>
> We might with a safe and expeditious voyage make naval incursions on Java and the other Dutch settlements, and we might with equal facility invade the coasts of Spanish America, and intercept the Manila ships laden with the treasures of the west. This check which New South Wales would be in time of war, on both those powers make it a very important object when we view it in the chart of the world with a political eye.[27]

Sir George Young reiterated this point to Pitt in 1784:

> *Botany Bay,* the part that is proposed to be first settled, is not more than twelve hundred leagues from the coast of New Spain, with a

fair, open navigation; and there is no doubt but that a lucrative trade would soon be opened with the Spaniards for English manufactures. Or suppose we were again involved in a war with Spain: here is a port of shelter and refreshment for our ships should it be necessary to send any into the South Seas.

From the coast of China, it lies not more than about seven hundred leagues, and nearly the same distance from the East Indies; from the Spice Islands about five hundred leagues, and about a month's run from the Cape of Good Hope.[28]

A convict colony in New South Wales, then, would meet the criteria enunciated by the Beauchamp Committee in July 1785, that it should 'promote the purposes of future commerce or future hostility in the South Seas'; and that, thereby, it should bring benefits as 'may be deemed of sufficient consequence to warrant the expense inseparable from such an undertaking'.[29]

*

The third benefit to be expected concerned cotton, which by the mid-1780s the British were intent on manufacturing in much greater quantities.

At this time, India was the heartland of cotton production. People had grown cotton on the flood plains of the Indus Valley since time immemorial and, using simple but highly effective technology, they had developed a very successful manufacturing industry. By the first century of the Common Era, Arab traders were selling cotton goods in Italy and Spain, and these had become available in Northern Europe by the Middle Ages.

When the English East India Company established a presence in India in the seventeenth century, its officials began sending fine fabrics back to England. Naturally they became aware of the extensive local export trade in 'piece goods' (i.e., bales of cloth) to China. One of the perennial bugbears of Britain's Eastern trade was that the Chinese showed no interest in European manufactured goods, which meant that the British were compelled to offer silver in exchange for tea, silk and porcelain, and that their ships therefore had little outward cargo. As discussed earlier, these problems might partly be solved if the British could manufacture cotton goods at home and export them to China. In the mid-1780s, the industrialization of spinning and weaving offered these prospects, and with them arose another grand scheme, this time overseen by Sir Joseph Banks.

This *Bounty* scheme developed over a dozen years and more, with West Indian planters first requesting a supply of breadfruit in the early 1770s.[30] As I have outlined, the intention was to provide more food to support more slaves, who would increase supplies of cotton to be manufactured in England. The first concrete plan for obtaining breadfruit plants involved Governor Phillip's sending a convict transport on from Botany Bay to one or other of the central Pacific islands. Banks accordingly drafted instructions for Phillip and the gardener who was to oversee the business at the beginning of March 1787; but then he decided that the ship would be better fitted out in England.

At the same time, Banks arranged for Anton Hove, whom he had sent out to southwest Africa on the *Nautilus*, to go to India. Ostensibly, Hove was to present himself to the Indians through whose territories he travelled as a poor student interested in medicinal plants. However, in 'private' instructions issued in March 1787, Banks told him that collecting plants for Kew Garden was a 'secondary' consideration, as 'the real object of your mission is to procure for the West Indies seed of the finer sorts of cotton'. A couple of weeks later, Banks added that Hove was particularly to seek out that variety of cotton having the colour of 'nankeen cloth which is imported from China'.[31]

Hove had a very chequered time in India. Going directly against Banks's advice, at the urging of local people he surrounded himself with a retinue of servants and guards, so that he far exceeded his budget. Still, he returned with seeds of some 170 species, including twenty-three varieties of cotton, and samples of dyes. He also returned with fourteen kinds of grain for 'food and fodder', which Banks considered 'might prove a greater blessing to the [West India] islands than the breadfruit'.

And he brought back 'the nutmeg of Banda, the balm of Gilead, and the mangosteen of Malacca', which Banks also considered might prove of 'inestimable value' if introduced into the West Indies.[32]

It was James Matra who had first suggested the possibility of growing cotton in New South Wales. Given the latitude, he pointed out, New South Wales should be capable of producing, as well as spices, 'tea, coffee, silk, cotton, indigo, tobacco, and the other articles of commerce that have been so advantageous to the maritime powers of Europe'.[33] A convict population might produce these items cheaply, and thereby obviate the need for Britain to purchase them from others.

*

The fourth benefit to be expected – albeit a less urgent and less immediate one – from a settlement in New South Wales was a supply of spices.

Strictly controlling the production of aromatics (cinnamon, cloves, nutmeg, etc.) on various islands in the East Indies, the Dutch had long enjoyed a virtual monopoly of the spice trade, which they guarded jealously. One of the Patriots' reasons for detesting the recent peace treaty was a clause that gave the British the right to a 'free' navigation through the eastern archipelago, which directly threatened this monopoly.

One means open to European nations wishing to lessen their dependence on the Dutch for spices was to harvest them themselves at settlements in the East Indies. In January 1785, the merchant George Smith stressed to Henry Dundas the advantage of forming an outpost at Acheen, partly because it already produced goods for which there was demand throughout India – pepper, beetle, gold, Benjamin (benzoin gum or oil), camphor and sugar; partly because with careful cultivation it might also produce coffee, indigo, cinnamon, cassia, cloves and nutmeg; and partly because it would form a base for warships on the eastern side of the Bay of Bengal, and for merchantmen going to and coming from China.[34]

Such a move, however, would inevitably create resentment that might lead to war. A less risky, though a more difficult and expensive, means of solving the problem was for European nations to cultivate spices in other suitable locations. In the 1760s and 1770s, the French botanist Peter Poivre began doing so in his botanical garden at Mauritius. Fifteen or so years later, production was promising to meet all of Europe's demand for cloves and nutmeg by the end of the century.[35]

Joseph Banks was very aware that, when it came to transferring plants from one hemisphere to another and managing their acclimatization, the French were decades ahead of the British, and he was determined to rectify the situation. As well as expanding the botanical gardens at Kew and on St Vincent in the West Indies, he oversaw the establishment of others on St Helena and at Calcutta, and he brought plants to them from all over the world. The *Bounty* voyage, for example, was intended to comprehend much more than the transfer of breadfruit. Banks directed Bligh to take on a range of Pacific island fruits, along with, from the East Indies, 'mangosteens, duriens, jacks, nancas, lansas, and other fine fruit trees of that quarter, as well as the rice plant which grows upon dry land'. If the French would permit it, Bligh was to leave examples of the breadfruit at Mauritius and take on spice trees in exchange.[36]

If Britain were to produce spices in New South Wales, it would not need to insist on the right to a free navigation among the East Indian islands, which would mollify the Dutch; and it might in time become independent of them for these desirable condiments.

It was James Matra again who pointed out this possibility:

as part of New South Wales lies in the same latitude with the Moluccas, and is even very close to them, there is every reason to suppose that what Nature has so bountifully bestowed on the small islands, may also be found on the larger: but if contrary to analogy it should not be so, the defect is easily supplied, for as the seeds are procured without difficulty, any quantity may speedily be cultivated.[37]

In the matter of spices, too, a colony of convicts, with their free labour, might make a contribution to Britain's economy.

*

These, then – naval materials, a new base and desirable products – were the specific external returns that the Pitt administration might reasonably expect from the necessarily substantial investment in a convict colony in New South Wales. In attending only to the domestic one of getting rid of the convicts, traditionalist historians have failed to understand a much more complex situation.

# 9.

# Towards a Decision: August 1786

THE FIRST DAYS OF AUGUST 1786 were difficult ones for Britain.

On Wednesday 2 August, believing that the kingdom had been stolen from her and that if it were not returned, 'England would be drowned in blood for a thousand generations', Margaret Nicholson attempted to assassinate King George III. The King escaped unharmed.[1]

This disturbing event preoccupied the administration for several days. Lord Sydney organized for Nicholson to be interrogated at length by Evan Nepean and William Fraser, who ran the secret service in Europe, to determine her motives for the attack. The Under-Secretaries of State decided that she was not the agent of a foreign power and the doctors who examined her concluded that she was mad. (It seems that she became disordered after a lover rejected her.) The Great Cabinet of the Privy Council confirmed these findings after a lengthy interrogation on 8 August and announced them to the nation. As news of the attack spread, Lord Sydney received dozens of petitions from individuals and corporations expressing horror at this dreadful attempt and relief at His Majesty's providential deliverance. As duty required, he laid these before the King and returned the monarch's gracious thanks to the petitioners.

'Deeply impressed with the protection of the Almighty', the King took a country tour to Oxford, to restore his and his family's agitated nerves – and also to avoid being in London on his profligate heir's birthday! Lord Sydney too retired to his country seat for the weekend to recover from this 'disagreeable and alarming event', which, as he told a correspondent, 'you will easily imagine must have taken up my whole time and attention'.[2]

Meanwhile, the *Nautilus* had returned from its voyage to Das Voltas Bay, sailing into Portsmouth on 23 July, and T.B. Thompson had immediately travelled to London to report the results. The need for the ministers to deal with the assassination attempt, however, meant that it was some weeks before he was able to tell Sydney officially that he had found 'no bay, river, or inlet' in the vicinity of Das Voltas Bay, and that he had followed a frequently fog-bound coast north to 16°S latitude 'without finding a drop of fresh water, or seeing a tree'. On 15 August, Thompson advised the Admiralty, 'I have received my dismissal from my Lord Sydney'.[3]

*

In August 1786, then, the Pitt administration needed to consider again where to send convicts sentenced to transportation. Within two weeks, the ministers had decided that this should be Botany Bay.

There are fundamentally two perspectives from which we can view this decision. The first is negatively, as one taken in a slough of despair – as Mackay put it, as 'a reckless act on the part of a desperate ministry'.[4] The second is positively – that is, as one taken in the belief that there were benefits (in addition to that of getting rid of the convicts) to be gained from colonizing New South Wales.

The first perspective rests on the claim that, in the whole globe, there was simply nowhere else to dump the convicts – as Shaw misquoted Sydney's earlier comment, 'the more I consider the matter, the greater difficulty I see in disposing of those people'.[5] This view would lose any substance it might have if it were to emerge that Botany Bay was not the only place the Pitt administration considered once it had received the disappointing information about Das Voltas Bay.

There is such evidence. In June 1786, as the administration awaited the results of the *Nautilus* survey, the *Edinburgh Magazine* reported that one of the ministers had drawn up a plan for 'regulating the quota [of convicts] that it is imagined might be sent without hazard to Quebec and Montreal, Halifax, Jamaica, and all the Leeward Islands; and also to the British settlements in Africa, in which last they are not designed to be soldiers, as heretofore, but in another way, in the commercial and inland trade'.[6]

On 8 August, the Portuguese envoy in London reported to his Court the results of the Das Voltas Bay survey. He added that the Cabinet ministers were now uncertain 'whether they might send the convicts to the Cunene River, without violating the rights of the Portuguese Crown, or whether they should transport them instead to Cape Breton'.[7] Whether the North American destination being considered was limited to Cape Breton (or Cape Breton Island) or was in fact the broader region identified in the *Edinburgh Magazine*'s report does not give any cause to doubt the general authenticity of Souza's information, which in all likelihood he had directly from Evan Nepean, who had repeatedly discussed the convict problem with him.

Simultaneously, John Blankett, a naval captain with political connections, wrote to Lord Howe: 'as I understand that the sloop from Africa is returned, without the success there was reason to expect, I may venture to suppose that the finding a proper place to send our convicts may again become a naval question'. He proposed Madagascar, because 'it would serve as an *entrepôt* between Europe and Asia for the refreshment of all ships going to and from India', and therefore become 'a great resource and recruit for the navy in India in any future wars', and a centre of trade with the countries facing the western Indian Ocean. Four days later, Blankett told Nepean of his suggestion, adding, 'I have reason to think that if it becomes a naval question that the idea will be adopted. I just hint it to you, in case you have any other plan which it might cross.' On 16 August, explaining that he believed that 'the Minister [i.e., the Prime Minister] might imagine it a naval question', Blankett wrote to Howe again about sending felons to Madagascar.[8]

'In disposing of the convicts,' Blankett observed, 'two objects seem to present themselves. The first is to send them from this country at the least expense possible; and the second [is] to make their future labour and subsistence serviceable to the state.'⁹ As this view of investment and return was the same as that being simultaneously enunciated by Evan Nepean in Heads of a Plan, it may be that Blankett and Nepean had discussed the matter. In any case, however, Blankett was well placed to know the administration's thinking. He was in close contact with Captain John Leveson Gower, Howe's protégé on the Admiralty Board; and in 1787 Nepean sent him as Phillip's replacement to spy in France. Most significantly perhaps, on 19 August, the day on which Cabinet decided for Botany Bay, Howe asked him if 'he would be willing to undertake the direction of the plan … in case the conduct of any similar voyage of discovery and settlement of the convicts should be tendered for his acceptance?'¹⁰

Then there was the proposal put forward in the autumn of 1785 by William Dalrymple and Henry Pemberton, and considered by Pitt, Dundas and Grenville, for a settlement on the southeast coast of Africa, in the vicinity of the Krome River. True, there is no explicit evidence that this proposal was under notice again in August 1786, but we might claim that it had dropped entirely out of sight only if there was no subsequent attention to it. In 1789, however, the administration planned another survey of islands and coasts of the southern Atlantic Ocean, including of the east African coast 'from the eastern limit of the Dutch possessions, to the Portuguese settlement at Mozambique'.¹¹

So, far from lacking alternative sites for convict transportation, in mid-August 1786 the Pitt administration had suggestions for at least seven:

1. Nova Scotia (or perhaps Lower Canada more generally)
2. The West Indies
3. West Africa
4. The area at the mouth of the Cunene River in southwest Africa (17°S latitude, 12°E longitude)
5. The southeast coast of Africa (east of Plettenburg Bay, in the Krome River area, c. 34°S latitude, 26°E longitude)
6. Madagascar
7. Botany Bay

While no purposeful analysis of the situation survives (if one was ever written down), we may plausibly suppose that the ministers would have viewed these alternatives with varying degrees of enthusiasm. For instance:

1. Nova Scotia was a comparatively short voyage from Britain, and ships sailed outwards regularly in the spring and summer, so it would be cheap to transport convicts there. However, there were no clear commercial advantages to be gained from doing so, and in any case the Canadians had already objected to the idea. A convict settlement in North America, moreover, would not meet Pitt's desire for a new base 'to the southwards of the Line'.

2. The West Indian islands were also a comparatively short voyage from Britain, and the route was a busy one, so again transportation to one or more of them would be comparatively cheap. However, these islands already possessed a slave labour force. If the response of the settlers at Honduras to convicts in 1784–6 was any indication, the West Indian ones might also object. Again, none of these islands was of any help to ships sailing to or returning from India.

3. The annual voyages of the slave traders to West Africa provided a ready-made method of transporting convicts to the Africa Company's forts, but these could not be sent there in sufficient numbers to solve the domestic problem, and there was abundant evidence of the perils of sending them in any numbers at all. And then, parliament's 1785 condemnation of the Lemain scheme really precluded any further attempts. Nor were these forts situated south of the equator.

4. A settlement on the southwest coast of Africa would certainly help British ships sailing to and from the Indian and Pacific oceans, but the Portuguese were likely to object to any settlement in or adjacent to Angola. Another survey would be needed, and transportation to the area would be significantly more expensive.

5. The same considerations applied to a settlement on the southeast coast of Africa. The Dutch might well object to it, and it would also

be within the territorial limits of the East India Company. A survey would be necessary, and, again, transportation there would be expensive.

6.  There were similar arguments for and against a settlement on Madagascar. It would give increased access to the Indian Ocean but, as Blankett himself observed, the East India Company would probably object.[12] A survey would be needed, and transportation would be expensive.

7.  New South Wales was very distant from Europe, so transporting convicts there would be even more expensive. However, Britain had a preliminary right to possess this territory, and Cook's, Banks's and Matra's descriptions rendered a further survey unnecessary.

Whatever the comparative advantages and disadvantages of each of these sites, the fact is that in August 1786 the Cabinet ministers had a number to consider – that is, they had a choice.

*

Beyond that of an individual site, however, these ministers had a much more profound choice to make.

Considering it as a whole, the scheme reported by the *Edinburgh Magazine* was essentially one in the old mode, since it would have involved using private contractors to ship convicts to places already under British control – places where some structures of authority already existed, where merchants and planters might make use of the convicts' labour, and where the contractors might obtain a return cargo. The government's involvement, and therefore the cost to it, would be minimal.

However, none of the individual destinations mentioned in the *Edinburgh Magazine*'s report, nor probably all of them together, would have been able to take convicts in the numbers required to solve the problem, particularly if each succeeding year brought hundreds more. On the other hand, a properly planned new convict colony might do so; but if begun from scratch and if located at a great distance from

Europe, it would cost the government a great deal of money. The site chosen therefore needed to be one that would offer returns on this investment.

*

It is now time to offer a detailed analysis of what made Botany Bay a suitable site for a convict colony. (In doing so, I draw only on knowledge available in 1786.)

First, it was thought to offer a sheltered anchorage, and one able to be fortified.[13] Cook had described it as 'capacious, safe and commodious', with an entrance through narrow-set heads and 'steep rocky cliffs next [to] the sea', and therefore 'tolerably well-sheltered from all winds'. It had a channel giving 2 to 2½ fathoms of water at low tide, and anchorages of from 5 to 7 fathoms.

Second, according to Cook's, Banks's and Matra's descriptions, the environs had the potential to meet the needs of the colonists and of ships that might visit. There were the native resources – on land, a kind of spinach, a kind of cherry, 'large quantities' of quails and parrots; and in the bay, a plethora of shellfish and fish. There were a number of streams, and while there were some areas of swampy ground, much of the land might be easily improved. The timbered areas were 'free from underwood of every kind and the trees are at such a distance from one another that the whole country, or at least great part of it, might be cultivated without being obliged to cut down a single tree'. Away from the marshes, the soil was 'a light, white sand' that produced 'a quantity of good grass'; and there were areas of a 'much richer ... deep black soil', which bore 'besides timber as fine meadow as ever was seen', and which might produce 'any kind of grain'. Colonists might cultivate these areas in 'the ordinary modes used in England', Banks said. 'In this extensive country', Cook wrote, 'it can never be doubted but [that] most sorts of grain, fruits, roots etc of every kind would flourish here were they once brought hither, planted and cultivated by the hand of industry, and here are provender for more cattle at all seasons of the year than ever can be brought into this country'. The large trees seemed to offer an abundant supply of fuel and building materials, and the stone was also 'very proper' for building.

It is worth digressing here, so as to lay to rest another of the enduring misconceptions of Australian history, which is that Cook falsely described the Botany Bay region, and that with the passage of time Banks overlaid the barren landscape with a romantic tinge. 'The fine meadows talked of in Captain Cook's *Voyage* I could never see, though I took some pains to find them out', John White complained bitterly in 1788. Two hundred years later, L.A. Gilbert suggested that the passing years 'had given New South Wales a new lustre in Banks's mind'.[14]

But consider. Unless weather patterns are disrupted by the *el niño* phenomenon, the Sydney region usually receives a good deal of rain in autumn. Cook, Banks and Matra were at Botany Bay in the first week in May 1770. Reflecting recent rains, there was abundant groundwater and fresh growth. Fish had come inshore to feed on the nutrients the flowing creeks were carrying into the bay, hence the presence of the large stingrays, come to feed on the fish, which the Europeans caught. (Their first name for the harbour was 'Stingray Bay'.)

The First Fleet, however, reached Botany Bay in late January 1788. There had obviously been little recent rain, for the ground was dry and creek-flows meagre, and, being at the end of their annual cycle, the native grasses had withered. Whether the local Aborigines were in the habit of burning off to encourage fresh growth when the rains arrived is unknown; but, if they were, this would have been another factor influencing the appearance of the country at different times of the year. Clearly, the landscape about Botany Bay in January 1788 was very different from that in May 1770. But rather than calling the accuracy of Cook's and Banks's descriptions into question, historians should have looked out their windows – or, if you like, attended to the state of the track at Randwick's autumn carnival!

Returning to our list and the third point in Botany Bay's favour, the region's climate appeared healthy. Cook observed that the Aborigines of New South Wales lived 'in a warm and fine climate and enjoy[ed] a very wholesome air'. Matra told the Beauchamp Committee that the

*Endeavour* people found the climate 'perfectly agreeable to [the] European constitution'. Clearly, Botany Bay should prove no 'white man's grave', in the manner of the Gambia or Batavia.

Fourth, the British might claim New South Wales without violating the decorums of European politics. Cook's discovery and charting of the continent's eastern coast were the first recorded by the representative of a European state. (We may discount here any prior discovery by Portuguese or Spanish navigators, for which there is no good evidence.) Cook's taking formal possession of the territory gave Britain a preliminary right among its neighbours to claim it. By settling it, Britain would make actual this preliminary right, thus precluding a claim by either the Dutch or the French.

The fifth attraction of Botany Bay was one that time and changed consciousness have rendered problematic. The British believed that there was only a sparse Aboriginal population in New South Wales. Banks reported that he and Cook had encountered only a few Aborigines at Botany Bay, never more that '30 or 40 together'. Although given to hostile gesturing, these had seemed not 'at all to be feared'. They had only the most insubstantial of dwellings and appeared nomadic. He believed that they wandered 'like the Arabs from place to place, set [their shelters] up whenever they met with [an area] where sufficient supplies of food are to be met with, and as soon as these are exhausted remove to another, leaving the houses behind, which are framed with less art or rather less industry than any habitations of human beings probably that the world can show'.[15] They did not keep domestic animals, and they did not plant. According to European ideas of the time, as they had not mixed their labour with the land, they had not established a right to possess it. New South Wales was for the claiming.[16]

Sixth, Botany Bay was adjacent to the route into the Pacific Ocean pioneered by Cook on his second and third voyages – that is, down the Atlantic Ocean to the Cape of Good Hope, east through the southern Indian Ocean, then east and north into the Pacific Ocean. Though longer than the Europeans' usual western one through the Straits of Magellan or round Cape Horn, this eastern route was significantly less arduous because of the direction of prevailing winds and currents. Ships might refresh their wood and water at New South Wales, Van Diemen's Land or New Zealand – and, with a bountiful colony, also replenish their food supplies.

And then, Botany Bay was not inconveniently far from the East Indies and India. Matra described it as 'about a month's run to the Cape of Good Hope; five weeks from Madras, and the same from Canton; very near the Moluccas, and less than a month's run to Batavia'.[17] Sir George Young told Pitt the same things. From Botany Bay, the British might attack the Dutch in the East Indies by a 'safe and expeditious voyage', and the Spanish in Manila with equal facility. Moreover, as Cook was returning from his second voyage, it took him just five weeks to sail from Princess Charlotte Sound in the south island of New Zealand to Tierra del Fuego – so that, as Young again told Pitt, a settlement at Botany Bay would facilitate trade with Spanish America and, in the event of another war, provide 'a port of shelter and refreshment for our ships, should it be necessary to send any into the South Seas'.[18] This was advice the Prime Minister kept in mind. Twenty years later, with war again imminent, he indicated places around the world that might be attacked, and by what means. Against Valparaiso in Chile he recorded: 'New levies or otherwise from New South Wales'.[19]

And, seventh, the islands in the southwestern Pacific offered the prospect of a supply of naval materials for ships in the eastern seas. These islands ranged from New Caledonia to New Zealand, but attention centred on Norfolk Island, about 1600 kilometres to the northeast of Botany Bay. This small island is of volcanic origin; it has two peaks of about 300 metres and is some 36 square kilometres in area. Its coastline is abrupt and jagged, and it offers a reasonable landing at only one spot – and then not when the sea is heavy. Shoals and reefs cluster about it. The French navigator Lapérouse, who was unable either to anchor or land there in 1788, described it as 'only a place fit for angels and eagles to reside in'.[20] But in the late eighteenth century, Norfolk Island had two most valuable attributes: towering pine trees rose above it, and the New Zealand flax plant spread over it. These were manna to a maritime nation which would send its ships into the oceanic reaches of the world.

\*

Traditionalist historians have been dismissive of the naval stores motive for the colonization of New South Wales. Documents from the time, however, show decisively that those involved in the Botany Bay decision were well aware of this likely benefit.

When the *Endeavour* reached New Zealand in 1769, Cook and Banks were struck by the towering trees of the River Thames region – 'the finest timber my eyes ever beheld', Banks wrote.[21] They were struck, too, by the flax plant that flourished in many places:

> But of all the plants we have seen among these people that which is the most excellent in its kind, and which really excels most if not all that are put to the same uses in other countries, is the plant which serves them instead of hemp and flax ... Of the leaves of these plants with very little preparation all their common wearing apparel are made and all strings, lines and cordage for every purpose, and that of a strength so much superior to hemp as scarce to bear a comparison with it. From the same leaves also by another preparation a kind of snow white fibres are drawn, shining almost a silk and likewise surprisingly strong, of which all their finer cloths are made; and of the leaves without any other preparation than splitting them into proper breadths and tying those strips together are made their fishing nets. So useful a plant would doubtless be a great acquisition to England ...[22]

On his second voyage, Cook also drew attention to the pine trees of New Caledonia and the Isle of Pines. But what particularly took his attention was Norfolk Island. He and his companion William Wales wrote that the flax was so abundant on the island's jagged shores that it was 'scarce possible to get through it', and that the 'spruce pines' grew in 'vast abundance and to a vast size, from two to three feet diameter and upwards', and were superior to those of New Zealand and New Caledonia for 'masts, yards, etc'. Here was an island, they said, 'where masts for the largest ships' might be obtained, and Cook fashioned one tree into a yard for the *Resolution*.[23]

Banks brought samples of New Zealand flax back to England. Furneaux, who returned from the second voyage before Cook, brought seeds, which Lord Sandwich sent to the King, saying that this 'remarkable flax plant ... is very likely to grow here', and that Banks advised that 'the sooner it is put into the ground the better'.[24] On the *Resolution*'s return in 1775, J.R. Forster, one of its naturalists, gave some specimens of the plant to a 'foreign lady' to work, and the result was 'a degree of fineness and whiteness which could be little expected'. When Forster showed the results to the Admiralty, they asked Cook to obtain some samples of seeds and plants on his forthcoming voyage, 'that farther experiments may be made of it'.[25]

In their published accounts of the voyages, Cook himself and a number of his companions (among them Sydney Parkinson, Georg Forster and John Matra) suggested that the islands of the southwestern Pacific Ocean might in future supply naval materials.

This perception was soon a commonplace in the secondary accounts of the voyage. Here are some examples to add to those I gave in the Introduction.

Immediately on the return of the *Endeavour* to England, the *Gentlemen's Magazine* reported that 'among the curiosities brought home by Mr Banks and Dr Solander, there is some hemp seed of a new species, which is reckoned to have twice the strength of any other yet discovered, and as it grows in a dry, light soil, it promises to be of the greatest utility to our agriculture and navigation'.[26] When John Hawkesworth's compilation of the recent Pacific voyages had appeared, this magazine borrowed from it to report that when the British landed in New Zealand 'the Indians laughed at their nets, and showed them one of theirs five fathom deep, and not less than three or four hundred fathom long, made of a kind of grass which is very strong'. Cook and Banks, the report continued,

found in the woods trees of an incredible size, one of which meas-
ured 19 feet 8 inches in the girt, 6 feet above ground, and from the
root to the first branch 89 feet, and as straight as an arrow, and
tapered but very little in proportion to its height. Between the woods
in which these trees grow, there runs a river not unlike the Thames,
where ships of any burden might ride in safety, and load with all
imaginable ease.[27]

In 1776, this magazine reported further that at Norfolk Island Cook
and his officers had found 'trees large enough for the masts of 3rd-rate
men-of-war'.[28]

Two years later, also summarizing Hawkesworth, C.T. Middleton
told readers:

Among all the trees and shrubs, of which there are many, bearing
beautiful flowers, and highly aromatic, there is not one that produces fruit; but there is a plant worth them all, serving the natives
instead of hemp and flax. Of this plant there are two species; one
bearing a deep red flower, the other a yellow. The leaves of both
resemble flags, but the blossoms are not so large, and their clusters
are more in number. They make all their clothes of the leaves of this
plant, and also all their strings and cordage, which are at once glossy,
elastic, and so strong, that nothing made of hemp can equal them.
From the same, by another process, they draw out long, slender,
strong fibres, white as snow, and shining as silk; of these they make
their better cloth; and, by slitting the leaves in proper breadths, and
tying them together, they make their fishing nets. This plant seems
to grow best in boggy grounds; there is every reason to believe that
it would thrive well in England, and could we transport it here, it
would be a great acquisition.[29]

In 1782, G.H. Millar advised that in New Zealand 'are forests of great
extent, crowded with trees, the straightest, cleanest, and largest ever
seen. They are rather too hard and heavy for masts; but if they could be

lightened by tapping, as it is probable they might, they would make the finest masts for shipping in the world'.[30]

What is especially significant here is the opinion of experts who had a hand in the Botany Bay business. For example, Brook Watson was commissary to the British army in America during the Revolutionary War and had very large trading interests in the Canadian colonies, including in naval stores. As Sheriff of London, he had frequent contact with Home Office officials, and as an MP he had close ties with Pitt. His firm, Rashleigh and Company, supplied some of the items sent on the First Fleet. In 1785, Watson told a Canadian acquaintance that if the flax from the southwest Pacific might 'be introduced and accord with your soil, it would be better than the mines of South America to Spain'. And in 1789, when he was assisting the Board of Trade to obtain details of a new French method of manufacture, he told Hawkesbury:

> The more I consider the nature of hemp, the capability of our country to produce it and the consequences of its being so produced, and the peculiar advantages which would accrue to our manufacturers from bringing it to them in its best form, by the mode recently discovered for doing it – the more anxious I am for its being carried to the highest pitch of improvement. To this desire your Lordship must attribute the repeated applications with which I trouble you. The specimens of New Zealand hemp which I have seen are so far superior to any other I have beheld that I most earnestly entreat your Lordship to take the best and most speedy means for procuring some of its seed from that country.[31]

\*

One of A.G.L. Shaw's reasons for rejecting Blainey's point about the significance of naval stores in the Botany Bay decision was that

> We might expect some contemporary commentators to have discussed the hopes, ill-founded though they may have turned out to be, of obtaining naval supplies from the Pacific. ... But no. Neither

the *Annual Register* nor the *Gentleman's Magazine*, for example, refers to hopes of naval stores from 'New Holland'.[32]

This claim is wrong. When London publications reported on the mounting of the First Fleet in October 1786, they did draw attention to the prospect of obtaining naval stores from the islands of the south-western Pacific Ocean. On 13 October, the *Morning Chronicle* advised that Botany Bay was 'within a fortnight's sail of New Zealand, which place is covered with timber, even to the water-edge, of such an enormous size and height, that a single tree would be much too large for the mast of a 1st rate man-of-war'. The next day, the *London Chronicle* told its readers:

To the other important benefits which the settlement of New South Wales affords, is to be added, that very valuable article of New Zealand hemp or flax plant, an object equally of utility and curiosity. Any quantity of it might raised in the settlement, in as much as it grows spontaneously in New Zealand. This plant is so admirably disposed by nature, that it will serve the various purposes of hemp, flax and silk, and is easier manufactured than any one of them. In naval affairs, it could not fail of being of the utmost consequence; a cable of ten inches being supposed to be of equal strength and durability with one of European hemp of eighteen inches. Some of this flax is now in England, and the manufacturers are of opinion, that canvas made of it would be infinitely superior in strength and beauty to any at present in use. … The advantages that might accrue from this article would be important beyond belief.

That newspapers considered it significant to report these things is another indication of the importance of naval materials to Britain's imperial and commercial endeavour.[33]

*

To understand how a convict labour force was relevant to the creation of a new source of naval materials, we need to know how hemp and flax were manufactured in the eighteenth century.

As I have discussed, the progressive expansion of the military and merchant marines of Western Europe created a constant, and indeed insatiable, demand for canvas, cables and cordage. While there was some cultivation of *Cannabis sativa* in England, Scotland, Holland, France, Spain and the lands behind the Adriatic coast, by far the most important region was that around the Baltic Sea, extending from what are now Germany and Poland into Russia. There, each year, farmers planted and harvested vast fields of hemp, selling it to merchants who in turn sold it to dealers and manufacturers in Holland, France, Spain and Britain.

Cut and bundled, the leaves or 'flags' of hemp were soaked in water ('retted'), until the hard outer layer (the 'harl') disintegrated, exposing the fibres. These were then beaten ('scutched') to remove the residual harl, then untangled and separated by being passed through a comb ('hackle'). Depending on their size and quality, these fibres were then either woven into canvas or kneaded and twisted into cordage and cables, which were 'tarred' (mostly with oil from Baltic pines) to make them impervious to water. An additional use of hemp came with the shredding of old ropes and cables to produce 'oakum', which was used to caulk ships' planks.

Dismissing the importance of the naval stores motive, David Mackay asserted that 'the beating and dressing of flax and hemp, and the manufacture of ropes and sailcloth were technically difficult and labour-intensive processes in the eighteenth century', with the implication that these would not have been considered suitable tasks for convicts.[34] Well, he was half-right. The manufacturing of hemp and flax and the 'picking' of oakum were certainly 'labour-intensive' work; but while they were dirty, they did not require particular skills.

How Mackay could make this extraordinary claim is mystifying, for by the 1780s there was a long tradition in Britain of setting the poor and criminals to this work. It was one of the duties of the overseers of the poor to provide 'a convenient stock of flax, hemp, wool, thread, iron and other ware and stuff' for those ordered to the parish workhouses to process.[35] In the course of his inspections in the 1770s, John Howard found prisoners beating and weaving flax and hemp and picking oakum in the London, Tothill Fields, Dartford, Cambridge, Warwick, Southwell, Peterborough and Thame bridewells.[36]

In 1779, the Bunbury Committee heard testimony that the setting of criminals to beating hemp and picking oakum was a frequent practice in local jails – for example, at Clerkenwell, Maidstone, Southwark and St George's Fields. It also received Benjamin Crook's proposal for employing convicts to make cordage for the navy. In turn, it recommended that those confined to the proposed new penitentiary houses should be employed at tasks

> *in which a competent knowledge may be acquired with little application, and to which no apprenticeship is necessary; in which many may be kept to labour by the supervision of few;* and in which it is difficult to embezzle the materials: such, for example, as the sawing of stone, the making of cordage, or picking of oakum.[37]

In line with this recommendation, in mid-1785 Sir Watkin Lewes, member of parliament and sheriff and alderman of the City of London, told the administration that he was willing to employ between 300 and 600 transport convicts in making annually 1500 tons of cordage for the Royal Navy.[38]

That convicts might be set to manufacturing the flax growing on distant Pacific islands was a natural extension of this thinking.

\*

Now, all this would be irrelevant if in the mid-1780s British authorities did not consider the possibility of obtaining naval materials from the islands of the southwestern Pacific Ocean. There is clear evidence that they did so.

1. There are the reports of the prospects by Cook and his companions on his three voyages, concerning the timber and flax growing on Norfolk Island and the New Zealand islands.
2. Then, there are the favourable opinions formed by experts in England, particularly of the virtues of the flax.
3. There is the attention drawn to the prospect in the proposals of Matra, Young and Call.
4. There is the specific adoption of these proposals. Nepean listed 'Matra's scheme' in the agenda for Cabinet's discussion of the available options; and it is seldom noticed that the mode of settlement pursued – a main colony on the coast of New South Wales and a secondary one on Norfolk Island – was that proposed by John Call.

*

As I show in the next chapter, there is abundant evidence that in August 1786 members of the Pitt administration hoped that the investment in a convict colony in New South Wales would result in those returns discussed in the previous chapter. Before proceeding to consider this evidence, though, I need to point out a peculiarity in the manner of this decision.

Normally, questions relating to colonization would have been referred to the Privy Council's Committee of Trade and Plantations, but there is no evidence that this was done in the case of New South Wales. In mid-August 1786, when the decision was taken, administrative arrangements were in a transitional state. In 1782, when it had become clear that the war in America was lost, the Committee of Trade and the Secretaryship of State for American Colonies had been abolished, with the new Home Office becoming responsible for colonies.

Then, in March 1784, finding that he had no adequate forum in which to discuss colonial questions, develop commercial policies and formulate trade agreements, Pitt had revived the Committee of Trade, this time as a standing committee of the Privy Council. By mid-1786, it had become apparent that the role of this body needed to be expanded, and that a more permanent structure was needed. The reconstituted

Committee of Trade and Plantations commenced on 23 August 1786, with Charles Jenkinson, raised to the peerage as Lord Hawkesbury, at its head.[39] (For convenience, I have used the modern title Board of Trade when referring to this committee.)

It seems that the administration was anxious to conclude some pieces of colonial business before this new committee took legal effect. On Wednesday 16 August, Sydney asked William Fawkener, the clerk of the Privy Council, to arrange for Hawkesbury to reach town 'on Friday morning early enough to hold a Committee of Trade before the Levée, to consider of Lord Dorchester's instructions'. Pitt, Sydney, Hawkesbury, Carmarthen, Grenville and Effingham accordingly met on the Friday and approved the Home Office's draft of those instructions.[40]

We must conclude that a decision about Botany Bay was part of this 'tidying-up' of colonial business, for the decision not to refer it to the new Board of Trade must have been deliberate. No known document casts any direct light on this puzzle. It may be that, on 18 August, when the Home Office was still formally responsible for colonies, the Cabinet ministers considered that this gave them sufficient authority to take a decision, and that they were in a position to do so because the proposal had been closely examined in 1785 by the House of Commons committee, and because Evan Nepean had subsequently developed detailed costings.

All this may have been so. Still, it is difficult to avoid the conclusion that something deeper was involved, something which caused the administration not to want the new Board of Trade to consider Botany Bay. Such consideration would have delayed the decision by months, perhaps by many months if other sites were proposed, during which time both the number of transport convicts and public resentment at the central government's failure to ship them out of the country would have increased. As parliament had risen and would not sit again until late January 1787, by taking the decision in mid-August the administration had six months to get the convicts away before there might be any sustained scrutiny of its decision for Botany Bay.

This analysis may seem cynical – but then, political machinations often justify a degree of cynicism. However, there are other things to keep in mind when trying to understand the Botany Bay decision. First, although again there is no explicit evidence for it, I think Pitt told his ministers what he wanted – i.e., to use the convicts to build a base south of the equator – and that they agreed. As I have shown, by mid-August 1786 the international political situation had become very threatening to Britain's situation in Europe and India. It had become important to secure possession of New South Wales and the adjacent islands with their naval materials before the French occupied them. Moreover, Pitt's extensive scheme for expanding British commerce in and about the Pacific Ocean would require bases if it were to succeed. Because of the certain domestic and international opposition that would arise once the parameters of this scheme became known (from the East India Company on the one hand, and France, Spain and Holland on the other), it is not surprising that the administration would have avoided publicizing its thinking. This does not mean, however, that these concerns were not important, or that they did not give an extra urgency to the Botany Bay decision.

It is, I know, all too easy to invoke secrecy to indulge fantasy. However, in the 1780s there *was* a deal of secrecy about plans to increase Britain's strategic resources along the India route. The commander of the *Swallow* was instructed to keep the purposes of his voyage 'as secret as possible'. In presenting his Das Voltas Bay proposal, Edward Thompson stressed: 'I could wish secrecy was observed in this matter and plan, for the moment it is divulged and committed to the public, the French will embrace the advantage and possess themselves of this country'. The Admiralty subsequently issued him with secret orders, and the *Nautilus*'s stores were augmented to eight months' supply at sea, so as to conceal the true length of its voyage. In presenting his plan for the Kaffir Coast, William Dalrymple said, 'What I write must be kept secret, as the Dutch would make every exertion to seize the country if they had the least idea of our intentions of setting in the neighbourhood.' And in passing this proposal on to Dundas, Devaynes said: 'I am of opinion if anything is done it should be *done secret and out of hand*', adding, 'I have sent a copy of it to Mr Pitt, and have not communicated [it] to our Court [of Directors] or any other person.'[41]

Similarly, there was a deal of secrecy about Botany Bay. Indeed, there is one curious newspaper report that the Pitt administration leaked rumours of the plan's having been modified or even abandoned, so as to conceal its real intentions.[42] Then there was the choice of Arthur Phillip as the colony's governor. Given his extensive covert career, Phillip was just the sort of 'able and discreet officer' whose appointment the Home Office had called for when it wrote to the Admiralty about the post.[43] Phillip spoke five European languages fluently. He had spied not only in Europe but also in South America, and had sailed on at least one secret expedition intended to subvert Spain's authority in its colonies.[44] The decision to appoint such a man as governor is significant.

There is also the uncommunicative manner in which Phillip conducted himself on the voyage out to New South Wales. David Collins, who sailed with the First Fleet as the colony's new deputy judge-advocate, reported to his father from Rio de Janeiro that:

> Our governor has not as yet announced himself as such, nor did he communicate any of his powers or instructions to Major Ross, until a week after our arrival here. Major Ross, I apprehend, will write to you, and if he does, no doubt he will inform you fully of these circumstances, indeed more amply than is in my power, for I am wholly in the dark respecting them. Neither know we anything of his future plans or intentions. We understand they are to be developed when we leave the Cape of Good Hope, between that port and New South Wales. I do imagine this secrecy is calculated to prevent any discovery of them by letter from the officers of the new settlement to their friends at home, until they begin to be put in execution. How far this is wise or necessary I will not take upon me to decide, but if any plan or design is kept secret now, I can only say it is the first circumstance of the kind to be met with in our history.[45]

Robert Ross complained bitterly that Phillip did not confide in him: 'I could not, I confess, but feel myself much hurt at his Excellency's not having given me the most distant hint of his intention [to go on ahead], prior to our quitting the Cape.' And Ross's friend Captain Campbell repeated this complaint: 'This man will be everything himself. [He] never, that I have heard of, communicates any part of his plan for establishing the colony or carrying on his work to anyone.'[46]

In what were evidently acrimonious exchanges with the marine officers, Phillip insisted opaquely that, as a consequence of its 'situation', the colony would 'in time become the Empire of the East', a view his opponents held in contempt; but then, they were not privy, as he was, to the administration's thinking.[47]

There are two more major points about the Botany Bay decision with need simple reiteration here. The first is the central role played by the Prime Minister, William Pitt. By late 1785, Pitt had clearly taken charge of the business of establishing a new convict colony, and Evan Nepean, the Under-Secretary at the Home Office, was working according to his direction. As was the case with the business of India, where convicts were concerned Lord Sydney had become invisible.

The second is that by this decision members of the Pitt administration shifted their thinking about where to send the convicts, from the Atlantic world to the much greater one beyond. In doing so, they abandoned the old mode of dealing with the problem, that is, exporting it, with the central government playing only a minimal role, and adopted a new one, in which the government's role would be dominant. This was a radical departure, which we may now see as an early manifestation of one of the most striking features of the modern state, which in the past two hundred years has progressively extended its control over the lives of its citizens.

# 10.

# *The Decision for Botany Bay*

AND SO TO BOTANY BAY.

By mid-August Evan Nepean was busy working up Duncan Camp-bell's earlier estimates of the cost of transporting 750 convicts, three marine regiments and a handful of officials to the harbour 33° south of the equator, on the coast of New South Wales, seen by Captain Cook, Sir Joseph Banks and James Matra in May 1770.[1] He considered the figures again and again, until he had worked out that, for the voyage out and in the first three years of the colony, the cost for a male convict would be about £32 per annum, or only about £4 more than that of keeping him on a hulk.[2]

Having arrived at this satisfactory figure, Nepean then drew up the document entitled 'Heads of a Plan for effectually disposing of Convicts, and rendering their Transportation reciprocally beneficial both to them-selves and to the State, by the establishment of a Colony in New South Wales'. This region, he wrote, seemed 'peculiarly adapted to answer the views of government'. Its climate was good, and its soil fertile enough for agriculture. The colonists might obtain livestock from the Cape of Good Hope and the Molucca Islands. If they were industrious, they should become self-sufficient in food in three years. In any case, when set against the 'great object to be obtained by it', the difference in cost between placing the convicts at Botany Bay and that of keeping them on the hulks was 'too trivial to be a consideration with government'. And

Botany Bay's remoteness meant that the convicts would scarcely be able to return to Britain without permission.[3]

The expedition to establish the colony should consist of a warship and a tender of about 200 tons and transport ships; officials, comprising a governor, lieutenant-governor, deputy judge-advocate, surgeons and others; marine guards and their officers; and convicts. After they had escorted the transports out, the governor might use the warships to obtain livestock, and perhaps Polynesian women to redress the sexual imbalance. The marines, who would maintain order among the colonists and protect them from the natives, should include skilled workmen – carpenters, sawyers, blacksmiths, potters and farmers.

Pitt and his ministers evidently decided for Botany Bay on Saturday, 19 August 1786. As the Prime Minister habitually held Cabinet meetings on Tuesdays and Fridays, this was an unusual day to meet. But there had been a royal Levée the previous day, which had continued much longer than usual owing to the numerous nobles who had attended to comfort the King after his ordeal, and the number of addresses His Majesty received from relieved corporations and citizens.[4]

On Monday 21 August, when he was back in the office, Evan Nepean drafted the letter announcing the decision, which went with Lord Sydney's signature and a copy of the Heads of a Plan to the Treasury. Nepean instinctively dated this letter the 21st, but then back-dated it to the 18th. This change was necessary because the Treasury Board had risen for its summer recess on 18 August – and then as now, government departments needed Treasury approval to spend money. Nepean's counterparts at the Treasury, George Rose and Thomas Steele, duly recorded Sydney's letter as having come before the Board on the Friday, and approval having been given the same day.[5]

*

So we come to the central question: why did the Pitt administration decide to establish a convict colony at Botany Bay? Traditionalist historians have long woven their explanations out of four strands: 1) the inability to continue transporting convicts to North America; 2) the domestic pressure caused by their accumulation in large numbers in local jails and on the hulks; 3) the sheer inability to find any other place in the whole world to which to send them; and 4) Botany Bay's distance from Britain, which would make it extremely difficult for these failed citizens to return.

It is here, however, that the point made decades ago by Dallas and Blainey becomes very relevant. While these factors may well explain why the British authorities decided to use convicts in the Botany Bay venture, only the last begins to account for the choice of site.[6]

To understand this choice, we have to look to the other factors, at the other historical contexts that I have analysed. These involved Britain's naval needs in the southern Atlantic, Indian and Pacific oceans, and included the roles a settlement at Botany Bay might play in trade or war, as outlined by James Matra and Sir George Young in 1783–4. It is true that, at the end of 1784, Earl Howe, the First Lord of the Admiralty, was sceptical about the envisaged benefits, although, significantly, he didn't entirely rule out such a move, for he began his advice to Sydney with: 'Should it be thought advisable to increase the number of our settlements on the plan Mr M. Matra has suggested …'.[7] However, between December 1784 and August 1786 there were a number of planning and political developments which combined to make a colony in New South Wales seem advantageous. Indeed, it may not be an overstatement to say that these developments made it necessary that the British establish a colony in the region so as to obtain formal possession of it.

As discussed, these developments included pressing military and material concerns, and the grand scheme formulated by Pitt, Dundas, Grenville, Mulgrave and Hawkesbury to promote a massive expansion of British trade in the Indian and Pacific oceans, including with the countries of eastern Asia, the Spanish colonies in the Americas and the inhabitants of the northwest Pacific coast and the Kamchatka peninsula. To bring this scheme to fruition the politicians needed to carry out a number of interrelated projects – surveys of coastlines and islands, the creation of new bases along shipping routes, liberal new trading agreements with European nations and China (and, they hoped, Japan), and the reduction or removal of the monopolies of the East India Company and the South Sea Company. As I have described in detail in *The Global Reach of Empire*, it would take thirty years and two global conflicts for this scheme to be achieved. Nonetheless, Pitt and his colleagues began the task in the mid-1780s and pursued it into the early 1800s. The colonization of New South Wales is part of this larger story.

\*

The traditional historians have repeatedly claimed either that there is no good evidence or no evidence at all to relate the Botany Bay venture to these very broad considerations. In this, they have been simply wrong. There is an abundance of relevant evidence.

Let me start by considering the Heads of a Plan and the letter that accompanied it when it was sent to Treasury. These documents have been the central exhibit in the long-running debate over the administration's motives. Signed by Sydney but written by Nepean, the letter begins:

> The several jails and places for the confinement of felons in this kingdom being in so crowded a state that the greatest danger is to be apprehended, not only from their escape, but from infectious distempers which may hourly be expected to break out amongst them, His Majesty, desirous of preventing by every possible means the ill consequences which might happen from either of these causes, has been pleased to signify to me his royal commands that measures should immediately be pursued for sending out of this kingdom such of the convicts as are under sentence or order of transportation.[8]

The Heads of a Plan begins:

> Heads of a Plan for effectually disposing of Convicts, and rendering their Transportation reciprocally beneficial both to themselves and to the State, by the Establishment of a Colony in New South Wales ...[9]

*Rendering their transportation reciprocally beneficial both to themselves and to the State* – yet the traditionalists would have us believe that the sole benefit to Britain from this venture, which might be effected only with great effort and at very considerable expense, given that Botany Bay was half a world away, would be the riddance of its criminals. In fact, however, the last three paragraphs of the Heads spell out three other advantages to be derived from it:

> It may not be amiss to remark in favour of this plan that considerable advantage will arise from the cultivation of the New Zealand hemp or flax plant in the new intended settlement, the supply of which would be of great consequence to us as a naval power, as our manufacturers are of opinion that canvas made of it would be superior in strength and beauty to any canvas made from the European material, and that a cable of the circumference of ten inches made from the former would be superior in strength to one of eighteen inches made of the latter. The threads or filaments of this New Zealand plant are formed by nature with the most exquisite delicacy, and may be so minutely divided as to be manufactured into the finest linens.
>
> Most of the Asiatic productions may also without doubt be cultivated in the new settlement, and in a few years may render our recourse to our European neighbours for those productions unnecessary.
>
> It may also be proper to attend to the possibility of procuring from New Zealand any quantity of masts and ship timber, for the use of our fleets in India, as the distance between the two countries is not greater than between Great Britain and America. It grows close to the water's edge, is of size and quality superior to any hitherto known, and may be obtained without difficulty.[10]

Let me deal with the middle of these paragraphs first. 'Asiatic productions' here means principally spices and cotton. As discussed, the Pitt administration was certainly interested in reducing Britain's dependence on the Dutch for these sought-after spices, and in supplying its cloth manufacturers with greater amounts of cotton.

The first and last of these three paragraphs have become famous in the historiography of the Botany Bay decision, as writers have argued over their status and the validity of the explanation they offer. The traditionalist historians have concluded that, coming as they do at the end of the document, and with their conditional verbs ('it may not be amiss …', 'it may also be proper to attend …'), they were merely 'tacked-on', a sort of 'window-dressing', and that the motive they announce is therefore inconsequential. These historians have also argued that the 'dumping of convicts' explanation, coming as it does at the start of the letter to the Treasury, is the only real and true one for the decision.[11] Those who have challenged the traditional view, however, – principally Geoffrey Blainey and I – see these paragraphs as most significant, for they clearly state a motive other than the convict one, and one, moreover, which accords with the needs of the time.

The traditionalists' stance here has been decidedly odd. They have implicitly downplayed the importance of Heads of a Plan because of its title, and have dismissed the significance of the final paragraphs because of their position within the document. But there are no logical grounds for doing so, unless one wishes only to confirm a deeply held view, and not to consider information that might contradict it. As a number of other such documents from the period demonstrate, the title 'Heads of a Plan' means precisely what it seems to – that is, a concise enunciation of the major points of a plan.[12] There are no grounds for giving more weight to one paragraph than to another according to their position within the document. And if we dismiss the significance of the third last and last paragraphs of the Heads, we obliterate from the record what Evan Nepean considered the principal benefits Britain was expecting to derive from the Botany Bay colony (apart from that of sending criminals out of the kingdom).

Nepean's view should not be dismissed as inconsequential. Far from being some underling requested to find an excuse for a fundamentally unjustifiable decision, he was the government official most involved in the decision and in the mounting of the First Fleet. If anyone other than Pitt and his closest advisers knew what the motives for these things were, it was Nepean.

In fact, the 'naval stores' paragraphs of Heads are perhaps the two most significant ones of all for understanding the business. As Bolton pointed out, they are very largely direct quotes from James Matra's 1783 proposal, which we know was considered by Cabinet at the end of 1784. Apart from these two instances, they appear nowhere else, and so are unique in the records of the Botany Bay decision.

On the other hand, the opening paragraph of the letter to the Treasury, with its alarmist notes concerning the convicts, appears again and again. I have found some nineteen examples of this generic paragraph in documents from the 1770s and 1780s. The first of these is in a January 1776 letter from William Eden to the Secretary of State:

> The number [of transport convicts] [was] so great in London that it became necessary in order to avoid pestilential disorders to remove near 140 aboard a vessel in the River; and I hear this morning that, exclusive of the inconvenience of keeping them in this severe weather, several have died aboard, in consequence of the complaints contracted in prison, and that it is much to be wished for the sake of all that the crowd could be lessened.[13]

Nepean used it again at the beginning of 1783, and while his letter is now seemingly lost, his Treasury colleague's reply indicates its tenor, and also conveys the historical fact it reflects:

> my Lords [Commissioners of His Majesty's Treasury] understanding that the jail of Newgate is crowded with prisoners to a very inconvenient degree and that an infectious distemper has broken out among them, are of opinion that it is highly important the convicts there should be removed immediately without waiting to settle the terms for transporting them to America ...[14]

In the mid-1780s, whenever the Home Office wrote to the Treasury or Admiralty boards or Duncan Campbell concerning the need to expand the hulks system or that to resume transportation, the writer – that is, Evan Nepean – invoked this generic paragraph to justify the request. It appears, for example, in North's letter to Campbell of 24 August 1783; in Sydney to Campbell, 23 January 1784; in Sydney to the Admiralty, 29 May, 9 and 11 June 1784, and 10 November 1785; in Sydney to the Treasury, 9 and 12 February, 20 March and 10 November 1785.

Neither is it always placed at the head of these letters. It appears in the body of Rose's letter to Nepean of 3 January 1783. Indeed – dare I mention it? – on one occasion it is placed *last*, in Sydney's letter to the Treasury of 10 November 1785: 'I will only beg leave further to mention to your Lordships, that the jails are in so crowded a state that it is absolutely necessary for the Public safety that this measure should be carried into execution.'[15]

Of course the danger of typhus fever on the hulks was real. There were repeated outbreaks between 1776 and 1786, most often when infected convicts arrived from county and local prisons, where they had been kept in very squalid conditions and their clothing had become infested with vermin. However, when we see the phrase 'may hourly be expected to break out' repeated over two years and more, we may understand the rote nature of the opening paragraph of the letter to the Treasury.

That is, this paragraph is mostly a rhetorical flourish, whereas the last paragraphs of Heads of a Plan give vital insight into the thinking of the Pitt administration. But having taken the opposite view, the traditionalists absolved themselves of any need to investigate the other historical contexts of the Botany Bay decision. They thereby failed to understand that the need for more, and more secure, naval supplies was indeed a major factor in it.

*

Some of Nepean's arrangements for the First Fleet and the colony once the decision had been taken confirm the centrality of this motive. In

October and November 1786, he asked William Sharrow, a Birmingham manufacturer, how the New Zealand flax should be worked.[16] He and other officials saw that the necessary equipment was sent on the ships, including 'the necessary articles for dressing flax' – viz., '9 hackles for flax; 9 hackle pins; 3 flax-dressing brushes; 127 dozen combs; 1 machine for dressing flax, with ironwork and brushes;' and a 'loom for weaving canvas complete'.[17] At the beginning of November, Brook Watson passed on to Nepean a recommendation that Lieutenant William Dawes go out to New South Wales, as someone competent to attend to 'the flax from New Zealand, or any other important article of commerce which that country may produce'. In addition to Dawes, a master weaver, Roger Murley or Morley, joined the expedition as a free man.[18]

Then, at the end of October, writing to the Irish government, Nepean outlined what the venture was to involve. According to those who had been with Cook when he visited the area in 1770, it offered a good climate, fertile soil, wood, water and seafood, and was therefore a suitable site for a settlement. The founding expedition would consist of two warships and transports for 750 convicts, 200 marines, the civilian officials and the stores. Upon arrival, the convicts would be employed in building and agriculture.

Nepean explained that the scheme was to be 'reciprocally beneficial'. 'Besides the removal of a dreadful banditti from this country,' he said, 'many advantages are likely to be derived from this intended settlement':

> Some of the timber is reported to be fit for naval purposes, particularly masts, which the fleet employed occasionally in the East Indies frequently stands in need of, and which it cannot be supplied with but from Europe. But above all, the cultivation of the flax plant seems to be the most considerable object. This plant has been found in that neighbourhood in the most luxuriant state, and small quantities have been brought to Europe and manufactured, and, from its superior quality, it will it is hoped soon become an article of commerce [i.e., export] from that country.[19]

This paragraph has an additional significance. Nepean states explicitly that the naval materials obtained in the Pacific would be sent to India – a detail not mentioned in the Heads of a Plan. India was the destination suggested by Young and Call in their June 1785 request for permission to colonize Norfolk Island. In giving this destination, Nepean revealed an evolution in the administration's thinking, whereby New South Wales had become part of the long-term policy being developed by the India Board to obtain materials for the India guardships 'on the spot, or in adjoining settlements'.[20] Nepean's comments also gainsay Manning Clark's assertion that 'everyone associated with the execution of the [Botany Bay] decision named the overcrowding in the jails as the only motive' – clearly, this simply isn't so.[21] There is no doubt that when they took their decision in August 1786, British authorities were interested in obtaining naval materials from the islands of the southwestern Pacific Ocean. In their eagerness to dismiss or downplay this interest, the traditionalist historians have either denigrated or simply ignored a considerable body of evidence.

*

There is also evidence that the Pitt administration's plans extended beyond Botany Bay. The Orders-in-Council that specified New South Wales as the place of transportation provided for one or more secondary colonies, stating as they did that the destination was to be 'Botany Bay, on the eastern coast of New South Wales, or some one or other of the islands adjacent'. And Phillip told Nepean in March 1787 that his instructions should include the provisos 'that I send one of the ships to Charlotte Sound, in the island of New Zealand, for the flax plant, and to the Friendly Islands for the breadfruit'.[22]

Then there are Phillip's instructions, which included these directions:

> Norfolk Island … being represented as a spot which may hereafter become useful, you are, as soon as circumstances will admit of it, to send a small establishment thither to secure the same to us, and prevent its being occupied by the subjects of any other European

power, and you will cause any remarks or observations which you may obtain in consequence of this instruction to be transmitted to our principal Secretary of State for plantation affairs for our information.

And:

as it has been humbly represented unto us that advantages may be derived from the flax plant which is found in the islands not far distant from the intended settlement, not only as a means of acquiring clothing for the convicts and other persons who may become settlers, but from its superior excellence for a variety of maritime purposes, and as it may ultimately become an article of export, it is therefore our will and pleasure that you do particularly attend to its cultivation, and that you do send home by every opportunity which may offer samples of that article, in order that a judgment may be formed whether it may not be necessary to instruct you further upon this subject.[23]

Phillip told Lieutenant Philip King on 1 February 1788 – that is, within a week of his hoisting the flag at Port Jackson and of Lapérouse's arrival, and before he had landed the bulk of the convicts and unloaded the ships – that he was sending him and a specialist party (which included the master weaver and convicts experienced in the business) to occupy Norfolk Island and commence harvesting the flax. King sailed fourteen days later, with orders that, 'after having taken the necessary measures for securing yourself and people, and for the preservation of the stores and provisions, you are immediately to proceed to the cultivation of the flax plant'.[24]

Finally, there are the comments of the officers when the hopes for Norfolk Island failed to materialize – as one reflected, 'the scheme of being able to assist the East Indies with naval stores, in case of a war, must fall to the ground'.[25] Clearly these hopes were real. There is more to the flax scheme, for, as with the breadfruit venture, British authorities did not give up their hopes when it did not initially succeed; but I have told you enough for you to know that it was an important motive in the decision to colonize New South Wales.

*

Cotton also figured in arrangements for the expedition. There are a number of indications in Phillip's letters that he began to consult Banks about the colony immediately on being offered the governorship of it in September 1786. On 30 October 1786, he reminded Nepean of the need to obtain cotton seeds. Nepean accordingly wrote to William Singleton, a Wigan manufacturer, who replied that he was sure 'cotton will thrive in [the] South Seas', and offered to supply different kinds of seed for trial plantings. Phillip subsequently took on more seeds and plants at Rio de Janeiro. Following Phillip's explicit instruction, King planted cotton immediately on landing at Norfolk Island, but this evidently did not succeed, for Phillip later reported that 'of the cotton seed brought from England very little vegetated'.[26]

Phillip also took on some cochineal insects and the nopal (prickly pear) plants they live on at Rio de Janeiro on the voyage out. The story of these insects and the reddish-purple dye derived from their bodies is a curious one. On conquering Mexico, the Spanish found the Aztecs using the dye, and, keeping its origins secret, they gained a monopoly of it. By the mid-eighteenth century, there was strong demand for it in Europe, where it sold for more than 14 shillings per pound. From 1759 onwards, the British Society of Arts, Commerce and Manufactures offered a prize to whoever might produce twenty-five pounds in a single year in Jamaica.

Then, at the beginning of the 1770s, the Portuguese found colonies of the insect on Santa Catarina Island off the southern coast of Brazil. The viceroy established a large plantation there, from which he dispensed plants and insects freely to ships and to other parts of Brazil. Phillip conducted breeding experiments in his cabin while in the Portuguese navy, but his insects died during the winter when he patrolled off Colonia in the River Plate. Nonetheless, his experiment convinced him that the insects might be 'carried into our West India islands and there bred to the great advantage of the nation, as well as to the very great profit of the planter'.[27]

On the way to New South Wales, Phillip repeated his experiment. Since there is no mention of them in New South Wales, these insects too presumably died during the voyage. But the purport of Phillip's having carried cotton seed and cochineal insects on the voyage out is clear. If cotton would grow in New South Wales, and if the insects could be established there, Britain would have another source of fibre for its manufacturing, and a sought-after dye, both of which might be produced cheaply by a convict labour force – in other words, New South Wales had a role to play in the *Bounty* scheme.

There is no overt evidence in the way in which the First Fleet was equipped that the Pitt administration intended to make New South Wales an immediate source of spices. When we consider the range of plants that Banks sent out to New South Wales on the First Fleet and later, though, and those that Phillip and others sent back to him, we may readily see that he intended the colony to participate in the global exchanges he was pursuing.[28] The introduction of spices and Asian fruits into the antipodean colony would have been a logical, and short, next step.

*

It is clear, then, that Pitt and his colleagues did indeed anticipate significant returns from the government's investment in a convict colony in New South Wales. Rather than a simple 'dumping of convicts' scheme, the plan bore on Britain's commercial and strategic endeavours in the vast oceanic world between the great capes.

It was a scheme that carried considerable risks and, given the distance from England and from other sources of supplies, and also the nature of the colonists, it might easily have failed. But it did not; rather, despite the early difficulties, it succeeded beyond expectation. When we consider modern Australia, we may see that the Botany Bay scheme has been the most striking penal experiment in history.

# CONCLUSION

THERE ARE A NUMBER OF CENTRAL points to be made about the Pitt administration's decision to establish a convict colony at Botany Bay.

First, the decision to resume transportation was a deliberate one. It was by no means inevitable that it should have been taken. In 1779, consequent upon the Bunbury Committee's recommendations, the North administration had begun preparations to build two large 'penitentiary houses', where men and women convicts would be forced to contemplate their misdeeds and set to useful tasks. True, by 1786 progress in building these had been so slow as to be almost non-existent. Still, the Pitt administration might have continued with the project, and thus advanced the emergence of the modern prison as represented by Millbank (1816) and Pentonville (1840–2) by some decades. This would have constituted a very significant change to British penal practice, which Pitt and his colleagues chose not to undertake. Rather, they decided to legislate the encompassing penal act of August 1784 (24 Geo III, c. 56), with its provision that convicts might be transported anywhere beyond the seas.

In part, this act represented a deliberate return to a long-established practice, that of 'exporting' an intractable social problem. It also represented an affirmation of William Eden's view that convicts 'might be compelled to dangerous expeditions; or be sent to establish new colonies, factories, and settlements on the coasts of Africa, and on small islands for the benefit of navigation'.[1] This rationale was endorsed in

1785, when the Beauchamp Committee recommended that a convict colony be established at Das Voltas Bay, but with the important qualification that this should be done 'so far only as the commercial and political benefits of a settlement on the southwest coast of Africa may be deemed of sufficient consequence to warrant the expense inseparable from such an undertaking'.[2]

With the 'in principle' decision to resume transportation, the real question became: to where? Honduras proved a fizzer; public opinion forced the administration to abandon the Lemain scheme; and Das Voltas Bay turned out to be unsuitable. As Pitt told parliament in February 1786, 'the great difficulty lay in fixing upon a fit place for the transportation of convicts'.[3] There is some evidence that, at this point, Pitt and his colleagues did contemplate making a permanent change to Britain's punishment for lesser felonies, with Pitt remarking that 'if it should happen that the mode prescribed by the act should not be thought literally practicable, His Majesty's servants would very soon substitute another mode of punishment in its stead'.[4]

But they did not do so. In choosing Botany Bay, Pitt and his colleagues signified that they thought it a suitable site for transportation. It is sometimes asked why they didn't send a survey ship out, as they did to Das Voltas Bay? The answer is straightforward. Cook was the finest navigator and chart-maker of his time, and Banks a pre-eminent naturalist. What reason did Pitt and his colleagues have to think their reports were unsound?

Neither was the decision for Botany Bay hastily taken. It developed over seven years, the idea having first been raised in by Banks in 1779, and thereafter considered at intervals until August 1786. It may even have had a longer gestation, given that it turned in part on knowledge produced by Cook's voyages, particularly the first (1768–71) and second (1772–5). It is noteworthy that both Cook and Banks pointed out that the Thames River area of the north island of New Zealand was suitable for colonization.[5]

As K.M. Dallas and Geoffrey Blainey said long ago, while the fact of the convicts may explain why they were used in the colonization, it does not explain the choice of the site – in Dallas's words, 'The First Fleet was a well-planned naval expedition sent to seize and fortify a naval base; the convicts were what they had always been – the servants of mercantilist interests'; and in Blainey's, 'Two questions should be involved in explaining why Botany Bay was settled in 1788. The first is why Britain in the 1780s sought an overseas place to which convicts could be sent … The second question is why Britain selected Australia rather than another land of exile'.[6]

*

The traditional account of the reasons for colonizing New South Wales developed in the nineteenth century. Advanced by the most notable historians of Australia's development, it had gathered great force by the middle decades of the twentieth century. The views of Dallas and Blainey did little to diminish this force and this old explanation has continued strong, despite mounting evidence of its severe limitations. More recently, it has been repeated by David Mackay, Alan Atkinson and Thomas Keneally.

And yet – to use an expression beloved of Manning Clark – it is fatally flawed. The major reason for this is that it does not connect the Botany Bay decision to anything other than the loss of the American colonies and the accumulation of British criminals at home. In one of the poems of his old age, when he thought his facility was fading, W.B. Yeats had the circus ringmaster plead, 'What can I but enumerate old themes?'[7] This is just what the traditionalist historians have done. With the old, supposedly tried and true, explanation in mind, they went to the documents in *Historical Records of New South Wales* and found it confirmed. The many complaints by county authorities to the Home Office and by local jailers to Duncan Campbell offered a second confirmation – if one were needed. And there the historians let their investigations rest. They did not seek among the voluminous records of the 1780s for other factors, specifically those of commercial ambition, international politics, strategic imperatives and naval needs. By neglecting these factors they were able to dismiss the significance of the last paragraphs

of the Heads of a Plan, and to deny that these other motives had anything to do with the decision to colonize New South Wales.

Within this severely limited perspective, there were many specific
instances of omission and blindness. Let me indicate some of these.

I'll start with the business of cost. In the mid-1780s, it was costing
the government about £28 per year to keep a male convict on a hulk in
the Thames (not taking into account the value of his labour). In August
1786, Evan Nepean produced figures to show that the cost over three
and a half years (i.e., a six-month voyage and three years in the settlement) of sending the initial draft of 750 convicts to New South Wales
would be about £34 per person per annum. By December, however,
responding to a request from Pitt for more details, he and Sir Charles
Middleton had revised this figure upwards to £45; and it increased further as more and more items were added to the First Fleet. By 1790, the
cost of this first expedition had risen to £63 per convict per annum.
(This last figure excludes the cost of the *Guardian*'s voyage.)[8]

Contrary to the traditionalists' claims, the Botany Bay venture was
an expensive one. Pitt knew this at the time the First Fleet was mounting; and he implicitly conceded as much in parliament in February
1791, when the Third Fleet was gathering and voices were raised against
continuing transportation to New South Wales. Having invested heavily in establishing the new colony, he argued, it made sense to continue
to use it:

> no cheaper mode of disposing of the convicts, he was satisfied, could
> be found. The chief expense of the establishment of the colony was
> already passed and paid. Why, then, were they, unless strong rea-
> sons indeed operated to enforce the measure, to begin *de novo*, and
> make a new colony? And where it could be made to more advantage
> he really was stranger.[9]

In one of those curious omissions the traditionalists are given to,
Shaw seized on only part of this statement, arguing: "'no cheaper mode
of disposing of the convicts could be found", declared Pitt in the House

of Commons, and that has to be explained by those who urge that other reasons were more important'.[10] But Pitt was speaking in 1791, not 1786, and he was discussing the cost of the Third, not the First, Fleet. His point was that the major expenses of establishing the colony having already been met, there was *now* no cheaper way of disposing of the convicts. The difference is significant.

When I was interviewed before receiving my first grant to research the Botany Bay decision in British archives, one member of the panel remarked that he hoped I would not spend (he meant, 'waste') my time going through files others had already investigated thoroughly. We know that the traditionalists had read through the files in the HO 42 series (Domestic Papers of George III), for these contain the many complaints from county officials about the government's failure to clear their jails of transport convicts. It's a good thing I did not heed this advice, for these files also contain Duncan Campbell's and Evan Nepean's calculations of the likely cost of the Botany Bay venture, calculations which show that the decision was not taken overnight, and that it was carefully prepared for.

The traditionalists missed more things in these and other files. There is Evan Nepean's suggestion that, in view of the opposition to Lemain, the administration look rather to Das Voltas Bay (HO 42/1). There is John Call's long proposal for the colonization of New South Wales or New Zealand, and Norfolk Island or New Caledonia, so as to obtain naval materials. This was published anonymously and incompletely in *Historical Records of New South Wales*, but the manuscript version was annotated by Nepean: 'Copy of a paper left with Lord Sydney by Colonel Call' (HO 42/7). There are the letters between Nepean and William Sharrow concerning how the New Zealand flax should be worked (HO 42/8, 9, HO 43/2). There is the version of the letter to the Treasury Board, drafted by Nepean on 21 August then backdated to 18 August (HO 35/7). Most notably, there is Nepean's letter of June 1786 to the Treasury Secretaries, in which he indicates that Pitt has determined that the convicts should be used to establish a settlement south of the equator (T 1/632). Why did the traditionalists not see these things?

In general, the traditionalists limited their enquiries to familiar things. Why did none of them analyse in detail how Duncan Campbell kept the convicts on the hulks? (Actually, it is only proper to point out that one person did. As a young man, Wilfrid Oldham went from Adelaide to London in the 1920s, and wrote a doctoral dissertation on transportation and the hulks system. However, this study was not published until 1990, long after his death. Oldham's conclusions were very similar to mine. I believe that if his study had been published earlier, it would have been impossible for Clark and his colleagues to write of the origin of the New South Wales colony as they did.)

Why did none of them investigate the actual situation concerning naval materials, in England and in India, to see if the paragraphs in Heads of a Plan reflected a clear historical need?[11]

Then there are the distortions. I have already given two instances by Shaw. Here are two more. Early in the first volume of *The Europeans in Australia*, Alan Atkinson ringingly dismisses the naval stores motive, declaring that 'Nothing could be further from the truth'. He then vaguely tells readers that the British occupied Norfolk Island 'during 1788'. Not until 141 pages later does he mention that Phillip had been instructed to do so; and he does not mention at all that this instruction was intended to prevent any other European power from possessing it. Neither does he point out that this threat was made real by the arrival of Lapérouse's ships at Botany Bay on 25 January 1788. Nor does he explain why European maritime nations should have been interested in Norfolk Island, a remote speck in the Pacific Ocean. If he had, he would have had to admit that it had only timber and flax to offer, and that these were therefore the only possible reasons for Britain's and France's being interested in it. Had Atkinson admitted these things, he would have been unable to write so dismissively: '[New South Wales] was so far from Europe that transported men and women would find it hard to get back. Also, it was useless. Because it was useless the people who were sent there would work for nothing but their own survival.'[12]

In his recent first volume of *Australians*, Thomas Keneally also briefly mentions the controversy over the naval materials paragraphs of

Heads of a Plan, only to conclude: 'The document declares itself at its opening sentence: "Heads of a plan for effectually disposing of convicts."'[13] His failure to give readers the second half of the title: 'and rendering their transportation reciprocally beneficial to themselves and to the state, by the establishment of a colony in New South Wales' must have been deliberate.

There are also plain errors in the traditionalist account. It was simply wrong for Shaw to claim, in rejecting Blainey's views, that flax 'played no particular part' in the consideration of a new commercial treaty with Russia. As I have shown, it was a central consideration in August and September 1786, at the time of the Botany Bay decision. It was also wrong of him to say that no one knowledgeable in the business of working flax went on the First Fleet.[14]

Then there are the outrageous statements reflecting nothing but prejudice and a desire to shock. Robert Hughes had no evidence for his calumny that Duncan Campbell was 'crooked'; and John Molony's statement that 'the British decision to send Governor Arthur Phillip to found a penal settlement at Botany Bay ... was made with breath-taking nonchalance and almost criminal negligence' was equally ill-considered.[15]

Publishers, too, have wilfully promoted these old and blinkered views. For example, Melbourne University Press keeps reissuing Manning Clark's *A History of Australia* in various forms, the first volume of which appeared in 1962. Some of the analysis in it was outdated at the time, and this situation hasn't improved in the succeeding decades. Clark's views are also regularly recycled in school texts and newspaper articles, as though no new insights have emerged since the mid-twentieth century.

*

What, you might well ask, enabled me to see past these old assumptions when the leading historians couldn't? The answer is curious.

As he responded to Blainey's arguments, Geoffrey Bolton grew more willing to entertain the possibility that there may have been motives other than the 'dumping of convicts' one, conceding at one point that he and his colleagues might 'have all missed a number of considerations obvious to a fresh mind coming to the question unencumbered by the presuppositions which specialists in the period may form'.[16]

I think that my having been trained in English literature put me in the way of doing so. Not having been educated in the prevailing view of modern Australia's origins, I was able to see its limitations, and to approach the records with a mind not directed by deep-seated assumptions. And, as I mentioned in the Introduction, these records proved very much more extensive than historians had previously known. Also, my reading of eighteenth-century geography books gave me the means to understand how informed people then viewed the world beyond Europe.

So far as I can tell, the traditional explanation of Botany Bay became so powerful because, with a strong sense of how the nation had developed socially, politically and economically, the historians looked back from the mid-twentieth century to its 1780s beginning and saw a mass of convicts. I have tried instead to put myself in the place of the economic and strategic planners and politicians who guided Britain's affairs in the last decades of the eighteenth century, and looked outwards from London – to Europe, with its intense national rivalries; about the watery Atlantic world, with its islands and coastlines and shipping routes and raw materials; far across the Levant to South and East Asia; and to the Pacific Ocean beyond, which then offered large opportunities for economic expansion.

Different perspectives can produce sharply different analyses, and our unexamined assumptions can limit historical understanding. As Philip Lawson has pointed out, if we go by the length of the relevant parliamentary debates and reports of public discussion in Hanoverian Britain, 'India took up far more time in public and private deliberation than America, at least up to 1774.' A preoccupation with America, Lawson thought, had quite distorted the study of Britain's mid-eighteenth-century history: 'The obsession with America has been evident in works on the eighteenth century since the last [i.e., nineteenth] century, and the justification for this bias is never questioned or ... even acknowledged.' Then, with the work of new generation of historians in mind, he asked:

> Is the American obsession to continue? If so, then scholars will continue to be victims of an old mythology. To break out of this tiresome framework, the scope of the debate needs expanding. The 1760s and 1770s are special not simply because of the American problem but also for the imperial questions raised elsewhere, India and Quebec in particular, which proved equally intractable and difficult to answer. In the narrow focus on America, historians have … been misleading their audience for far too long.[17]

The same general point can be made about the mid-1780s and the Botany Bay decision: historians have overlooked India, strategic needs and commercial ambitions in their preoccupation with the convict problem. It was not accidental that Pitt should have made his first major task the legislating of a satisfactory system for the government of India. Nor was it mere idiosyncrasy that led Henry Dundas, effectively if not formally the Secretary of State for India,[18] to tell Sydney, the nominal head of the new India Board, that they must take it 'for granted that India is the quarter to be first attacked', that they 'must never lose sight of keeping such a force there, as will be sufficient to baffle all surprise'; nor to tell parliament after Nootka Sound that the administration had been 'contending not for a few miles, but a large world'.[19]

With the notable exceptions of Dallas and Blainey, what the historians of the Botany Bay decision have missed is its imperial dimension. It was always wrong of the traditionalists to proceed on the assumption that Botany Bay was entirely unconnected to concerns and activities elsewhere. They would probably respond that they were simply not persuaded by the evidence of other motives. To continue this disbelief into the twenty-first century, however, is to fly in the face of now-abundant information.

Still, such distortion has a long history in Australia. After two and a half years of effort at Sydney, in the face of an initially recalcitrant labour force, surly marine officers, the wreck of supply ships and a long *el niño*-induced drought, Phillip had achieved some social cohesion and made substantial progress in establishing a food supply for the colony. In July 1790, he told Banks that he had had 'many as fine figs as ever I tasted in Spain or Portugal'. In April 1792, he wrote that 'all our fruit trees thrive well, and I have this year gathered about three hundredweight of very fine grapes ... I have oranges but they are not yet ripe ... We have now vegetables in abundance. At Parramatta they are now served daily to the convicts.' 'Still', he cautioned, 'you may be told that the country will not produce a cabbage.'[20]

In 1792, on his way to Sydney, Major Grose met some disgruntled officers at the Cape of Good Hope, who told him he was going to a place of dearth and despondency. On arrival, he found the reality quite different. Indeed, he was astonished by the verdant and productive state of the colony – as he reported to Nepean, 'instead of the rock I expected to see, I find myself surrounded with gardens that flourish and produce fruit of every description. Vegetables are here in great abundance, and I live in as good a house as I wish for. I am given the farm of my predecessor, which produces a sufficiency to supply my family with everything I have occasion for.'[21]

*

There is a lesson here. Only when we have replaced clichés repeated without examination from one generation to the next with accurate analysis of the full documentary record, and broadened our perspectives to include the imperial dimension, shall we at last have an authentic understanding of the beginnings of modern Australia.

In its intricacies and its extensions, the real story of the Botany Bay decision is very different from the meagre one the traditionalist historians have told, and much more interesting. I hope you have enjoyed it.

# Acknowledgments

All reasonable efforts have been made to locate copyright holders. Where they have held the copyright, the directors and/or governing bodies of the institutions listed in the bibliography have kindly given permission to cite and to quote from original sources.

I have specifically to thank: The Direcção-Geral de Arquivos, Lisboa; the Curator, Early Modern and Osborn Collections, Beinecke Rare Book and Manuscript Library, Yale University; the Keeper of Special Collections, Bodleian Library, University of Oxford; the Trustees of the British Library, London; the Director, William L. Clements Library, University of Michigan; the Trustees of the Royal Botanic Gardens, Kew; the Trustees of the Natural History Museum, London; the Director, National Library of Australia; the Archive and Manuscripts Manager, National Maritime Museum, London; the Director, Perkins Library, Duke University; the Keeper of the Public Records, Public Records Office, National Archives, Kew; the Librarian and Director of the John Rylands University Library, University of Manchester; the State Librarian and Chief Executive, State Library of New South Wales, Sydney; the Director of the Sutro Library, the San Francisco branch of the California State Library.

Some sections of this work were first published (in somewhat different form) in *Convicts and Empire: A Naval Question, 1776–1811* (Oxford University Press, Melbourne, 1980) and *Botany Bay Mirages: Illusions of Australia's Convict Beginnings* (Melbourne University Press, Melbourne, 1994). The publishers have kindly agreed to my including them here.

\*

During a long career – and mine now comprehends fifty years – an academic writer learns from many people and accumulates many debts, some obvious, but others obscure. It were an impossibility for me now to list all of those – friends and opponents (in an intellectual sense) – to whom I am indebted for numbers of the insights I offer here. However, there are some people whom I do wish to thank explicitly.

Geoffrey Blainey has steadily encouraged me to develop my views, and I have also benefited from discussing them with Geoffrey Bolton. Extended conversations with Bernard Bailyn have enabled me the better to place the Botany Bay decision in the context of the Atlantic world of the 1780s. Isabel Moutinho has helped me to uncover the Portuguese dimension of British thinking about what to do with the convicts.

For forty years, John Salmond has interested himself in my work and been a sterling friend. So, too, has Inga Clendinnen. The generous encouragement and hospitality that Glyndwr Williams and Sarah Palmer have offered over many years have made my periods of research in England so much more pleasurable than they otherwise would have been.

In the recent past, I have also had the pleasure of discussing my work with Gary Sturgess, who knows the records well and who is not shy about disagreeing. And then, there has been the collaboration with Natasha Campo in the transcription and editing of the documents, a business inevitably full of tedium (which Natasha bore ever cheerfully), but one which has also brought large rewards. I have also warmly to thank the editorial and production staff at Black Inc., in particular Chris Feik and Denise O'Dea.

*

I have been in the curious situation of being a historian of Australia who has had to travel repeatedly to overseas archives to study the circumstances of our beginnings. These research trips would have been impossible without financial support from La Trobe University and the Australian Research Council, and the writing up of results would have been even more protracted without periods of leave from teaching given by La Trobe University. I thank both organizations warmly.

Even in being grateful for the substantial help I have had, however, I must also express my deep regret about how the university world has changed in recent decades. It would now be virtually impossible to commence a research project such as this, one that would take thirty-five years to complete. Universities and external funding bodies would require results within two to three years; and the concomitant regimens of grant applications and reporting requirements would mean that you would have to present your findings without the benefit of the leisure to reflect on them and on what you might still discover. And without efficient 'performance', you would find it progressively more difficult to obtain the further research grants you would need to complete the project. Universities – and scholarly pursuits more generally – are not businesses or government departments, and they shouldn't be regulated as though they are. In measure as they are, so is our intellectual life diminished.

# Endnotes

## 1. Archives and Files

ANTT: Arquivo Nacional da Torre do Tombo (Lisbon)
 MNE: Ministério dos Negócios Estrangeiros
Beinecke: Beinecke Rare Book and Manuscript Library, Yale University
 Osborn: James Marshall and Marie-Louise Osborn Collection
BL: The British Library
 Add. MS: Additional Manuscripts
 Egerton: Egerton Manuscripts
 OIOC: Oriental and India Office Collections
 B: Minutes of the Court of Directors
 D: Committee of Correspondence
 E: General Correspondence
 F: Board of Control Records
 G: Factory Records
 H: Home Miscellaneous Series
 I: Europeans in India
 L/MAR: Marine Records
 L/PS: Political and Secret Department Records
Brotherton: Brotherton Library, University of Leeds
 Sydney: Sydney Papers
Clements: William L. Clements Library, University of Michigan (Ann Arbor)
 Nepean: Nepean Papers
 Shelburne: Shelburne Papers
 Sydney: Sydney Papers
Kew: Kew Gardens Herbarium
 JBK: Banks Papers
NH: The Natural History Museum (London)
 DTC: Dawson Turner transcripts of Banks Papers
NMM: National Maritime Museum (London)
 ADM/A, B, BP, C: Navy Board Papers
 HOW: Howe Papers

MID: Middleton Papers
SAN: Sandwich Papers
THM: Thompson Papers
NLA: National Library of Australia (Canberra)
NAS: National Archives of Scotland
    GD: Gifts and Deposits
Perkins: William Perkins Library, Duke University (Durham, NC)
    Dundas: Dundas Papers
    Grenville: Grenville Papers
    Pitt: Pitt Papers
PRO: Public Record Office, The National Archives (London)
    ADM: Admiralty
    BT: Board of Trade
    CO: Colonial Office
    FO: Foreign Office
    HO: Home Office
    PC: Privy Council
    PRO: Public Record Office
    SP: State Papers
    T: Treasury Papers
    WO: War Office
Rylands: The John Rylands University Library, University of Manchester
    English: English MSS
SLNSW: State Library of New South Wales (Sydney)
    Bonwick: Bonwick transcripts
    Dixson: Dixson Library
    Mitchell: Mitchell Library
SRNSW: State Records of New South Wales (Sydney)
Sutro: Sutro Library, California State Library (San Franscisco)
    Banks: Banks Papers
    EN: Entomology
USNA: The National Archives of the United States (Washington)

### 2. Printed Sources

*Banks*: The 'Endeavour' Journal of Joseph Banks, ed. J.C. Beaglehole, 2 vols
    (Angus and Robertson, Sydney, 1963).
*Bligh*: William Bligh, A Voyage to the South Sea (London, 1792).
*Colenbrander*: H.T. Colenbrander, ed., De Patriottentijd, vol. 3: Appendix
    (Martinus Nijhoff, [n.p.], 1899).
*Collins*: David Collins, An Account of the English Colony in New South Wales,
    ed. B. H. Fletcher (A.H. and A.W. Reed, Sydney, 1975 [1798]).

*Cook*: *The Journals of Captain James Cook on his Voyages of Discovery*, ed. J.C.
Beaglehole, 3 vols in 4 parts (Hakluyt Society, Cambridge, 1955–68).

*Cornwallis*: *Correspondence of Charles, First Marquis Cornwallis*, ed. Charles
Ross, 3 vols (John Murray, London, 1859).

*Despatches Despatches from Paris, 1784–1790, vol. 1: 1784–1787*, ed. O Browning
(Camden Society, 3rd series, vol. 16: London, 1909).

*Dropmore*: *Report on the Manuscripts of J.B. Fortescue, Esq., Preserved at Dropmore*, 10 vols (Historical Manuscript Commission, London, 1892–1927).

*Eden*: [William Eden], *Principles of Penal Law* (London, 1771).

*Fielding*: Henry Fielding, *An Enquiry into the Causes of the Late Increase of
Robbers and Related Writings*, ed. Malvin R. Zirker (Clarendon Press,
Oxford, 1988 [1751]).

*George III: Correspondence*: *The Correspondence of George III*, ed. Sir John
Fortescue, 6 vols (Frank Cass, London, 1967 [1927–8]).

*George III: Later Correspondence*: *The Later Correspondence of George III*, ed.
A. Aspinall, 5 vols. (Cambridge University Press, Cambridge, 1966–70).

*Howard*: John Howard, *Prisons and Lazarettos, vol. 1: The State of the Prisons
in England and Wales*, 4th ed. (Patterson Smith, Montclair, NJ, 1973
[1792]).

*HRA*: *Historical Records of Australia*, 4 series (Commonwealth Parliament,
Sydney, 1914–1925).

*HRNSW*: *Historical Records of New South Wales*, 7 vols (Government Printer,
Sydney, 1892–1901).

*Hunter*: John Hunter, *An Historical Journal, 1787–1792*, ed. John Bach (Angus
and Robertson, Sydney, 1968 [1793]).

*Instructions*: *British Diplomatic Instructions, vol. 7: France, vol. 4: 1745–1789*, ed.
L.G.W. Legg (Camden Society, 3rd series, vol. 49, London, 1934).

*Janssen*: Stephen Janssen, *This Sheet Contains Three Tables, from 1749 to 1771*
(London, 1772).

*JHC*: *Journals of the House of Commons*

*King*: *The Journal of Philip Gidley King: Lieutenant, RN, 1787–1790*, ed. P.G.
Fildon and R.J. Ryan (Australian Documents Library, Sydney, 1980).

*Lapérouse*: Jean-François Galaup de la Pérouse, *A Voyage Round the World*, ed.
L.A. Milet-Mureau., 2 vols (London, 1799).

*Nagle*: *The Nagle Journal: A Diary of the Life of Jacob Nagle, Sailor, from the year
1775 to 1841*, ed. J.C. Dann (Weidenfeld and Nicolson, New York, 1988).

*PH*: *Parliamentary History*

*PR*: *Parliamentary Register*

*Sandwich*: *The Private Papers of John, Earl of Sandwich: First Lord of the
Admiralty, 1771–1782*, ed. G.R. Barnes and J.H. Owen, 4 vols (Navy Records
Society, London, 1932–8).

*Smith*: Adam Smith, *An Enquiry into the Nature and Causes of the Wealth of Nations*, ed. R.H. Campbell and A.S. Skinner, 2 vols (Clarendon Press, Oxford, 1976 [1776]).

*William Smith*: *The Diary and Selected Papers of Chief Justice William Smith, 1784–1793*, ed. L.F.S. Upton, 2 vols (Champlain Society, Toronto, 1963).

*Tench*: Watkin Tench, *A Narrative of the Expedition to Botany Bay* (1789), in *Sydney's First Four Years*, ed. L.F. Fitzhardinge (Library of Australian History, Sydney, 1979 [1789]).

*White*: John White, *Journal of a Voyage to New South Wales*, ed. A.H. Chisholm (Angus and Robertson, Sydney, 1962 [1790]).

*Winslow*: [Edward Winslow], *Winslow Papers, AD 1776–1826*, ed. W.O. Raymond (New Brunswick Historical Society, St John, 1901)

INTRODUCTION

1. Barrington, pp. 5–7.
2. Lang, p. 23.
3. Flanagan, vol. 1, pp. 20–22.
4. Sutherland, p. 14.
5. Blair, p. 91.
6. 'The Day We Were Lagged', *Bulletin*, 21 January 1888, p. 4.
7. The Bonwick Transcripts now constitute one of the treasures of the State Library of New South Wales.
8. Hancock, p. 11.
9. O'Brien (1937), pp. 159, 179.
10. Crawford, pp. 34–5.
11. Crowley, pp. 1–3.
12. Shaw (1966), p. 49.
13. Clark, p. 69.
14. Seeley, p. 8.
15. Clark, p. 70.
16. Rusden, vol. 1, pp. 14, 17.
17. Gonner, pp. 629, 632.
18. Barton, vol. 1, pp. 1–9.
19. Rutter, p. 14.
20. Hancock, p. 11.
21. Dallas, pp. 4–12.
22. Blainey (1966), pp. 16–37.
23. See Shaw (1968), Bolton (1968, 1969), and Blainey (1968(1) and (2)). Many of the contributions to the debate were summarized or reprinted in Martin (1978).
24. Anna Seward, *Elegy on Captain Cook*, 1st ed. (London, 1780), pp. 11–12.

25. F.W. Martyn, *The Geographical Magazine*, 2nd ed. (London, 1785-7), vol. 1, p. 578.

26. See the various essays in Martin; and Gillen (1982), Mackay, and Frost (1985).

## 1. *Eighteenth-Century England: Crime*

1. Edmund Burke, *Reflections on the Revolution in France* (1790), in *The Writings and Speeches of Edmund Burke, Vol. 8*, ed. L.G. Mitchell (Clarendon Press, Oxford, 1989), pp. 146-8.

2. *Fielding*, pp. 143-44.

3. *Boswell's Life of Johnson*, ed. G.B. Hill, rev. L.F. Powell (Clarendon Press, Oxford, 1971 [1934]), vol. 3, p. 178.

4. Wordsworth, *The Prelude* (1805 version), Book 7, ll. 184-310.

5. Diary entry, 27 December 1784, *William Smith*, vol. 1, p. 176.

6. Chambers and Mingay, pp. 3, 15, 34-5.

7. William Cobbett, in the *Political Register*, 15 March 1806, cols 361-2.

8. Ibid, 12 July 1817, col. 463.

9. Briggs, pp. 18, 23.

10. Rodger, p. 206.

11. Nagle, p. 209.

12. Malcolmson, p. 85.

13. Ibid, pp. 85-127.

14. William Paley, *The Principles of Moral and Political Philosophy* (London, 1785), quoted in Beattie, p. 148.

15. 'The Felon's Muster Roll', *Edinburgh Magazine*, vol. 2 (1785), pp. 42-3.

16. Quoted in Beattie, pp. 157-8.

17. Quoted ibid., p. 156; and *Bath Chronicle*, 18 January 1787.

18. *Bath Chronicle*, 11 January 1787.

19. Beattie, p. 152.

20 Thompson (1971); Thompson (1975).

21. *PH*, vol. 19 (for 1777-8), col. 970.

22. Quoted in Beattie, p. 138.

23. Quoted ibid., p. 151.

24. *Bath Chronicle*, 8 January 1784, 18 January 1787.

25. Thompson (1975), pp. 225-7.

26. P. Cromp to Sydney, 17 January 1785, HO 42/6, fos 31-2.

27. Janssen, as quoted in Langbein, p. 110 and Beattie, p. 22.

28. Cited by Beattie, pp. 227-8.

29. *Salisbury Journal*, 6 October 1783 (quoted in Beattie, p. 228).

30. *Fielding*, p. 75.

31. E.g., [Anon.], *An Account of the Endeavours that have been used to Suppress Gaming-Houses* (London, 1722), p. 20.

32. Camplin to [Germaine], quoted in Beattie, p. 138; Thomas Robertson to [Sydney], 30 November and 10 December 1782, HO 42/1, fos 360, 379; quoted in Malcolmson, p. 87; quoted in Reece, p. 182.

## 2. Eighteenth-Century England: Punishment

1. Langbein, pp. 96, 118.
2. Quoted in Beattie, p. 467.
3. See Ekirch (1987), pp. 17–18, 70–71.
4. Campbell's memorandum, in C.R. Freire to Sá e Mello, 7 September 1784, ANTT, NME caixa 706, no. 66.
5. Suffolk, Warrant, 28 December 1775, SP 44/91, pp. 446–7.
6. Sydney to Shortland, 8 May 1787, HO 13/5, p. 185.
7. *JHC*, vol. 40 (1784–5), pp. 1161–2.
8. *William Smith*, vol. 1, p. 173. (9 Geo. 1, c. 22, passed in 1723, became known as the 'Black Act'.)
9. See Beattie, pp. 183, 333, 426.
10. For Ryder, see Langbein, pp. 98, 111–3.
11. Ibid., p. 112.
12. Ibid., pp. 111–2.
13. Janssen (as cited in Langbein, p. 110).
14. Rochford to the Norfolk Justices, 23 September 1772, SP 44/92, pp. 52–3.
15. Sydney to the Oxford Justices, 12 April 1787, HO 13/5, pp. 130–3.
16. See below, pp 51–52.
17. Nepean to Sydney, 9 November 1786, SLNSW, Mitchell MS An 53/1.
18. Nepean to Astley, 9 October 1786, HO 13/4, p. 231.
19. Arnold and others to Moore, and Moore to Nepean, 24 April 1784, HO 42/4, fos 163–4.
20. See Beattie, passim.
21. *The Proceedings of the Old Bailey* (Online), T 1783 0430-64; Gillen (1989), p. 131.
22. Ibid., T 1786 1213-35; Gillen (1989), pp. 148–9.
23. Ibid., T 1785 0511-3; Gillen (1989), p. 150.
24. Ibid., T 1782 0109-8; Gillen (1989), pp. 155–6.
25. Ibid, T 1782 1204-68; Gillen (1989), p. 155.
26. Ibid, T 1783 0910-50; Gillen (1989), pp. 221–2.

## 3. Dealing with the Convict Problem

1. This evocative phrasing is from the prologue supposedly spoken at the first play performed at Sydney. See Geoffrey Ingleton, ed., *True Patriots All* (Angus and Robertson, Sydney, 1952), p. viii.
2. William Eddis, *Letters from America*, ed. A.C. Land (Belknap Press,

Cambridge, Mass., 1969), p. 36.

3.  Morgan, pp. 201–27; Ekirch (1987), pp. 97–132.

4.  *JHC*, vol. 36 (1776–8), p. 927.

5.  This analysis is based on Campbell's letterbooks in SLNSW, Mitchell MSS ZA 3225–3232, and on his returns and related correspondence in the HO 42 and T 1 and T 54 series.

6.  Campbell to Eden, [mid-1776?], SLNSW, Mitchell MS ZA 3231, p. 3.

7.  Campbell to Cooper, 14 February 1782, SLNSW, Mitchell MS ZA 3231, pt 2, p. 51; to Rose, 12 January 1785, T 1/622, no. 210.

8.  Campbell to Iain Campbell, 14 February 1767, SLNSW, Mitchell MS ZA 3231, pt 1, p. 13.

9.  Eden to the Recorder of London, 29 November 1775, SP 44/91, p. 437.

10. Eden to [Weymouth?], 16 June 1776, BL Add. MS 34413, fos 11–12; and see Oldham, pp. 33–4.

11. Eden to Campbell, 12 December 1776, SP 44/93, pp. 126–7; Campbell to Robinson, 19 December 1776, Mitchell MS ZA 3226, pp. 2–3.

12. Scott, p. 39.

13. Crawford, p. 33.

14. Crowley, p. 4.

15. Clark, pp. 64, 69.

16. Shaw (1966), p. 43.

17. Conway, p. 50.

18. Hughes, p. 62; Molony, pp. 2–3; Mackay, pp. 13, 16.

19. Quoted in Bain Attwood, *Possession: Batman's Treaty and the Matter of History* (The Miegunyah Press, Melbourne, 2009), p. 168.

20. [William Eden], *Principles of Penal Law* (London, 1771), pp. 28–9.

21. Campbell to Eden, [mid-1776?], SLNSW, Mitchell MS ZA 3231, pt 2, pp. 3–5.

22. Campbell, Testimony, April 1778, *JHC*, vol. 36 (1776–8), p. 926; Campbell to Treasury, 11 March 1777, T 1/529; to Eden, 17 March 1777, SLNSW, Mitchell MS ZA 3226, pp. 34-5, and *JHC*, vol. 36 (1776–8), p. 927; Campbell to Akerman, 8 March, to Eden, 4 June 1777, SLNSW, Mitchell MS ZA 3226, pp. 38, 55–6; Campbell and Treasury, Agreement, 2 February 1778, T 54/42, pp. 442-7; and *JHC*, vol. 36 (1776–8), p. 927.

23. Campbell to Fraser, 24 July 1778, SLNSW, Mitchell MS ZA 3226, pp. 218–9; to Treasury, c. 27 July 1778, T 1/539, fo. 242.

24. Bunbury, Report, 1 April 1779, *JHC*, vol. 37 (1778–80), pp. 306–14.

25. Campbell and Treasury, Agreement, 5 November 1779, T 54/43, pp. 143–9.

26. 'An Account of the whole Number of Convicts on board the several Hulks … in each Year from 12 July 1780 to the 31 December 1790', [undated], CO 201/5, fo. 339.

27. Report, 15 April 1778, *JHC*, vol. 36 (1776–8), pp. 927–9.

28. Ibid, pp. 926–9.

29. Ibid; and Campbell to Hill, 20 February 1786, SLNSW, Mitchell MS ZA 3229, p. 128.

30. Report, *JHC*, vol. 36 (1776–78), pp. 929–30. Bentham's report is printed in an abridged form in Oldham, pp. 201–2.

31. Ibid.

32. Report, *JHC*, vol. 37 (1778–80), pp. 308–9; Campbell to Bunbury, 21 April 1779, SLNSW, Mitchell MS ZA 3226, p. 306; and Campbell's Returns, variously in T 1/539, 548, 564, 578, 594.

33. Campbell's Returns, variously in T 1/619, 622, 626, 630, 634, 637.

34. E.g., Campbell to Clayton, 21 August 1777, SLNSW, Mitchell MS ZA 3226, p. 77.

35. Campbell to Rose, 12 January 1785, T 1/622, fo. 210.

36. Campbell to Robinson, 6 July 1778, SLNSW, Mitchell MS ZA 3226, p. 216.

37. Campbell to Eden, 15 October 1776, SLNSW, Mitchell MS ZA 3225, pp. 494–5.

38. Campbell to Eden, 26 October 1776, ibid., p. 544.

39. Campbell to Treasury, [c. 27 July 1778], T 1/539, fo. 242.

40. Quoted in W.B. Johnson, *The English Prison Hulks*, 2nd ed. (Phillimore, London, 1970), p. 5.

41. Report, *JHC*, vol. 36 (1776–8), pp. 927, 932; Campbell, Return, 11 January 1779, T 1/539, pt 2, fo. 310.

42. Campbell to Hill, 20 February 1786, SLNSW, Mitchell MS ZA 3229, p. 127.

43. Quoted in Johnson, p. 5.

44. Report, *JHC*, vol. 36 (1776–8), p. 928; Campbell to Suffolk, 1 October 1778, SLNSW, Mitchell MS ZA 3226, pp. 248–50; Report, *JHC*, vol. 37 (1778–80), p. 309.

45. Reports, *JHC*, vol. 36 (1776–8), pp. 928, 932, and vol. 37 (1778–80), pp. 309, 313; Campbell, Return, 3 December 1778, T 1/539.

46. Nepean, Memoranda, 1789, CO 201/4, fos 154, 183, 192.

47. Campbell to Eden, 4 June 1777, to Fraser, 8 and 25 May and 6 July 1778, to the Ordnance Board, 24 September 1778, Mitchell MS ZA 3226, pp. 55–6, 201–2, 205, 214–15, 248.

48. Campbell, 'Observations on the Act for punishing Convicts by Labour on the Thames', with Campbell to Eden, 12 January 1778, SLNSW, Mitchell MS ZA 3231, pt 2, p. 13; Reports, *JHC*, vol. 36 (1776–8), p. 928, and vol. 37 (1778–80), p. 309.

49. See O'Brien (1937), p. 133; Shaw (1966), p. 42.

50. Reports, *JHC*, vol. 36 (1776–8), p. 928, and vol. 37 (1778–80), p. 309.

51. Campbell to Eden, 12 January 1778, SLNSW, Mitchell MS ZA 3231, pt 2, pp. 13–15; Johnson, p. 5.
52. Reports, *JHC*, vol. 36 (1776–8), p. 928, and vol. 37 (1778–80), p. 309; Campbell to Eden, 5 December 1777, SLNSW, Mitchell MS ZA 3226, p. 126.
53. See, e.g., 'State of Bounties and Clothing . . .', July 1785–July 1786, T 1/637.
54. Campbell to Fraser, 24 July and 17 December 1778, SLNSW, Mitchell MS ZA 3226, pp. 218, 302; Suffolk, Warrants, 31 July and 26 December 1778, SP 44/93, pp. 277, 313–4.
55. Campbell to Lance, 13 August 1778, and to Eden, 6 October 1779, SLNSW, Mitchell MSS ZA 3226, p. 236, ZA 3227, p. 6.
56. Campbell to Porten, 1 June, to Fraser 23 and 24 August and 16 December 1780, SLNSW, Mitchell MS ZA 3227, pp. 143–4, 167, 244.
57. Campbell to Philips and Nash, 26 November 1781, SLNSW, Mitchell MS ZA 3227, p. 372; Return, 9 October 1781, T 1/564, fo. 334; to Fraser, 27 December 1781 and 4 February 1782, SLNSW, Mitchell MS ZA 3227, pp. 389, 415; Stormont, Warrants, 8 January and 12 February 1782, SP 44/96, pp. 187–8, 195–6; Campbell to Buller, [June 1782], SLNSW, Mitchell MS ZA 3228, p. 50.
58. Reports, *JHC*, vol. 37 (1778–80), p. 309, and vol. 40 (1784–8), p. 1161.
59. Weymouth, Warrant, 18 December 1770, SP 94/91, p. 27, and Warrant, 16 January 1776, SP 44/93, pp. 3–4.
60. Campbell to Eden, 10 February 1777, SLNSW, MS ZA 3226, p. 27; Campbell to Fraser, 6 July, 7 September and 14 October 1780, to Porten, 8 November 1779 and 31 October 1780, to Stormont, 5 and 6 June 1781, SLNSW, Mitchell MS ZA 3227, pp. 33, 156–7, 179, 192, 222, 304, 307.
61. Brown to Amherst, 13 March 1779, WO 1/1137.
62. See Conway.
63. John Roberts to Gilbert Ross, [c. January 1785], HO 42/5, fo. 465.
64. Buller to Shelburne, 1 July 1782, Clements, Shelburne, vol. 152, no. 40.
65. Rose to Nepean, 3 January 1783, HO 35/4; North to Campbell, 24 August 1783, Sydney to Campbell, 23 January 1784, HO 13/1, pp. 173–4, 316–7.
66. The 1778 House of Commons committee stated that: 'The Yearly Average of the Felons, who were ordered for Transportation during a Period of Six Years and an Half, from the 1st of *November* 1769 to the 1st of *May* 1776, amounts to 960, of which a Fourth being deduced for Women, which is nearly the Proportion that appears from the Accounts given to your Committee of Persons transported in the said Six Years and an Half, there remain 720 Males liable to the Punishment of hard Labour on the River *Thames*.' *JHC*, vol. 36 (1776–8), p. 932.
67. Report of the Debate, 11 March 1784, *PH*, vol. 24 (for 1783–8), col. 756.

## 4. *The Atlantic World and Beyond*

1. Bailyn, pp. 31, 55.
2. The literature concerning the Atlantic slave trade is vast. Some recent studies are Falola and Roberts (2008), and Richardson (2009). Then there is the massive electronic resource, www.slavevoyages.org, whose attendant *Atlas of the Transatlantic Slave Trade* is forthcoming.
3. Anderson to North, 20 November 1783, HO 42/3, fo. 176; Bouverie to Nepean, 4 December 1783, HO 12/3, fo. 266; Bailey to [Nepean], 26 January 1784, HO 42/4, fos 44–5; Carter to Sydney, 20 May 1784, HO 42/4, fo. 235; Lygon to Sydney, 10 June 1784, HO 42/4, fo. 279; Kent to Sydney, 2 November 1784, Simpson to Sydney, 8 November 1784, HO 44/40, pp. 101, 103.
4. Sydney to Spencer, 18 December 1784, HO 42/5, fo. 375.
5. Wallis to Sydney, 29 December 1784, HO 42/5, fo. 384; Sedley to [Nepean], 6 February 1785, HO 42/6, fo. 64; Higgins to [Nepean], 9 February 1785, HO 42/6, fo. 68; White to [Nepean], 12 April 1785, HO 42/6, fo. 189; More to Sydney, 20 April 1785, HO 42/6, fo. 205.
6. Hurford to Shelburne, 27 July 1782, Clements, Shelburne, vol. 152, no. 44.
7. For instance, Wright to [Nepean], 24 August 1782, HO 42/1, fos 290–3, and Robertson to Sydney, 30 November and 10 December 1782, HO 42/1, fos 360, 429–30.
8. Lewes to [?], [c. May 1785], HO 42/7, fos 28–33.
9. [?] to [?], [undated], HO 42/7, fos 40–5.
10. Report, 1 April 1779, *JHC*, vol. 37 (1778–80), p. 312.
11. Shelburne, Memorandum, c. July 1782, Brotherton, Sydney R 8.
12. Buller to Shelburne, 2 April 1782, Clements, Shelburne vol. 152, no. 39.
13. African, Committee Minutes, 28 September and 2 October 1782, T 70/145, pp. 153, 154; to Nepean, 28 September 1782, T 70/69, p. 307; to Sydney, 2 October and to Miles, 6 November 1782, T 70/69, pp. 307, 309.
14. African Committee, Minute, 6 November 1782, T 70/145, p. 159.
15. Miles to African Committee, 1 February 1783, T 70/33, pp. 53–5.
16. Ibid.
17. African Committee, Minute, 22 December 1784, T 70/145, pp. 253–4; to Sydney, 22 December 1784, T 70/69, p. 330.
18. W.H. to [Nepean?], c. 27 December 1782, and Campbell to [Nepean], 27 December 1782, T 1/581, nos 92a and b.
19. Privy Council, Order-in-Council, 27 April 1785, PC 2/130, pp. 156–7.
20. North to the King, 11 July 1783, the King to North, 12 July 1783, *George III: Correspondence*, vol. 6, pp. 415, 416.
21. North to the King, 18 July 1783, ibid., p. 418; North, Warrant for transpor-

tation, 12 August 1783, HO 13/1, pp. 173–4; to Governor Parr, 12 August 1783, CO 218/25, pp. 430–1.

22. Hurford to Campbell, c. 22 June 1782, Clements, Shelburne vol. 152, no. 41; Campbell to Buller, 28 June 1782, SLNSW, Mitchell MS ZA 3228, p. 63; Shelburne, Memorandum, [undated], Brotherton, Sydney R 8; Buller to Shelburne, 1 July 1782, Clements, Shelburne vol. 152, no. 40.
23. Pinto de Sousa to Sá e Mello, 3 October, Sá e Mello to Pinto de Sousa, 26 October 1782 (draft), ANTT, MNE caixa 705, no. 561, and livro 129.
24. Thompson to Shelburne, 9 October 1782, Clements, Shelburne vol. 152, no. 27.
25. Thompson to Rose, 1 August, to Sydney, 8 August 1784, NMM, THM 6.
26. Houghton to Sydney, 24 February 1783, CO 267/20, fos 349–56.
27. Morse to North, 6 March 1783, CO 267/7.
28. 23 Geo. III, c. 65.
29. North to Admiralty, [c. 15 September 1783], SP 42/66, fos 420–2; African Committee to Nepean, 16 September 1783, CO 267/20, fo. 245.
30. Morse to Sydney, 23 June 1784, CO 267/8.
31. Thompson, Description of St Thomas, and to Rose, 1 August 1784, NMM, THM 6.
32. Clarke to Pitt, 17 March 1785, PRO 30/8/363, fos 56–66.
33. Bindley to [Sydney], 16 September 1782, HO 42/1, fos 334–5.
34. Matra to [North], 23 August 1782, CO 201/1, fos 57–61.
35. See Ehrman, pp. 140–1.
36. Report of the Debate, 2 March 1784, *JHC*, vol. 39 (1782–4), p. 968.
37. Matra to Sydney, Supplement, 6 April 1784, CO 201/2, fos 64–5.
38. Attorney-General to Sydney, [c. 11 August 1784], HO 42/6, p. 56; Memorandum, [c. 11 August 1784], Clements, Sydney vol. 11.
39. Matra to Fox, 7 August 1784, BL, Add. MS 47568, fos 240–6.
40. Call to [Sydney], [c. 1 September 1784], HO 42/7, fos 49–57. I have given this approximate date for this paper, because Call wrote to Warren Hastings on 3 September 1784: 'I have lately suggested to the ministry the sending of our criminals to an establishment on New South Wales, or on New Zealand.' BL, Add. MS 29166, fo. 27
41. Young to Pitt, [c. 1 September 1784], PRO 30/8/342, fos 283–4.
42. Matra to Nepean, [1November 1784], CO 201/1, fo. 65.
43. Young, Revised proposal, [before 13 January 1785], Arden to Sydney, 13 January 1785, Matra to Nepean, [13 January 1785?], CO 201/1, fos 51, 53, 66.
44. Matra to Nepean, 1 [November] 1784, CO 201/1, fo. 65.
45. C.R. Freire to Sá e Mello, 31 August and 7 September 1784, Sá e Mello to Freire, 2 October 1784 (draft), ANTT, MNE caixa 706, nos 65, 66, and livro 125, fo. 46.

46. Holdsworth to Milbanke, 14 April 1784, HO 28/4, fo. 130.

47. Daniel Hill, Deposition, 4 July 1788, CO 123/11, pp. 319–30.

48. Sydney to Clarke, 5 October 1784, CO 137/84, fo. 147.

49. What Shaw quoted was: 'The more I consider the matter, the greater difficulty I see in disposing of those people.' Shaw (1966), p. 45.

50. 24 Geo. III, c. 56.

51. [Roberts] to Ross, [c.1 January 1785], HO 42/5, fos 465–9.

52. Sydney to African Committee, 5 January 1785, CO 267/21, fos 1–2; Ross to Nepean, 5 January 1785, HO 42/6, fos 23–4.

53. Barnes to [Nepean], 4 February 1785, HO 35/1.

54. Howe to Pitt, 25 December 1784, PRO 30/8/146, fos 209–10; to Sydney, 26 December 1784, HO 28/4, fo. 386.

55. [Nepean], 'Memo. of matters to be brought before Cabinet', [undated, but c. 27 December 1784], SLNSW, Dixson MS Q 522.

56. The *General Advertiser* for 28 December 1784 recorded that Cabinet had met the previous day at Lord Gower's house; and Nepean to Nichol, 29 December 1784, HO 42/5, fo. 461.

## 5. *The Lemain Fiasco of 1785*

1. Nepean to Nichol, 29 December 1784, HO 42/5, fo. 460.

2. Bradley to Nepean, [c. 1 January 1785], HO 42/1, no. 26.

3. Thompson, Journal entry, 3 January 1785, BL, Add. MS 46120, fos 45–6; to Nepean, 10 January 1785, CO 267/9.

4. Thompson, Journal entry, 31 July 1783, BL Add. MS 46120, fo. 7.

5. [Dalrymple], 'Memorandum communicated to the Chairman of the India Company in January 1782', and 'Heads of Instructions given by the Secret Committee to the Captain of the *Swallow*, September 1783', CO 77/25, fos 119–22, 123–5.

6. Thompson, 'Some account of the Country on the West Coast of Africa between 20° and 30° of South latitude ...', 9 March 1785, CO 267/9; Thompson, Journal entries, 20 February and 21 March 1785, BL, Add. MS 46120, fos 55, 62.

7. Wilson to Nepean, 31 January 1785, CO 267/21, fos 6–8.

8. These documents went as enclosures to Sydney's letter to the Treasury Board, 9 February 1785, T 1/614, no. 335. There is a copy of this letter in HO 35/1.

9. Sydney to the Treasury Board, 9 and 12 February 1785, T 1/614, nos 335, 339a; Rose to Navy Board, 23 February 1785, T 27/37; Navy Board to Rose, 28 February 1785, T 1/616, no. 447a.

10. Sydney to the Lord President of the Privy Council, 3 March 1785, HO 43/2, pp. 17–18; Privy Council, Orders-in-Council, 11 March 1785, PC 2/130, pp. 75–80.

11. Campbell to Nepean, 5 March 1785, T 1/619; Sydney to Treasury, 20 March 1785, T 1/619, no. 856a.
12. Report of the Debate, 16 March 1785, *PH*, vol. 25 (1785–6), cols 391–2.
13. Report of the Debate, 11 April 1785, ibid., cols 430–1.
14. Ibid.
15. Beauchamp Committee, Minutes, HO 7/1, from which I have taken the witnesses' order of appearance. The quotations, however, are from the Report printed in *JHC*, vol. 40 (1784–5), pp. 954–60. I have modernized spelling, punctuation and capitalization. Details not in the printed report are from the minutes.
16. Beauchamp, Report, 9 May 1785, *JHC*, vol. 40 (1784–5), pp. 954–60.
17. Beauchamp Committee, Minutes, HO 7/1.
18. There is a copy of this printed version at CO 201/8, fos 152–3.
19. Memorandum, [undated], HO 42/6, pp. 53–4.
20. This letter is evidently lost.
21. Report of the Debate, 29 June 1785, *PH*, vol. 25 (1786–8), col. 906.
22. Nepean, Memorandum, [undated], HO 42/1, p. 462.
23. Sydney to Cavendish, 20 May 1785, Beinecke, Osborn no. 14753 (1).
24. Privy Council, Orders-in-Council, 13 May 1785, PC 2/130, pp. 219–21, 221–2.
25. See above, pp. 97–8, 110. It may be that Call did not present the committee with the complete text of his proposal.
26. The manuscript copy in HO 42/6, fos 449–67 was annotated by Pitt, 'June 1785', and by another person '21 June 1785'. The printed version, from which the following quotations are taken, was presented to the House of Commons on 28 July 1785. *JHC*, vol. 40 (1784–5), pp. 1161–4. There are no substantive differences between the texts.
27. Sydney to Admiralty, 22 August 1785, HO 28/5, fos 118–20.
28. Thompson to Howe, 29 December 1784, NMM, THM 6.
29. Admiralty to Thompson, Instructions and Secret Instructions, 15 September 1785, ADM 2/1342.
30. Blagden to Banks, 3, 10 and 15 September 1785, Kew, JBK nos 201, 203, 204; Banks, 'Heads of Instructions to be given by Captain Thompson ... to Mr Hove', [c.15 September 1785], ADM 2/1342.
31. Pemberton to Dundas, [c. 15 September 1785], BL, OIOC G/9/1, pp. 18–25.
32. Diana Dalrymple to Devaynes, [c. 17 September 1785], PRO 30/8/128, fos 64–5.
33. Devaynes to Dundas, 17 September 1785, NAS, GD 51/3/17, fos 1–3; William Dalrymple to Dundas, 2 October 1785, T 1/624, fos 93–4; Pitt to Grenville, 2 October 1785, *Dropmore*, vol. 1, p. 257.

## 6. *Thinking about the Whole Globe*

1. Baugh, p. 341.
2. Newcastle to Holdernesse, 25 July 1758, BL, Add. MS 32882, fo. 65.
3. See, e.g., Pocock to Clevland, 7 December 1758, ADM 1/161, fo. 292; Cornish to Clevland, 24 June 1761 and 5 April 1762, ADM 1/162, pt 1, fo. 129, pt 2, fos 17–18; Harland to Stephens, 20 September 1773, ADM 1/163, fo. 240.
4. See H.M. Scott.
5. *Sandwich*, vol. 3, p. 170
6. Hughes to the Bombay Council, EIC, 27 January 1784, BL, OIOC H 178, p. 917; to Stephens, 10 September 1784, HO 28/5, fo. 30.
7. The characterizations of Gower and Camden are Ehrman's, p. 184. The others are by W. W. Grenville, 'Commentaries on my own Political Life and of Public Transactions connected with it', Perkins, Grenville book 6, pp. 3–6.
8. Sydney to Pitt, 24 September 1784, PRO 30/8/181, fo. 261; Dundas to Cornwallis, 29 July 1787, *Cornwallis*, vol. 1, p. 321; *William Smith*, Diary entry, 5 July 1786, vol. 2, p. 124.
9. Quoted in Ehrman, p. 303.
10. India Board, Secret minute, 26 August 1786, BL, OIOC L/P&S/2/1, no. 14; Dundas to Hawkesbury, 16 September 1786, BL, Add. MS 38192, fo. 44; Dundas to Eden, 28 September 1786, BL, Add. MS 34466, pp. 353–5.
11. Dundas to Lowther, 25 July 1806, quoted in C. Matheson, *The Life of Henry Dundas* (Constable, London, 1933), p. 375.
12. Chairmen, EIC, to Hillsborough, 25 October 1781, BL, OIOC H 154, pp. 119–20.
13. Hughes to Bombay Council, EIC, 27 January 1784, BL, OIOC H 178, pp. 916–7.
14. For Suffrein's views on Acheen, see George Smith to Dundas, 27 January 1785, BL, OIOC H 434, pp. 49–54; Carmarthen to Hailes, 23 December 1784, BL, Egerton MS 3499, pp. 75–6.
15. Dundas to Sydney, 2 November 1784, PRO 30/8/157, fo. 6.
16. Howe to Pitt, 25 December 1784, PRO 30/8/146, fos. 209–10; to Sydney, 26 December 1784, HO 28/4, fo. 386.
17. India Board, Secret minute, 9 April 1785, BL, OIOC L/P&S/2/1, no. 3; and Draft of secret despatch, 9 April 1785, BL, OIOC L/P&S/5/583.
18. HO 42/6, fos 462, [468].
19. India Board, Secret minute, 27 June 1785, BL, OIOC L/P & S/2/1, no. 6; Draft of secret despatch, 27 June 1785, BL, OIOC I/1/13.
20. Clark, p. 69; Bolton (1968), p. 15; and particularly Atkinson (1997).

21. Barnes, Testimony, 2 May 1785, HO 7/1.
22. Nepean to Middleton, 12 December 1786, CO 201/2, fo. 53; Middleton to Nepean, 13 December 1786, CO 201/2, fo. 54; Middleton to Pitt, 13 December 1786, (privately owned); Stephens to Middleton, 14 December 1786, NMM, MID 1/177; Rogers to Nepean, 21 December 1786, CO 201/2, fos 66–7; Stephens to Nepean, 28 December 1786, CO 201/2, fos 41, 43.
23. Phillip to Sydney, 1 March 1787, CO 201/2, fo. 114.
24. Banks to Barrow, 12 August 1815, NHM, DTC vol. 19, pp. 174–8; to Nepean, 9 September 1787, HO 42/12, no. 115.
25. Turnbull, Macaulay and Gregory to Nepean, 10 May, Calvert to Nepean, 1 June, Nepean to Steele, 10 June 1786, T 1/632, fos 35–40.
26. India Board, Draft of Cathcart's instructions, undated but before 30 November 1787 (the date of the finalized version), BL, OIOC G/12/18, pp. 121–34.
27. *Smith*, vol. 2, p. 631.
28. Ibid.
29. E.g., Rough Minutes, [June 1786?], BT 6/226; and Minutes, 14 November 1786, BT 5/4, pp. 75–7.
30. See Frost (2003), pp. 168–9.
31. Nepean to Sackville Hamilton, Draft, 24 October 1786, HO 100/18, fos 372–3.
32. India Board, Memorandum, 25 May 1787, PRO 30/8/360, fos 108–14.
33. Banks to Dundas, 15 June 1787, PRO 30/8/361, fos 33–5.
34. For details of the Nootka Sound alarm, see Frost (2003), ch. 9.
35. Board of Trade, Minutes, 20 January 1791, BT 6/95, pp. 391–2, and BL, Add. MS 38390, fos 9–10.
36. Board of Trade, Minutes, 21 January 1791, BT 5/7, pp. 21–3; and Southern Whalers to Fawkner, 24 January 1791, BT 6/95, p. 395.
37. Grenville to Westmoreland, 13 January 1791, *Dropmore*, vol. 2, p. 14.
38. Board of Trade, 'Confidential Paper', 14 February 1791, BT 6/227, and Minutes, 14 February 1791, BT 5/7, p. 52–4, and BL, Add MS 38393, fos 26–7.
39. Select Committee, EIC, Memorandum, 17 March 1791, BT 6/227.
40. Lushington to Cottrell, 17 March, Cottrell to Dundas, 18 March 1791, BL, OIOC G/32/164; Memorandum, undated, but c. 21 March 1791, BT 6/227.
41. Writing in July 1804, Dundas recalled that 'it is almost twenty years since I first had occasion to consider that subject, and I had much conversation with Sir Charles Middleton upon it when he was comptroller of the navy'. Dundas to Wellesley, 4 July 1804, BL Add. MS 37275, fo. 260.
42. India Board, 'Observations on the Account of Materials that may be procured in India for Ships of any Size', 15 January 1788, PRO 30/8/360, fos 116–18.
43. See Frost (2003), Ch. 11.

44. Report of the Debate, 14 December 1790, *PH*, vol. 28 (1789–91), col. 979.

45. Phillip to Sydney, 15 May 1788, CO 201/3, fos 6-7; to Lansdowne, 3 July 1788, SLNSW, Mitchell MS 7241, p. 3; to Middleton, 6 July 1788, [privately owned].

## 7. *Voices Prophesizing War*

1. Secret Committee, EIC, to Bengal Council, 9 and 19 September 1783, BL, OIOC L/P & S/1/9, fos 223-33, 234-47, 253-66.

2. Carmarthen to Storer, 1 January 1784, FO 27/11, pp. 1-2.

3. Pitt to Carmarthen, 10 April, Howe to Carmarthen, 11 April 1784, BL, Egerton MS 3498, fos 30, 178.

4. Hailes to Carmarthen, 2 June and 21 July 1785, BL, Egerton MS 3499, fos 116, 128-9; 4 August and 1 December 1785, FO 27/17, pp. 782, 930.

5. Carmarthen to Hailes, 28 May 1784, FO 148/4, no. 12.

6. Dorset to Carmarthen, 1 July 1784, FO 27/12, p. 768.

7. Hailes to Carmarthen, 2 September, Dorset to Carmarthen, 7 October 1784, *Despatches*, pp. 19, 23; Carmarthen to Dorset, 19 October 1784, FO 27/13, pp. 1158-9.

8. Phillip to Stephens, 14 October 1784, ADM 1/2307, and Register of Officers on leave abroad, ADM 6/207, fo. 8; Nepean, Entry, 11 November 1784, Clements, Nepean, Secret Service Ledger ; Phillip to Nepean, January 1785, FO 95/4/6, pp. 499-500.

9. Hailes to Carmarthen, 28 April 1784, FO 27/11, p. 597; Dorset to Carmarthen, 22 July 1784, *Despatches*, pp. 4-5, 16; Dorset to Carmarthen, 30 June 1785, FO 27/16, pp. 672-3; Keith to Carmarthen, 7 December 1785, FO 7/11, pp. 631-2.

10. [Baldwin], 'Speculations on the Situation and Resources of Egypt, 1773–1785', [3 May 1785], BL, Add. MS 38346, fos 256-7.

11. 'Heads of [a] Conversation between Mr Dundas and Mr Baldwin in February 1784', PRO 30/8/360, fos 287-91; Mulgrave, Memorandum on the transmission of despatches via Suez, [undated], PRO 30/8/360, fos 338-45; India Board to Carmarthen, and Draft of Instructions for Baldwin, 19 May 1786, BL OIOC F/2/11, pp. 74-119; Baldwin to Carmarthen, 24 June 1786, BL, OIOC G/17/6, fo. 20.

12. Dundas to Sydney, 2 November 1784, PRO 30/8/157, fo. 6.

13. For Suffren's views, see George Smith to Dundas, 27 January 1785, BL, OIOC H 434, pp. 53-4.

14. Carmarthen to Dorset, 23 December 1784, FO 27/13, pp. 1368-70; to Hailes, 23 December 1784, BL, Egerton MS 3499, fos 75-6.

15. Dorset to Carmarthen, 28 December 1784, FO 27/13, pp. 1398-9; Hailes to Carmarthen, 13 January 1785, BL, Egerton MS 3499, fo. 85.

16. Carmarthen to Dorset, 15 February 1784, BL, Add. MS 28060, fos 99-100,

16 February 1784, FO 27/11, pp. 249–51, 2 July 1784, FO 27/12, pp. 758–60, 1 October 1784, FO 27/13, p. 1068; Carmarthen to Dorset, 1 November, and Dorset to Carmarthen, 2 December 1784, FO 27/13 (after pp. 1211 and 1331).

17. Carmarthen to Hailes, 4 June 1784, Hailes to Carmarthen, 10 June 1784, FO 27/12, pp. 689–92, 715–7; Carmarthen to Harris, 14 January 1785, Harris to Carmarthen, 4 March 1785, FO 37/6.

18. Hailes to Carmarthen, 10 June 1784, FO 27/12, pp. 715–7; Carmarthen to Dorset, 27 July 1784, *Instructions*, p. 251; Dorset to Carmarthen, 8 and 22 July, 19 and 26 August 1784, *Despatches*, pp. 18, 19.

19. Harris to Carmarthen, 19 August 1785, FO 37/7, no. 42.

20. Harris to Carmarthen, 23 September 1785, FO 37/8, no. 60; Pitt to Grenville, 4 October 1785, *Dropmore*, vol. 1, p. 257.

21. Harris to Carmarthen, 9 and 16 September 1785, FO 37/8, nos 52, 55; 8 November 1785, FO 37/9.

22. Grimoard to Vergennes, 18 and 30 September 1785, and Castries, 'Observations relative à la Hollande', 8 October 1785, *Colenbrander*, pp. 10–16.

23. Carmarthen to Dorset, 17 February, Vergennes to Dorset, 1 April 1786, FO 27/18; Carmarthen to Harris, 24 February 1786, FO 37/10.

24. This account is based on the documents in *Colenbrander*, pp. 1–34.

25. [      ], Memorandum, 15 May 1785, BL, Add. MS 28060, fo. 342.

26. Harris to Carmarthen, 3 February 1786, BL, Add. MS 28061, fo. 21.

27. Macpherson to the Secret Committee, EIC, 23 September and 27 October 1785, BL, OIOC L/P & S/1/9, fo. 140, and H 555, pp. 283–9; Hailes to Carmarthen, 22 June 1786, FO 27/18.

28. Article 13, Treaty of Versailles, 3 September 1783, FO 93/33/2.

29. Bengal Council to the Secret Committee, EIC, 10 and 27 January and 4 February 1786, BL, OIOC L/P & S/5/20, nos 8, 9, 10; and Secret Committee, Minutes, 23 June 1786, BL, OIOC L/P & S/1/9, fos 144–5.

30. Bengal Council to the Secret Committee, EIC, 10 January 1786, L/P&S/5/20, no. 8.

31. Harris to Carmarthen, 1, 4 and 8 August 1786, FO 37/11, nos 68, 70, 72.

32. Sydney to the King, and the King's reply, 16 August 1786, *George III: Later Correspondence*, vol. 1, p. 244.

33. 'Private Instructions …', 'Plan of the Voyage', 'Extract from the general instructions', and 'Memoir drawn up by the Academy of Sciences', in *Lapérouse*, vol. 1, pp. 11–43, 119–35.

34. Dorset to Carmarthen, 5 May and 9 June 1785, FO 27/16, pp. 553, 605–6; Dalrymple to Carmarthen, 8 June 1785, BL, Egerton MS 3501, fo. 39.

35. Carmarthen to Fitz-Herbert, 23 June 1785, FO 97/340.

36. Bolton (1968), p. 6.

37. Fitz-Herbert to Carmarthen, 17 January 1786, FO 97/340.

38. Fitz-Herbert to Carmarthen, 18 February 1786, ibid; Carmarthen to Fitz-Herbert, 17 November 1786, FO 97/341.

39. William Richardson to Hawkesbury, 8 September 1786, BL, Add. MS 38220, fos 11-14.

40. [    ], *The Public Advertiser*, 19 August 1786.

41. Forster and Thornton, Testimony, 24 August 1786, BT 5/4, fos 2-4.

42. Board of Trade, Minute, 25 August 1786, BT 5/4, fo. 9; Navy Board, 'An Account of the Average Prices . . .', 21 March 1787, ADM BP/7.

43. Middleton to Pitt, 29 August and 5 September 1786, PRO 30/8/111, fos 129, 132.

44. Mitchell to Hawkesbury, 21 September 1786, BL, Add. MS 38220, fos 81-2.

45. See above, ch. 6, pp. 142-3.

46. Sydney to the Chairmen, EIC, 15 September 1786, BL, OIOC E/1/79, no. 187.

47. George III, Instructions to Phillip, 25 April 1787, CO 201/2, fo. 35.

## 8. *An Overseas Convict Colony: Investment and Return*

1. Letter, 11 February 2010.

2. Eden, pp. 28–9.

3. See above, ch. 4.

4. Pitt to Grenville, 2 October 1785, *Dropmore*, vol. 1, p. 257.

5. Thompson, 'Some account of the Country on the West Coast of Africa . . .', 9 March 1785, CO 267/9.

6. Report, *JHC*, vol. 40 (1784–5), p. 1164.

7. [Nepean], Heads of a Plan, [c.15 August 1786], T 1/639, no. 2176.

8. Blainey (1966), p. 28.

9. Sandwich, Memorandum, c. 31 December 1781, *Sandwich*, vol. 4, p. 282.

10. Palliser, Memorandum, ibid., p. 308.

11. These details are taken from the voluminous Navy Board records in the ADM 106 series, with the figures for the mid-1780s coming from Navy Board to Admiralty, 21 April 1804, BL, Add. MS 37275, fos 302–3. For other details, see Frost (2003), chs 4 and 11.

12. 'Account of Masts made 1780, 1781, 1782, 1783', [1784], ADM 106/3321, fo. 30.

13. Jervis, Reasons for Peace, [1783], Clements, Shelburne vol. 72, no. 91.

14. Durno to Stormont, 13 January 1780, FO 64/1; Stormont to the Admiralty, 24 January 1782, Admiralty to Stormont, 11 March 1782, FO 64/3; Middleton to Pitt, 29 August 1786, PRO 30/8/111, fo. 129.

15. Hughes to Stephens, 23 April 1780, ADM 1/164, fo. 187.

16. Hughes to Stephens, 20 March 1781, ibid., fo. 222.

17. Most of the following details are from Hughes's Letterbooks, ADM 7/733, 734.

18. Richmond, pp. 253, 258–9.

19. Hughes to Stephens, 12 August 1782, ADM 1/164, fo. 347.

20. Hughes to the Bombay Council, EIC, 27 January 1784, BL, OIOC H 178, fo. 917; to Stephens, 10 September 1784, HO 28/5, fo. 30.

21. Deptford Officers to Navy Board, 20 August 1788, ADM 106/3322, fo. 17.

22. Navy Board, Minute, 1 August 1786, ADM 106/2621.

23. Young to Pitt, [c. 1 September 1784], PRO 30/8/342, fo. 284.

24. Hughes to Stephens, 10 September 1784, HO 28/5, fo. 30.

25. Young and Call, Memorial, 21 June 1785, BL OIOC E/1/76. no. 213.

26. EIC to Bengal Council, 6 May 1791, BT 6/101.

27. Matra, Proposal, 23 August 1783, CO 201/2, fo. 60.

28. Young to [Pitt], [c. 1 September 1784], PRO 30/8/342, fo. 283.

29. Beauchamp Committee, Report, 28 July 1785, JHC, vol. 40 (1784–5), p. 1164.

30. Morris to Banks, 19 April 1772, BL, Add. MS 33977, fo. 18.

31. Banks, Instructions to Hove, [ ] March and 3 April 1787, BT 6/246. 'Nankeen', named after Nankin, the southern capital of Kiangsu province, was made of yellowish cotton.

32. Banks to Hawkesbury, 28 August and 16 November 1789, BT 6/246.

33. Matra, Proposal, 23 August 1783, CO 201/1, fo. 57.

34. Smith to Dundas, 27 January 1785, BL, OIOC H 434, fos 43–54.

35. Banks to Yonge, 15 May 1787, PRO 30/11/13, fos 322–7.

36. Admiralty, Instructions to Bligh, 20 November 1787, in *Bligh*, pp. 5–8; Nepean to Fraser, 17 June 1787, FO 27/21, fo. 430.

37. Matra, Proposal, 23 August 1783, CO 201/1, fos 59–60.

## 9. *Towards a Decision: August 1786*

1. *Annual Register*, vol. 28 (1786), pp. 233–4.

2. The King to Hertford, 7 August 1786, *George III: Later Correspondence*, vol. 1, p. 242; Sydney to Lansdowne, 12 August 1786, Clements, Sydney vol. 13.

3. Thompson, Log of the *Nautilus* voyage, 8 April and 17 May 1786, ADM 55/92; to Stephens, 15 August 1786, ADM 1/2594.

4. Mackay, p. 57.

5. Shaw (1966), p. 45.

6. *Edinburgh Magazine*, vol. 3 (June 1786), p. 473.

7. Pinto de Souza to Mello e Castro, 8 August 1786, ANTT, MNE caixa 706, no. 698.

8. Blankett to Howe, 6 and 16 August 1786, NMM, HOW 3; to Nepean, 10 August 1786, HO 42/9, fo. 94.

9. Blankett, Memorandum, [undated, but August 1786], NMM, HOW 3.

10. Howe to Blankett (draft), 19 August 1786, NMM HOW 3.

11. Memorandum, 17 June 1789, CO 77/25, fos 127–8; Grenville to Admiralty

Board, and Heads of Instructions, 3 October 1790, ADM 1/4154, no. 43, and ADM 1/4155, after no. 59.

12. 'Madagascar might become highly advantageous, but it is probable the India Company would make obstacles to such an establishment': to Howe, 6 August 1786, NMM, HOW 3.

13. The following details are from, variously, *Cook,* vol. 1, pp. 304–13; *Banks,* vol. 2, pp. 53–61; Banks's testimony to the 1779 and 1785 House of Commons committees, HO 42/5, fos 111-13 and HO 7/1; Matra's proposal, 23 August 1783, CO 201/2, fos 59-61, and his testimony to the 1785 House of Commons committee, HO 7/1.

14. *White*, p. 110; L.A. Gilbert, 'Plants, politics and personalities in Colonial New South Wales', in *People and Plants in Australia*, ed. D.J. and S.G.M. Carr (Academic Press, Sydney, 1981), pp. 220–21.

15. *Banks*, Testimony to the 1785 House of Commons committee, HO 7/1; and *Banks*, vol. 2, p. 128.

16. For an extended analysis, see Frost (1994), pp. 176–89.

17. Matra, Proposal sent to Fox, 7 August 1784, BL Add. MS 47568, fo. 245.

18. Young, Proposal, [c. 1 September 1784], PRO 30/8/342, fo. 283.

19. Pitt, Memorandum, 17 September 1804, PRO 30/8/196, fo. 88.

20. White to Skill, 17 April 1790, *HRNSW*, vol. 1, pt 2, p. 333.

21. *Cook*, vol. 1, p. 206; *Banks*, vol. 1, p. 436.

22. *Banks*, vol. 2, p. 10.

23. *Cook*, vol. 2, pp. 565–6, 868–9.

24. Sandwich to the King, 16 July 1774, *George III: Correspondence*, vol. 3, p. 118.

25. Stephens to Cook, 20 July 1776, in *Cook*, vol. 3, p. 1513.

26. *Gentleman's Magazine*, vol. 41 (1771), p. 425.

27. Ibid., vol. 44 (1774), p. 21.

28. Ibid., vol. 46 (1776), p. 119.

29. Middleton, *A New and Complete System of Geography* (London, 1777–8), vol. 2, p. 519.

30. G.H. Millar, *The New, Complete, Authentic, and Universal System of Geography* (London, 1782), p. 206.

31 Watson to Winslow, 6 March 1785, *Winslow Papers*, ed. W.O. Raymond (New Brunswick Historical Society, St John, 1901), p. 274.

32. Shaw (1968), p. 202.

33. *Morning Chronicle*, 13 October 1786; *London Chronicle*, 14 October 1786.

34. Mackay (1985), p. 65.

35. *Fielding*, p. 100.

36. *Howard*, passim.

37. *JHC*, vol. 37 (1778–80), pp. 307, 310, 314. (My emphasis.)

38. Lewes to [Sydney?], [mid–1785], HO 42/7, fos 28–9, 32–3.

39. Board of Trade, Minutes, 23 August 1786, BT 5/4, p. 1.
40. Fawkener to Hawkesbury, 16 and 17 August 1786, BL, Add. MS 38219, fos 349–51; BT, Minutes, 18 August 1786, BL, Add. MS 38389, fo. 262. Dorchester had been appointed governor of the Canadian provinces.
41. 'Heads of Instructions given by the Secret Committee to the Captain of the *Swallow*, September 1783', CO 77/25, fo. 123; Thompson, 'Some account of the Country on the West Coast of Africa ...', 9 March 1785, CO 267/9; Admiralty, Secret Instructions to Thompson, 15 September 1785, ADM 2/1342, and Tripp to Stephens, 24 March 1786, HO 28/5, fo. 228; Dalrymple to Devaynes, c. 17 September 1785, PRO 30/8/128, fo. 65; Devaynes to Dundas, 17 September 1785, T 1/624.
42. *Morning Herald*, 6 December 1786. (I am grateful to Gary Sturgess for this reference.)
43. Nepean/Sydney to Admiralty, 31 August 1786, ADM 1/4152, no. 25, [p. 2].
44. For an extended account of Phillip's career, see Frost (1987).
45. Collins to General Collins, 19 August 1787, SLNSW, Mitchell MS 700, no. 8.
46. Ross to Stephens, 10 July 1788, ADM 1/3824, fo. 48; Campbell to Ducie, 12 July 1788, SLNSW, Mitchell MS AC 145, p. 3.
47. Campbell to Ducie, [November 1788], SLNSW, Mitchell MS AC 145, pp. 3–4 (of this letter).

## 10. *The Decision for Botany Bay*

1. Botany Bay's precise co-ordinates are 33°58'S lat., 151°13'E long. However, as 33°S is what appears in the documents, I shall use it as a shorthand form.
2. These undated estimates, which were drawn up before 18 August 1786, are in HO 42/7, fos 23–4, CO 201/2, fos 15–21, and HO 42/10, pp. 426–7. Concerning the annual cost of keeping a convict on a hulk at this time: according to the returns in T 1/626, 630, 634, 637, in 1786 Campbell received a total of £13,732 for the 490 convicts he had contracted to keep on the *Justitia* and *Censor* hulks in the Thames, or £28 per man per annum.
3. There are seven copies of 'Heads of a Plan' extant. That in CO 201/2, fos 11–13 seems the earliest – though it is worth noting that none of these copies is a draft.
4. For the fullness of the Levée, see the *Daily Universal Register*, 19 August 1786; and for Cabinet's meeting on the Saturday, see ibid., 21 August 1786.
5. Sydney to the Treasury Board, 18 [21] August 1786, HO 35/7 and T 1/639, no. 2176; Treasury Board, Minutes, 18 [21] August 1786, T 29/58, pp. 22–4.
6. Blainey (1968 (1) ), p. 204; Dallas, pp. 4–5.
7. Howe to Sydney, 26 December 1784, HO 28/4, fo. 386.
8. [Nepean/Sydney] to the Treasury Board, 21/18 August 1786, T 1/639, no. 2176.

9. [Nepean], Heads of a Plan, [c.15 August 1786], CO 201/2, fo. 11.

10. Ibid., fo. 13.

11. Clark saw that 'in a perfunctory, slapdash way, some of the commercial arguments for New Holland were tacked on to the Botany Bay solution for the evil of the over-crowded jails': p. 69. Bolton explained the presence of these paragraphs as the work of a Home office clerk 'confronted with the task of putting together a memorandum to justify the choice of New South Wales as a convict colony': (1968), p. 10. Shaw found it 'curious that Sydney should have placed these paragraphs, if they are so important, at the end rather than in the forefront of a lengthy document, and that he omitted them altogether from the detailed letter which he wrote to the Treasury explaining his "plan"': (1968), p. 195. Blainey characterized this generic approach as seeing the paragraphs only as 'quaint displays of window-dressing': (1966), p. 27.

12. E.g., when Thomas Robertson send his 'Abstract ... of [a] plan for employing the convicts in His Majesty's Royal Navy', to Sydney at the end of 1782, he referred to 'the heads of my plan' (HO 42/1, fos 28–31). In September 1785, Banks drew up the 'Heads of Instructions to be given by Captain Thompson ... to Mr Antoni Pantaleon Hove' (ADM 2/1342). In 1787, Mulgrave composed a 'Sketch of the Heads of a Treaty of Defensive Alliance ...', PRO 30/8/360, fos 199–212. About June 1786, the Board of Trade drew up the 'Heads of a Plan for opening Free Ports in the Island of Bermuda and in the Bahama Islands' (BT 6/226). When Pitt sent a draft to Carmarthen concerning commercial negotiations in Paris in September 1786, he termed it 'Heads of a Despatch' (Bodleian, English Letters, d. 122, fo. 146). On 30 January 1787, *The Daily Universal Register* reported that Pitt had presented to the House of Commons 'a small packet of papers, relative to the convicts intended for Botany Bay. The general heads of those papers being read ...'. In October 1789, the Admiralty Board drew up 'Heads of Instructions to be given to the Commander of the Vessel to be appointed to examine Isla Grande, Tristran da Cunha, etc.' (ADM 1/4155, after no. 59).

13. Eden to [Weymouth?], 16 January 1776, BL, Add. MS 34413, fo. 11.

14. Rose to Nepean, 3 January 1783, HO 35/4.

15. Sydney to the Treasury, 10 November 1785, T 1/616.

16. Nepean to Sharrow, 27 October 1786, HO 43/2, fo. 175; Sharrow to Nepean, 30 October 1786 and undated, HO 42/9, fo. 92, HO 42/8, no. 12.

17. Thomas, 'Additional Tools and Utensils ...', USNA, Record group 45/446, fo. 143a; 'Articles sent by the First Fleet to Botany Bay', *HRNSW*, vol. 2, p. 388; Sever, Log of the *Lady Penrhyn*, ibid, p. 407.

18. Twiss to Watson, 29 October 1786; Watson to Nepean, 2 November 1786, HO 42/10, fos 393–4. Hunter identified Murley as a 'weaver': *Hunter*, p. 201.

King, who took him to Norfolk Island, described him as 'an adventurer, [who] had been a master weaver': *King*, p. 40. Murley served as an AB on the *Sirius* (entered 8 December 1786) during the voyage out.

19. Nepean to Sackville Hamilton, Draft, 24 October 1786, HO 100/18, fos 369–72. Nepean annotated: 'This clause [i.e., paragraph] left out in the letter written to Mr Hamilton'. I don't think that its omission from the version sent lessens in the slightest degree its significance, for what it gives is the considered view of the administration official most involved in the Botany Bay decision and the mounting of the First Fleet. It may be that, on reflection, Nepean thought he should not advertise some of the venture's motives; but his omitting it does not reduce its importance as a statement of his understanding of the business. (Michael Roe (1952) first drew attention to this draft letter, and pointed out its significance.)

20. See above, ch. 6, pp. 154–8

21. Clark, p. 69.

22. Phillip to Nepean, 1 March 1787, CO 201/2, fo. 115.

23. Privy Council, Instructions to Phillip, 25 April 1787, CO 201/2, fos 35–6.

24. *King*, p. 37; Phillip to King, Instructions, 12 February 1788, CO 201/3, fo. 27.

25. *Tench*, p. 74.

26. Phillip to Nepean, 30 October 1786, HO 42/10, fo. 301; Singleton to Nepean, 5 November 1786, HO 42/10, fo. 383; Phillip to Banks, 2 September 1787, SLNSW, Mitchell MS C 213, p. 5; Phillip, Instructions to King, 12 February 1788, CO 201/3, fo. 27; *King*, pp. 56, 106; Phillip to Nepean, 17 November 1788, CO 201/3, fo. 166.

27. Phillip, Journal, Clements, Sydney vol. 17.

28. See Frost (1993).

CONCLUSION

1. *Eden*, pp. 28–9.

2. Beauchamp Committee, Report, 28 July 1785, *JHC*, vol. 40 (1784–5), p. 1164.

3. Report of the Debate, 7 February 1786, *PR*, vol. 19 (1787), p. 54.

4. Report of the Debate, 7 February 1786, *Gentleman's Magazine*, vol. 56 (1786), p. 168.

5. *Cook*, vol. 1, p. 278; *Banks*, vol. 2, p. 4.

6. Dallas, p. 5; Blainey (1968 (2)), p. 204.

7. Yeats, 'The Circus Animals' Desertion'.

8. I am providing details in *The First Fleet: The Real Story*.

9. Report of the Debate, 9 February 1791, *PH*, vol. 28 (1789–91), cols 1223–4.

10. Shaw (1984), p. 90.

11. Here, I acknowledge that A.G.L. Shaw did make an extensive examination of hemp and flax papers and references in the Board of Trade collections.

My point is rather than he and others didn't look at commodores' reports and Navy Board statistics to ascertain the need for naval materials and the quantities actually in store.

12. Atkinson (1997), pp. 58, 72, 213. It is also telling that Atkinson does not include the subheadings 'flax' and 'timber' in his 'Norfolk Island' entry in the index.

13. Keneally, pp. 43–4.

14. Shaw (1968), pp. 196, 199.

15. Hughes, p. 70; Molony, p. 1.

16. Bolton (1969), p. 70.

17. Lawson.

18. In 1787, Dundas told Lord Cornwallis, the governor-general of India, that Pitt intended to reconstitute the India board, so as to make him 'not only in reality but declaredly … the Cabinet minister for India' – Dundas to Cornwallis, 27 July 1787, *Cornwallis*, vol. 1, p. 245.

19. Dundas to Sydney, 2 November 1784, PRO 30/8/157, fo. 6; Report of the Debate, 14 December 1790, *PH*, vol. 28 (1789–91), col. 979.

20. Phillip to Banks, 26 July 1790 and 2 April 1792, SLNSW, Mitchell MS C 213, pp. 58–9, 87–8.

21. Grose to Nepean, 2 April 1792, *HRNSW*, vol. 1, part 2, p. 613.

# Select Bibliography

R.G. Albion, *Forests and Sea Power: The Timber Problem of the Royal Navy,*
*1652–1862* (Harvard University Press, Cambridge, Mass., 1926).

Alan Atkinson, *The Europeans in Australia, 1: The Beginnings* (Oxford
University Press, Melbourne, 1997).

Bernard Bailyn, *Atlantic History: Concept and Contours* (Harvard University
Press, Cambridge, Mass., 2005).

George Barrington, *The History of New South Wales* (London, 1802).

G.B. Barton, *History of New South Wales from the Records,* 2 vols (Charles
Potter, Government Printer, Sydney, 1889–94).

Daniel Baugh, *British Naval Administration in the Age of Walpole* (Princeton
University Press, Princeton, NJ, 1965).

J.M. Beattie, *Crime and the Courts in England, 1660–1800* (Princeton University
Press, Princeton, NJ, 1986).

Geoffrey Blainey, *The Tyranny of Distance: How Distance Shaped Australia's*
*History* (Sun Books, Melbourne, 1966).

Geoffrey Blainey, 'A Reply: I came, I Shaw …', *Historical Studies*, vol. 13 (1968),
pp. 204–6.

Geoffrey Blainey, 'Botany Bay or Gotham City?', *Australian Economic History*
*Review*, vol. 8 (1968), pp. 154–63.

David Blair, *The History of Australasia* (McCreedy, Thompson and Niven,
Glasgow, Melbourne and Dunedin, 1878).

G.C. Bolton, 'The Hollow Conqueror: Flax and the Foundation of Australia',
*Australian Economic History Review*, vol. 8 (1968), pp. 3–16.

G.C. Bolton, 'Broken Reeds and Smoking Flax', *Australian Economic History*
*Review*, vol. 9 (1969), pp. 64–70.

John Brewer, *The Sinews of Power: War, Money and the English State, 1688–1783*
(Unwin Hyman, London, 1989).

Asa Briggs, *The Making of Modern England, 1783–1867*: The Age of Improvement (Harper and Row, New York, 1965 [1959]).

J.D. Chambers and G.E. Mingay, *The Agricultural Revolution, 1750–1880*
(Batsford, London, 1966).

C.M.H. Clark, *A History of Australia, vol. 1* (Melbourne University Press,
Melbourne, 1962).

Stephen Conway, 'The Recruitment of Criminals into the British Army, 1775–81', *Bulletin of the Institute of Historical Research*, vol. 58 (1985).

R.M. Crawford, *Australia* (Hutchinson, London, 1952).

F. K. Crowley, 'The Foundation Years, 1788–1821', in *Australia: A Social and Political History*, ed. Gordon Greenwood (Angus and Robertson, Sydney, 1955).

K.M. Dallas, 'The First Settlement in Australia, considered in relation to sea-power in world politics', *Tasmanian Historical Research Association: Papers and Proceedings*, no. 3 (1952).

John Ehrman, *The Younger Pitt: The Years of Acclaim* (Constable, London, 1969).

A. Roger Ekirch, 'Bound for America: A Profile of British Convicts Transported to the Colonies, 1718–1775', *William and Mary Quarterly*, 3rd series, vol. 42 (1985).

A. Roger Ekirch, *Bound for America: The Transportation of British Convicts to the Colonies, 1718–1775* (Clarendon Press, Oxford, 1987).

Toyin Falola and Kevin D. Roberts, eds, *The Atlantic World, 1450–2000* (Indiana University Press, Bloomington, 2008).

Roderick Flanagan, *The History of New South Wales*, 2 vols (London, 1862).

Alan Frost, 'Botany Bay: An imperial venture of the 1780s', *English Historical Review*, vol. 100 (1985).

Alan Frost, *Arthur Phillip, 1738–1814: His Voyaging* (Oxford University Press, Melbourne, 1987).

Alan Frost, *Sir Joseph Banks and the Transfer of Plants to and from the South Pacific, 1786–1798* (The Colony Press, Melbourne, 1993).

Alan Frost, *Botany Bay Mirages* (Melbourne University Press, Melbourne, 1994).

Alan Frost, *The Global Reach of Empire* (Melbourne University Publishing, Melbourne, 2003).

Mollie Gillen, 'The Botany Bay Decision, 1786: convicts, not empire', *English Historical Review*, vol. 97 (1982).

Mollie Gillen, *The Founders of Australia: A Biographical Dictionary of the First Fleet* (Library of Australian History, Sydney, 1989).

E.C.K. Gonner, 'The Settlement of Australia', *English Historical Review*, vol. 23 (1888).

Sir W.K. Hancock, *Australia* (Ernest Benn, London, 1930).

Robert Hughes, *The Fatal Shore: A History of the Transportation of Convicts to Australia, 1787–1868* (Harvill Collins, London, 1987).

W. Branch Johnson, *The English Prison Hulks*, 2nd ed. (Phillimore, London, 1970).

Thomas Keneally, *Australians, vol. 1: Origins to Eureka* (Allen and Unwin, Sydney, 2009).

J.D. Lang, *An Historical and Statistical Account of New South Wales*, 2 vols (Cochrane and M'Crone, London, 1834).

John H. Langbein, '*Albion*'s Fatal Flaws', *Past and Present*, no. 98 (1983).

Philip Lawson, 'The Missing Link: The Imperial Dimension in Understanding Hanoverian Britain', *The Historical Journal*, vol. 29 (1986).

David Mackay, *A Place of Exile: The European Settlement of New South Wales* (Oxford University Press, Melbourne, 1985).

R.W. Malcolmson, '"A set of ungovernable people": The Kingswood colliers in the eighteenth century', in *An Ungovernable People: The English and Their Law in the Seventeenth and Eighteenth Centuries*, ed. John Brewer and John Styles (Rutgers University Press, New Brunswick, NJ, 1980).

Ged Martin, ed., *The Founding of Australia: The Argument about Australia's Origins* (Hale and Iremonger, Sydney, 1978).

John Molony, *The Penguin Bicentennial History of Australia: The Story of 200 Years* (Viking, Melbourne, 1987).

Kenneth Morgan, 'The Organization of the Convict Trade to Maryland: Stevenson, Randolph and Cheston, 1768–1775', *William and Mary Quarterly*, 3rd series, vol. 42 (1985).

Eris O'Brien, *The Foundation of Australia (1786–1800): A Study in English Criminal Practice and Penal Colonisation in the Eighteenth Century* (Sheed and Ward, London, 1937; 2nd ed., Angus and Robertson, Sydney, 1950).

Wilfrid Oldham, *Britain's Convicts to the Colonies* (Library of Australian History, Sydney, 1990).

Bob Reece, *The Origins of Irish Convict Transportation to New South Wales* (Palgrave, Basingstoke, 2001).

David Richardson, 'Cultures of Exchange: Atlantic Africa in the Era of the Slave Trade', in *Transactions of the Royal Historical Society*, 6th series, vol. 19 (Cambridge University Press, Cambridge, 2009).

Sir Herbert Richmond, *The Navy in India, 1763–1783* (Ernest Benn, London, 1931).

N.A.M. Rodger, *The Wooden World: An Anatomy of the Georgian Navy* (Naval Institute Press, Annapolis, 1986).

Michael Roe, 'Motives for Australian Settlement: A document', *Tasmanian Historical Research Association: Papers and Proceedings*, no. 4 (1952).

Michael Roe, 'Australia's Place in the "Swing to the East", 1788–1810', *Historical Studies*, vol. 8 (1958).

G.W. Rusden, *History of Australia*, 3 vols (Chapman and Hall, London, 1883).

Owen Rutter, ed., *The First Fleet* (Golden Cockerel Press, [n.p.], 1937).

Ernest Scott, *A Short History of Australia* (Oxford University Press, London, 1916).

H.M. Scott, 'The Importance of Bourbon Naval Reconstruction to the Strategy of Choiseul after the Seven Years' War', *Imperial History Review*, vol. 1 (1979).

J.R. Seeley, *The Expansion of England* (Macmillan, London, 1883).

A.G.L. Shaw, *Convicts and the Colonies: A Study of Penal Transportation from Great Britain and Ireland to Australia and Other Parts of the British Empire* (Faber and Faber, London, 1966).

A.G.L. Shaw, 'The Hollow Conqueror and the Tyranny of Distance', *Historical Studies*, vol. 13 (1968).

A.G.L. Shaw, 'The Reasons for the Foundation of a British Settlement at Botany Bay in 1788', *ARTS*, vol. 12 (1984).

Babette Smith, *Australia's Birthstain* (Allen and Unwin, Sydney, 2008).

Alexander and George Sutherland, *The History of Australia from 1606 to 1876* (George Robinson, Melbourne, 1877).

E.P. Thompson, 'The moral economy of the English crowd in the eighteenth century', *Past and Present*, no. 50 (1971).

E.P. Thompson, *Whigs and Hunters: The Origin of the Black Act* (A. Lane, London, 1975).

# Index

Lightning Source UK Ltd.
Milton Keynes UK
UKOW03f1848210713

214126UK00007B/103/P